Sir Harry and Lady Oakes   Meyer Lansky

Alfred de Marigny   Nancy Oakes

KING'S X

King's X (probably short *for king's excuse*):
used as a cry in children's games
to claim exemption from being tagged
or caught or to call for a time out
  Webster's Third New International Dictionary

KING'S X

Common Law and the Death of Sir Harry Oakes

Marshall Houts

WILLIAM MORROW & COMPANY, INC., NEW YORK 1972

Endpaper photos by permission UPI

Printed in the United States of America.
Library of Congress Catalog Card Number 77–170247

3   4   5   75   74   73

to Tim

CONTENTS

1

The Dead Baronet

Major Gray Phillips, impeccably dressed in the uniform of the Black Watch, hesitated a third time in front of the royal bedroom. He was the Duke's equerry; and his friendship and unofficial service reached back past the frustrated beginnings of World War II, through the humiliations of the postabdication years, into the senselessly precipitated abdication crisis itself, the truncated ten-month reign as king, and the faded brilliance of the Prince of Wales era. At seven in the morning, Phillips knew that His Royal Highness and the Duchess would still be sound asleep. Never early risers, they would resent being disturbed regardless of the provocation, even though the dazzling Caribbean sun was already far along in its orbit, and a cooling breeze following the night's violent storm had cleared air and sky and sea to blend all into a startling blue.

Major Phillips reluctantly brought his clenched fist against the bedroom door, first cautiously and then with sufficient strength to be heard. The muted grumblings from behind the door came soon; and some minutes after the royal aide identified himself, the Duke, attired in white silk robe, the Royal British Coat of Arms embroidered in azure, red, silver, and gold on the pocket, his brownish hair in total disarray, opened the door.

From her half-wakened position in bed, the Duchess

heard the two men discussing murder,* and she was shocked. Sudden death always startles; violent death repels and overwhelms. When the victim enjoys celebrity status, the death becomes sensational, and rational action by all who are intimately associated with the case is substantially diminished.

The Duchess, now fully awake, heard Major Phillips tell the Duke that the number one citizen of the Bahamas, Sir Harry Oakes, had been bludgeoned to death as he lay asleep in his bed; and as if this were not enough, the murderer had attempted to set fire to the body.

We have no way of knowing all that happened in the royal bedroom during the next several hours on that morning of July 8, 1943, but we can be assured that neither the Royal Governor nor his duchess wife attempted a return to sleep. There was a developing awareness—perhaps it originated with the Duchess and perhaps not—that the Royal Governor must act, and take principal charge of the investigation of his friend's murder so that it could be disposed of with a minimum amount of unpleasant publicity. The Duke undoubtedly was perceptive enough to wonder whether the arrangement he had earlier approved with Sir Harry and Harold Christie, the number-two citizen of the Bahamas, might have something to do with Sir Harry's death; and the more he thought of this possibility, the greater his fear became. Fear also thwarts rational action.

Characteristically, the Duke either acted precipitously in every crisis of his life, committing himself boldly to a course from which he stubbornly refused to retreat, regardless of consequences, or he dallied indecisively in a manner unbecoming in great leadership. He now decided to dawdle, probably because he feared the consequences of his own involvement, so no crucial decision was made, at least no definitive action taken, for three hours and fifty minutes, until he personally telephoned the Miami Police Department at 10:50 A.M.

We have no way of knowing all that happened during this

---

* See p. 346, *The Heart Has Its Reasons*, The Memoirs of the Duchess of Windsor (New York: David McKay Company, Inc., 1956).

critical interval; but we can presume that while he considered his options, he thought back on his relationship with the murdered baronet, the man who had captivated and intrigued him, whose life story he enjoyed repeating to friends and guests as part of his conversational leadership.

No man in the Islands could be oblivious to Harry Oakes, in life or in death. He was reputedly the richest baronet in all the British Empire. Someone dubbed him "the Cinderella Prospector"; to some he was philanthropist and benefactor; to others, bastard, robber, boor, and cruel oppressor. Few could speak of him in anything resembling neutral terms.

As is true of many men who attain celebrity status, myth and truth often merge imperceptibly.

Legend had it that Harry Oakes could write a check for $200,000,000 any time he wished, and his bankers would be only too happy to honor it. The truth was that since he discovered his Lake Shore mines in the province of Ontario, Canada, in 1912, over $200,000,000 in gold ore had been extracted from the ground for a net profit considerably in excess of $100,000,000. He shunned the stock market but owned half-a-dozen homes in and around Nassau, a mansion in Palm Beach, Florida, a spacious summer estate in Bar Harbor, Maine, a chalet at Kirkland Lake near the Canadian bonanza; and he had given away his $500,000 estate at Niagara, on the Canadian side of the Falls. There were also the London town house for formal society functions and the country estate in Sussex for weekend parties.

Harry Oakes did not start out as a British subject. His father was one of five brothers admitted to the bar in the state of Maine, sons of a proud, independent, defiant family that traced its origins back to Revolutionary days. Harry was the middle of five children born to this squire of Sangerville, Maine, who also taught school, served as a member of the school board, and enjoyed the outdoors as a land surveyor when he could.

From the beginning, Harry Oakes was an introspective

daydreamer, short and wiry, whose adult height barely reached 5 feet 6 inches. A lone wolf, he roamed the woods, fished the streams, and hunted the forests without a single close friend to his credit.

His father sent him to Bowdoin College in Brunswick, Maine, which had much earlier established its reputation for academic greatness. A small school with a captivating, ivy-covered campus nestled among great virgin oaks, it had produced a President of the United States, cabinet officers, senators and congressmen, doctors, lawyers, judges, and the likes of Nathaniel Hawthorne and Henry Wadsworth Long-fellow. Although he joined Zeta Psi fraternity, Harry Oakes continued as a 135-pound introvert, a shy, tongue-tied wan-derer who neither drank nor caroused, swore nor whored. His only concession to sociability was his wardrobe, which was immaculate.

If psychological clichés had been the vogue at the time of Harry Oakes' graduation from Bowdoin College in 1896, someone might well have alleged, "His grasp on reality is rather tenuous." When he talked at all, it was always about the great fortune he would make; but he would not even speculate on the plan he would employ to amass great wealth. His daydreams were psychotic in proportion; and his withdrawal from Syracuse Medical College after two years on the stated reason that the profession of medicine would not permit the amassing of great wealth attests to his eco-nomic immaturity.

Along with millions of others, Harry Oakes was fired by the gold news from the Yukon Territory—and Dawson City, Klondike, Bonanza Creek, were names that soon tempted tens of thousands from every walk of life to break from the anonymity and monotony of their current existences, to strike out for something different on the excuse of seeking fame and fortune.

The uniqueness of Harry Oakes' plunge into the mystic world of the gold prospector is that it came about with the encouragement and financial blessings of his family. Father, mother, and working siblings all contributed to his stake and

promised never to abandon him financially, no matter where
he was or what might be the lapse of time. His entire family
held the faith that he could not be denied his inalienable
fortune, provided he persevered with determination and intelligence to find it; and Harry would persevere.

The gold camps of the era were filled with drop-outs, mal-
contents, sociopaths, homosexuals, lesbians, prostitutes, alco-
holics, and psychotics. They were the ultimate in escapism.
Literally from nowhere, five, ten, twenty, and sometimes
thirty thousand people appeared in some wilderness creek
bottom or trail crossing, at a spot not marked on even the
most detailed maps, without housing, food, sanitary facilities,
or medical provision. The mass assemblage offered a sort of
group sanction for immoral, amoral, and asocial coexistence.
The announced goal was "gold," just as "love" is the benevo-
lent license for many hippie gatherings.

Harry Oakes spent the winter of 1898–99 in Skagway as a
hospital orderly in a makeshift shed where fugitive doctors
"treated" frostbite, gangrene, venereal disease, tuberculosis,
cirrhosis of the liver, pneumonia, and malnutrition. When the
spring thaw converted ice to slush, he made his way to
Dawson City, its massed riffraff making it the largest Canadian city west of Winnipeg. Harry Oakes quickly realized
that he was competing with thousands of other amateurs, so
he treated Dawson City as a learning experience only, vow-
ing to elevate the techniques of prospecting to a plane of
skill and science, to remove it from blind fool's luck.

Harry Oakes was considerably more mobile than the great
majority of his compatriots because he possessed money. He
made one promising strike in the Yukon; but it was a will-
o'-the-wisp, playing out just about the time that Nome, Alaska,
became the gold dreamer's delirium. With twenty thousand
other unfortunates, Oakes landed on the rocky coast of this
sleeping Eskimo village on the edge of the Bering Sea.
Legend has it that Oakes' boat was blown over during a storm
to the Siberian coasts of Russia, where he was actually captured by Cossack guards; and Oakes repeated this story as
gospel during his later years.

In a milieu where a partner was frequently essential to survival, Oakes still found that he could work only alone. If anything, his physical privations and the obsession that drove him to exhaustion for twelve, fourteen, and sixteen hours a day, seven days a week, made him more introspective. His eighty-pound pack was substantially heavier than half his total body weight. He endured the 50-degree-below-zero temperatures in the sunless winter. He tolerated the flies and mosquitoes of the long summers which were virtually without darkness. He did not drink. He did not gamble. What he did about women is not known. The life of the gold prospector in Alaska around the turn of the century could not help but leave an indelible imprint on this asocial Bowdoin Yankee, the erstwhile medical student with the psychotic compulsion that somehow, some way, some day, he would possess one of the world's great fortunes.

For fourteen incredible years, Harry Oakes pursued his quest.

After a realistic appraisal that his chances of success around Nome were nil, he worked his way back to Seattle, where he caught a boat for the Philippines. Not much is known about his activities in these islands, which the United States had just acquired as a dubious prize of war from Spain.

He next arrived in Australia, where the talk was of Lasseter's Reef, a story for all the world like dozens more about lost gold mines in the western part of the United States. Harry Oakes prospected the desert wastes of Western Australia, where the temperatures burned as high as 115 degrees and where the fight to stay alive was even more treacherous than in the subzero temperatures of the Yukon and Alaska.

The payoff from Australia equaled that from Nome, so he crossed over into New Zealand.

His older sister, Gertrude, perhaps served as his only continuing link to reality. Dumpy and fat, a characteristic of the Oakes clan, and completely devoid of femininity, Gertrude knew early in life that she would never marry. Working as a government secretary in Washington, D.C., she wrote Harry regularly and forwarded a stipend out of almost every monthly check. He probably could have survived without Gertrude's money, but nothing could have kept him from developing into a babbling psychotic without her spiritual support.

He headed for California and for a year prospected the hell-like formations of Death Valley, where the altitude was 280 feet below sea level, and the adversaries were not only rattlesnakes but human desert rats who took rifle shots at all who threatened their territories.

Gold was now announced in the Belgian Congo, and Harry Oakes was immediately on his way, drawn by some unseen magnet whose pull was stronger than gravity. The Belgian Congo yield paralleled those of the Yukon, Nome, Australia, California, and New Zealand; so the restless wanderer found himself again in Alaska. Geoffrey Bocca describes him at this stage as "a dehumanized man without friends." [*] He roamed Alaska for four fruitless years; and finally, in a funk of hopeless desperation, he reached Toronto.

Harry Oakes could no more turn back from his search than a massive glacier can stop its flow down the mountain sides, but his wanderings were now aimless, without direction. He had no faith whatsoever in the gold potential of Ontario, but there was no place else for him.

Myth and truth coalesce in their account of Harry Oakes' famous strike. The truth is that it occurred on Kirkland Lake in northern Ontario, east of the trading post of Swastika, some two years after Oakes' arrival in Toronto. We know that it was the second largest gold mine in the Western Hemisphere, second only to the Homestake mine in South Dakota, which served as the financial base for the William Randolph Hearst fortunes.

The manner of the golden hit suffers from bifurcation in the telling.

Years later Harry Oakes fumed at the stories that depicted his discovery as nothing more than the luck of a tattered hobo: He was thrown off a train by an irate conductor near

[*] *The Life and Death of Sir Harry Oakes* (Garden City, New York: Doubleday & Company, 1959).

Kirkland Lake because he did not have money for his ticket; he was thrown off the train at the same place by the same conductor because he was drunk; he bought the Kirkland Lake claim for five dollars from a starving Chinese cook; he merely poached the claim from a crazed prospector who asked only a crust of sourdough and a plate of rancid beans; he and a fellow prospector, George Tough, collapsed in exhaustion, and when they revived, Oakes clutched a high-grade nugget in his hand.

Throughout his life Harry Oakes vehemently insisted that the Kirkland Lake strikes were the result of scientific prospecting techniques developed through a dozen years, which entirely eliminated the element of luck. He had carefully analyzed the claims of other prospectors and their accompanying assayer's reports, and deduced that the ore veins ran toward the center of the lakes as spokes to the hub of a wheel. The great concentration of ore, ergo, would be in the formations near and under the waters. Other, less perceptive prospectors had made their mistake by not pursuing the thickening veins into the waters of the lakes.

Whether his theory was prescient or postfact rationalization, his two veins toward and under Kirkland Lake far exceeded his wildest daydreams. His rewards were somewhat dampened though by the incongruous fact that he had been forced into a makeshift partnership with four brothers, the Tough Boys, because he did not have enough cash to file his claims; and the Tough Oakes mine went into limited production in the fall of 1912, within days of Woodrow Wilson's first election.

Oakes' troubles were only beginning.

During the fourteen years of his ceaseless Grail, he swore to himself day by day and night by night that when he did find his bonanza, he would develop it himself. He had crossed paths with dozens of prospectors who had actually experienced the one strike of a lifetime, only to sell out million-dollar claims for a few hundred dollars for provisions money so that another ceaseless quest could begin immediately.

Harry Oakes organized the Lake Shore Mines Limited in 1914 with a capitalization of two million shares. He kept one million for himself and paid off past debts with another 300,000 shares, debts including the advances from his family, especially sister Gertrude. He immediately began scheming to eliminate the Tough Boys, whom fate had forced on him at a most inopportune time.

If Harry Oakes was an accomplished prospector, he was but an amateur mining engineer. Hundreds of thousands of dollars of sophisticated equipment to sink shafts, bring up the ore, and mill it for its gold content were required. The coffers of the Oakes family were bare of cash. The Canadian newspapers refused Oakes advertising space to promote his mining stock on the ground that it was hyperspeculative. Bankers and financial houses turned him down cold. World War I came and went with no notice whatsoever from Harry Oakes, except the realization that it deprived him inconveniently of machinery and manpower.

A series of lawsuits and countersuits between Harry Oakes and the Tough Brothers, as well as a brokerage house, ran up a bill of a quarter-million dollars in attorneys' fees. Finally, by 1921, some eleven years after his first strike at Kirkland Lake, Harry Oakes was one of the wealthy men of the world, twenty-three years after he had left Syracuse Medical College to accumulate his great fortune. In a short time, the shares in Lake Shores Mines Limited which he could not sell a few years earlier for ten cents climbed to a high of $64.50.

But Harry Oakes had paid dearly for his financial pinnacle. Anything resembling manners, grace, and charm which he had possessed when he left Maine were spilled along the frozen wastes of the Yukon and the burning sands of Australia and Death Valley. He was now a boorish man, crude in both language and demeanor. At the table he spit out grape seeds and fruit pits with the same reckless abandon that had characterized his animal-like meals in Dawson City and Nome. Since a knife was the proper eating tool for beans and bacon in Western Australia, there was no reason why it should not be used in the best hotels in Toronto. His language, liberally laced with four-letter words, remained vulgar.

He built a respectable chalet near the mine at Kirkland Lake, but then a period of pathological restlessness set in. He took a trip around the world, and then a second one; and on this second cruise he met Eunice MacIntyre. At twenty-four, she was exactly half his age, and his opposite in every way.

Eunice was three inches taller than Harry. Her soft blue eyes set off a plain, oval face formed around a straight, medium nose. She was slender and lithe, her movements instinctively poised. Her father was a government employee in Sydney, Australia, and Eunice worked as a stenographer in a bank. She smiled often and easily and Oakes fell immediately under her spell.

By this time he was paunchy, like a bloated athlete who adds great bulk quickly after hanging up his spikes and deserting the regimen of the training table. His face, particularly about the eyes, was a mass of fine lines, the insults of cruel years in arctic cold and desert heat. The wide-set eyes with their hard, intransigent glare fenced in a long, bulbous, beak-like nose. His nose stopped only a quarter inch above thin, fine lips that locked defiantly above a jutting, belligerent jaw. Perhaps his most noticeable feature was a full head of wavy hair, only slightly lined with gray.

Neither Harry nor Eunice permitted the ardor of their shipboard romance to cool as they hastened to Sydney, where they were married in 1923. Each possessed qualities to fill gaping voids in the other.

Their first child, Nancy, was born while they lived in the chalet near the mine; but the desolate area was repugnant to Eunice. They moved to Niagara immediately, into a sprawling, renovated castle where Edward VII once spent the night.

The world was now midway through the Roaring Twenties. Harry Oakes, rough, ruthless, uncouth, without taste or graciousness, perhaps the richest man in Canada, decided that

it was expedient for him to renounce his American national-
ity and become a Canadian citizen.

He lived as the total autocrat, enforced his mere word as
a royal command, and flew into tantrums and fits of rage
when his wishes were questioned; only Eunice could control
him and calm his fierce temper. Without her, it was unfortunately true that Harry Oakes made far more enemies than
friends.

Four more children were born over the next eight years.
They were cared for by nurses and governesses as they traveled with their parents throughout the world. It was a regal
life station without royal designation, but it lacked purpose
or challenge.

Harry Oakes' boredom increased after the Canadian elec-
tions of 1930. Following a contribution of $250,000 to the
campaign chests of the Conservative party, he hoped for appointment as senator, a lifetime prestigious honor; but the
spoils that year went to the Liberal party, which downed the
Conservatives handily at the polls. By this time Oakes' income from Lake Shore Mines Limited was being taxed at a
confiscatory rate of 85 percent; and he was now threatened
with an even greater increase in the tax structure. There was
no doubt that he was the largest single taxpayer in all of
Canada, and he complained vigorously and loudly of his
persecution.

At his Palm Beach home shortly after his Canadian disen-
chantment became complete, Harry Oakes met a real-estate
promoter from Nassau named Harold Christie, who set about
to convince Oakes that he should renounce Canada for the
Bahamas. One of Christie's arguments was irrefutable: The
Bahamas had never enacted any form of income taxation, nor
did they exact death duties or inheritance taxes. Regardless
of the unpleasantness of the thought, Harry Oakes was now
approaching sixty years of age, so he had to think in terms
of inheritance taxes. If he died a citizen of Canada, domiciled
there, the tax rate on his estate would exceed 90 percent.

After denouncing Canadian political philosophy and its

tax structure as it stringently affected him, Harry Oakes was soundly thrashed in the Canadian press, which called him "ingrate" and "tax dodger"; but after complicated legal maneuvering that transferred the management and owner-ship of Lake Shore Mines Limited to several interlocking holding companies, Harry Oakes moved with Eunice and their five children into a twenty-room mansion on the edge of the Bahamas Country Club. It was in this house, called West-bourne, where the body of Harry Oakes was to be reported by Harold Christie on the sultry Thursday morning of July 8, 1943.

Within a matter of months after his arrival in Nassau, working with Harold Christie, with whom he spent half his time, Oakes soon owned approximately one-third of the 21-by-7-mile island of New Providence. He built the golf course on which Westbourne abutted; and to entice Pan American Airways into a regular semiweekly stop, he leveled and graded Oakes Field. His holdings included the Moorish pink-stucco British Colonial Hotel, which rumor claimed he bought in spite so that he could fire the maître d' who once relegated him to a second-rate table in the rear of the dining room.

He developed a bus line to haul black workers from their hovels in Grant's Town and built them a waterworks. He gave a million dollars to Island charities: the Milk Fund for Un-derprivileged Children, the Fund for the Care of Unwed Mothers, and sporadic funds for the improvement of the facilities of the Royal Hospital and the public schools for black children.

Soon after acquiring the British Colonial, he ordered that only blacks should be employed, except in half-a-dozen top-echelon positions. When informed that there were not enough trained blacks to serve as waiters, porters, cooks, and chambermaids, an edict established a training school as part of the hotel operation.

At some point either Harry or Eunice Oakes, perhaps both, decided that he should have a baronetcy, this title of privi-lege and prestige near and dear to the heart of every Britisher around the world in the days before rapidly approaching World War II. Harry and Eunice spent considerable time in England, entertaining political people lavishly in Eunice Oakes' relaxed style in both their London town house and on the country estate in Sussex. Harry Oakes gave $500,000 in two bequests to St. George's Hospital in London. In short, he purchased the coveted title that was conferred upon him as part of the Honors List for George VI's birthday in 1939. Sir Harry and Lady Oakes should not be unduly criticized for the purchase of the title, as it was more or less standard procedure. One of the great criticisms leveled at World War I Prime Minister David Lloyd George, for example, during the last years of his active political power was that he sold the titles indiscriminately and with poor taste.

Sir Harry and Lady Oakes decided while still in London that they needed yet another honor to complete their dominant position in the Bahamas. Harry Oakes wished to be elected a member of the Bahamian House of Assembly, but no vacancy was readily available. The expedient soon devised was the elevation of a member of the elective House to the appointive nine-man Executive Council which served directly under the royal governor, an appointee of the king. The man chosen to move from Assembly to Executive Council was a promising young black barrister by the name of Alfred Adderley.

Sir Harry Oakes' election to the House of Assembly was a foregone formality. His opponent was a nameless black who received only a handful of votes while Sir Harry remained safely in London, his sole electioneering for his only attempt at elective office being a small amount of cash to insure the machinations of the elective process.

Now the honored baronet lay dead in his own bed, the violent end to a turbulent life. His intimates knew that over the years he had made dozens of enemies capable of inflicting the fatal wounds.

2

The Royal Governor

Decision-making was never the former king's great forte. It must have been close to nine o'clock before he remembered his censorship powers under the Emergency War Powers Act; so he moved to keep Sir Harry's murder a secret known only to Bahamian residents. His delay had not reckoned with the panicky actions of Harold Christie, who, in his rash of telephoning between seven and seven-thirty from Westbourne, called Étienne Dupuch, the Bahamian publisher with whom Sir Harry and Christie were to go on a sheep-inspection tour that morning. Dupuch recognized Christie's frantic reports as a major international news story and cabled it to the far corners of the earth.

This information stunned the Duke, who again retired with his Duchess into the solitude of their bedchamber at Government House to conjure up his next option. As never before, they cursed their plight in this moment of their second exile, now hoping only for a safe deliverance that would permit them to escape unharmed.

Had anyone dared suggest a scant seven years earlier that the king of the greatest throne in the world would one day be serving as royal governor of a relatively insignificant crown colony, he would have been considered mad. But that same king was indeed the royal governor with the responsibility to preside over an investigation of the sordid murder of one of his friends, a vicious killing in his own bailiwick that threatened to worry him more than all his errors of commission and omission in the past. Nothing in his training or background equipped him to decide what to do.

Over and over again, he undoubtedly asked himself how and why he should even be physically in Nassau, much less its royal governor, who must attempt to extricate himself from a highly vulnerable position. His unlikely official presence can perhaps best be explained by understanding that he was both product and victim of a generation gap.

One of the most revealing of all family portraits ever taken shows the future Edward VIII, clothed in white-lace dress twice the length of his body, resting apprehensively on the massive lap of his great-grandmother, the incomparable Queen Victoria. To the right stands an aging, rotund, and bearded figure in morning cutaway, the future Edward VII, Edward VIII's grandfather; opposite him, a slightly smaller, younger, and more handsome king-model, the epitome of formality and decorum, is the future King George V, Edward VIII's father. As for great dynastic houses, Victoria appears as the last ruler of the House of Hanover, Edward VII the only representative of the House of Saxe-Coburg-Gotha, with George V destined to become the first monarch of the House of Windsor. Although Victoria and Edward VII were honored with eras named for them, George V was perhaps more Victorian and Edwardian than even his grandmother and father.

Edward VII readily admitted that he was awed by and feared his mother; George V was awed by and feared Edward VII; Edward VIII was terrified of George V, specifying his "quarter-deck manner" acquired during his navy days when George hoped only for a full-time career in the Royal Navy. Although indelibly born and bred into these great dynastic houses, Edward VIII managed to evade their regimenting clutches, primarily because of the world-shattering changes wrought by World War I; but there is another reason: It is inconceivable that the tiny babe in the long flowing white dress can possibly be of the same species as the three great mastodons in the family portrait dominated by Victoria.

Known to the family as David, this eldest sibling of four

other boys and one girl born to George V and Mary was not
an intellectual by his own admission. Because of his father's
experiences and prejudices, David was preordained for the
Royal Naval College at Osborne where, even making allow-
ance for his status as heir apparent, he scored almost at the
bottom of his class. It was a technical curriculum emphasizing
mathematics, compass reading, signaling, and other mechanical trade-school chores; geography, history, and modern lan-
guages were ignored, which left a permanent gap in his
education for his subsequent approach to the problems of
kingship.

By 1910 Edward VII was dead; George V was on the
throne; and David was Prince of Wales at age sixteen.

He thought it an unkind cut when his father, departing
from naval tradition, ordered him to Oxford, where he
entered Magdalen College. His failures as a scholar undoubtedly caused him grave apprehensions and self-doubts;
so he compensated socially by being "a regular fellow," this
in itself a difficult goal in view of his privileged position:
personal valet, special quarters, helpful tutors, and all the
accouterments of the heir apparent to the greatest throne in
the world in pre-World War I England.

Whether in oral or written form, his communications from
his parents formed a single drumbeat: Duty! Duty! Duty! He
was a man apart from all other men. Already his life fell into
a precise and rigid mold; no alternative to enforced conformity lay ahead.

He was permitted four months in France by his father as
a "broadening" experience, but he made no progress whatsoever in mastering the French language. A contrasting visit
to Germany as the guest of his many German relatives (Kaiser
Wilhelm II was his first cousin once removed) permanently
burned itself into both mind and personality. He loved the
German people, admired their preoccupation with fatherland,
was able to master their language. He thought them basically
good and superb, regardless of their leadership of the moment.
In short, he became a permanent Germanophile, once and
for all.

Under the circumstances, his service in World War I as an

Army officer turned out surprisingly well. For one thing it saved him from Oxford, of which he said, "Oxford failed to make me really studious." Nor did he ever learn to read for pleasure.

By now he had attained his maximum height of 5 feet 7 inches, and while his build could never be described as skinny or slight, it was far from heavy and robust. At this stage a contemporary described him as "handsome in a soft sort of way." He forced his unruly golden hair to conform to a part on the left side. There were smile lines near his eyes, the nose turned up slightly, and the blue eyes were sad with a melancholy, faraway look. His rather expansive brow already showed wrinkles; thin, severe lips formed an almost feminine mouth. The ambivalent result of the whole could be construed as either weak, subservient submission or stubborn defiance.

When he protested to Lord Kitchener, then Secretary of State for War, that he should be allowed to go to the front since he had three brothers to take his place if he was killed, Kitchener candidly replied that he would not restrain him from the trenches if he could be sure that he would be killed; what he desperately needed to guard against was the Germans' taking him prisoner.

Over the years following World War I, Edward VIII's tours as Prince of Wales became legendary. Received enthusiastically by shouting hordes in Canada, Australia, New Zealand, South Africa, and finally South America, with occasional visits to the United States, he became undoubtedly the first of the great international celebrities, the object of far more obeisance and adulation than any military hero, head of state, or Hollywood star in history.

Back in Britain after his triumphant tours, he said: "It was especially in my relations with the family that I realized how much my outlook had changed. My life had become one of contrast and commotion; whereas order and perfection ruled my father's." His father railed at the short skirts and bobbed hair of the flappers; the Prince of Wales found them inviting, stimulating, and acceptable.

An aide once told him, "Life should be lived to the fullest";

and this became his personal creed, his rite, his duty to play hard after working hard. He complained vigorously that while many men might be chained to a desk, he was chained to the banquet table; and each night of the week, after some boring but official state function which he tolerated, frequently without enthusiasm, he ended the day at one of his favorite night-clubs: the Café de Paris, Ciro's, the Kit-Kat Club, or his own special Embassy Club. Here he danced the Charleston, the black bottom, and other jazz imports from America in an escapism known the world over as the Roaring Twenties; and his father lectured him blisteringly about his dancing until six o'clock every morning, "including Sundays."

His romantic escapades became legion, while tens of thousands of his unsettled World War I contemporaries idolized him as the vigorous leader of a long pent-up rebellion against Victorian and Edwardian inhibitions; and his personal family position automatically converted him into the apostle of "liberalism," which was looked upon with much the same disdain and dismay as the philosophy of the New Left was viewed by veterans of World War II.

Unfortunately, Edward VIII was possessed of a hyperabundance of one of the greatest of all human frailties: *rationalization*. He was to say later that during this period of the Roaring Twenties, he decided to "bring the monarchy, in response to new conditions, ever nearer to the people." Anything and everything that he did, therefore, he rationalized in soul-saving fashion within this framework of modernizing the monarchy and taking it to the people. It was, of necessity, perfectly all right for him to speak out boldly, perhaps rudely, on social and economic conditions, although historically the monarch has the constitutional power only to "suggest" and "advise."

It mattered not that his outbursts into political arenas became terrible tactical blunders, offensive not only to his father but also to the prime minister, members of the Cabinet, and members of Parliament. The inevitable result was that when his own constitutional crisis came, there were no more than two or three politically important personages in all of the

Empire to whom he could turn for advice and help; and for
the most part, he embarrassed these potential allies unmerci-
fully. If it was all right for him to butt into state matters that
his father, grandfather, and great-grandmother would never
even have thought of, there was no reason why he could not
conduct his personal life beyond the pale of prescribed traditions.

For the Prince, the Roaring Twenties blended imperceptibly
into the Depression-ridden Thirties. After barely surviving one
serious illness and a series of minor ones, George V exhibited
his frailness. Still, the heir apparent showed no signs of
settling into a more conformist pattern. Many of his subjects
and especially his mother and father were appalled by his
failure to take a wife. The restless Prince of Wales, like his
contemporaries everywhere throughout the world, could not
mature and grow into adult responsibility. The gross practical
jokes and the bizarre scavenger hunts for which the Prince
was dubiously famous appeared highly inappropriate to men
who could not find work, whose families existed on the public
dole.

The Prince's compromise at maturing was a rather amateurish attempt to show himself as "a prince with a social conscience." He traveled extensively in the coal-mining villages
and industrial centers where unemployment with its attendant
miseries ran high; and his ministers interpreted this unprecedented intervention as a frontal attack on their inability to
cure the Depression. He proposed massive public-housing
projects, offering some of his own personal estates and funds
to back them, only to see them scuttled by both Conservative
and Socialist leaders alike. He blasted away at what he called
the "unrealism" of the League of Nations while his foreign
ministers were striving valiantly to marshal public support
for it, to make it viable and capable of policing Europe's
aggressors. He flew headlong into the face of the pacifist
movement of the early Thirties by urging rearmament. It was
immaterial that a member of Parliament in political eclipse,
one Winston Churchill, espoused the same rearmament cause.
A member of Parliament was expected to advocate such

causes; a prince of the blood royal and the immediate heir apparent to the throne was constitutionally barred from injecting himself into the political arena.

The Prince finally decided to bow to tradition and take unto himself a wife and a helpmate. There was a substantial complication to this facet of his maturing program: The woman he selected was then married to another man; and if this were not enough, she had already divorced a previous husband. He knew that he could never marry her during his father's life because the Royal Marriages Act of 1772 gave the king a veto power over the choice of a wife by any prince of the blood royal. The Prince of Wales knew that the old Victorian and Edwardian would never consent to his marrying Wallis Warfield Spencer Simpson.

Had the Prince been in reasonable touch with reality, he would have realized that after his father's death he faced the real and highly dubious problem of whether he could ram Mrs. Simpson as queen down the throats of his still conforming British subjects. But since he dealt in unreasoning and unrealistic rationalizations, he concluded, probably reasonably enough for him, that a twice-divorced queen, and an American one at that, would be merely a modernization and democratization of the monarchy which was his prime goal after all. He would find out to his personal tragedy and disaster just how far off target his calculations were, which also included his sickening discovery that the survival of the individual monarch is not a prerequisite to the stability of the monarchy itself.

The Prince claims he met Mrs. Ernest Simpson at the country estate of mutual friends in 1931; she belabors the point that it was 1930. She was married, ergo, fair game for this particular prince; and it would have been totally out of character for her not to lead him on.

If not with Ernest Simpson's approval, at least with his silent acquiescence, the Prince of Wales took over his wife. She became his regular weekend guest at Fort Belvedere, the Prince's own "Grace and Favour" castle outside of London. At the beginning, Ernest submissively tagged along for the sake of appearances, but discovered all too soon that his presence was not necessary. The Prince became such a regular (nightly) fixture at the Simpson flat on Bryanston Court that Ernest developed the admirable trait of meekly retiring to his bedroom to work on the family budget and the ledgers of account shortly after the Prince's arrival.

Mrs. Simpson became the Prince's constant "companion," and there was an understanding arching of eyebrows and special inflection of voice when the knowing used the word "companion."

She was off to Kitzbühel in Austria with the Prince for a skiing vacation; on the spur of the moment the Prince decided that they should tour Vienna; and then without warning, they swayed under the spell of gypsy violins in dimly lit bistros in Budapest. She was with him on trips to Biarritz which progressed to cruises on the yachts *Cutty Sark* and *Anne*. All the time Ernest Simpson played his role perfectly, although Wallis complains that he once slammed his door with a bang when she elected to go off on a European jaunt with the Prince rather than accompany her husband on a business trip to New York.

It probably could never happen again, but during all this time the British press never once mentioned Mrs. Simpson, other than occasionally to print her name as part of the guest list in the *Court Circular*, which appeared daily. Grounded in the concept of fair play, which meant that members of the Royal Family were precluded by etiquette from answering any criticism against them, custom and usage prohibited any derogatory comments about the royal personages, particularly those comments that insinuated gossip concerning private lives. The relationship of Wallis Warfield Spencer Simpson to the Prince of Wales was, therefore, bantered about in the form of mouth-to-mouth rumor, oftentimes far more destructive than a straight news story could ever be. For example, one of the least vulgar of the stories making the rounds was: "What's the Prince of Wales's latest naval station?"

Answer: "I don't know, what is it?"

Reply: "He's the third mate on an American tramp!"

Good old staid, bourgeois, middle-class England was at first intrigued but then appalled at the rumors; and when George V fell desperately ill in late 1935, "What about the Prince? What will he do?" became even a more immediate topic of conversation than bread lines at home or Hitler and Mussolini on the Continent.

George V, undoubtedly realizing that his end was near, poured out his concern over the future King and his American "companion" to Cosmo Gordon Lang, Archbishop of Canterbury, the Primate of all England, and, next to the Royal Family itself, the ranking personage in the unremitting order of protocol. Lang reassured the dying sovereign that his son would undoubtedly come to his senses when he became king; at least the Church, whose tenets were unalterably opposed to divorce, would never permit a twice-divorced woman with two other living husbands to assume the role of queen.

Secure within the blinders of his own self-centered rationalization, if he saw any warning signals at all, the Prince elected to ignore them. When his father died on January 20, 1936, Edward VIII once more broke with tradition to watch himself proclaimed king by the Accession Council as he stood at the window of an apartment in St. James's Palace. An enterprising newsreel photographer held his breath until his film was developed: He had captured for posterity substantial footage of Mrs. Ernest Simpson standing next to the King, their arms locked in warm embrace, while the heralds proclaimed this advent of the second Windsor to the Crown.

Edward VIII has always vigorously insisted that he wanted to remain on the throne; but in analyzing his actions during the ten-and-a-half months of his reign, albeit in hindsight, it is difficult to imagine a course of conduct more completely demanding his ouster. If we accept his outrageous tactical and strategic decisions as consistent with a genuine desire to remain on the throne, then it is impossible to escape the conclusion that he is endowed with an appalling lack of sensitivity that has few rivals in all the pages of history.

In May, he arranged a formal dinner so that Prime Minister Stanley Baldwin, the tenacious old bulldog of the Conservative party, and Mrs. Baldwin could meet Mrs. Simpson. Ernest submissively agreed to come along to this state function for appearances' sake. Edward privately explained to Wallis that the purpose was to permit the prime minister "to meet my future wife!"

During the summer, Edward literally flaunted Mrs. Simpson to the world, the stage being the yacht *Nahlin* on which they cruised the Dalmatian coast, stopping in whatever village struck their fancy of the moment. The world's press captured shots of Edward, in bathing trunks, in compromising poses with Wallis, also attired only in a bathing suit. Ministers and college presidents throughout the United States railed against the King's "carrying on" in such a flagrant manner with a married woman, but, inconceivably, the British press remained silent on the King and Mrs. Simpson.

There can be no doubt that Edward himself precipitated the constitutional crisis that cost him his throne. His coronation was scheduled for the following May; a waiting period of six months was required in a divorce proceeding after the temporary decree *nisi* before the final decree *absolute*. They would be cutting it rather fine, but if Wallis proceeded immediately with a divorce action against Ernest, the decree absolute could be entered the following April; barely in time for the royal marriage before the pomp and circumstance of the coronation.

In one of the most convenient explanations of all time, Wallis discovered a letter addressed to her that should have been addressed to Ernest; she doesn't explain how, but this was sufficient to permit her conclusion that Ernest was involved with another woman. The King was most sympathetic to her plight and instructed his own personal solicitor to put her in touch with Theodore Goddard, a London solicitor, to handle her case. The complaint was filed; and surprisingly enough, Solicitor Goddard experienced no difficulty whatsoever in obtaining leading barrister Norman Birkett to present her case in court.

All agreed that less publicity would attend the case if it could be disposed of at the Ipswich assizes; so Mrs. Ernest Simpson was inconvenienced by having to take up residence in Felixstowe, a seacoast village east of London.

On October 27, everything appeared to be set up for the divorce hearing at Felixstowe; but neither His Majesty the King, nor his "'companion," nor the "guilty party" to the divorce proceeding had reckoned on the innate independence of the Common Law judges. Then, the only ground for divorce was adultery; and as with every form of extreme proscription, dubious evasive devices came into play. Barrister Birkett began to present his "usual" evidence of adultery. The clerk of the Hotel de Paris in Bray-on-Thames produced the registration card bearing Ernest Simpson's signature. He had registered in room 312. The hotel chambermaid testified that the following morning, when she took tea to the room, Ernest Simpson was in bed with a woman not his wife; she could not see beneath the covers, but their clothes were strewn all about the room.

It was the normal way of proving adultery in a divorce action: The divorce solicitor sent his client to an agency; the agency directed him to one of the hotels catering to the divorce trade; he was introduced to a girl who specialized in it. After the "guilty party's" registration at the hotel, the girl would go upstairs to the bedroom where the two spent a decorous night (he agreed to penalties if he attempted advances against his collaborator); just before the chambermaid's arrival, the two parties undressed and crawled under the covers, preparatory to the "surprise" by the maid as she brought the tea. The room clerk and the chambermaid were experienced witnesses in the courtroom. No problems were encountered, *unless* collusion between husband and wife could be proved. This was enough to vitiate the evidence.

Now, Justice Hawke smelled collusion, and it upset him.

Why, the justice asked, was the case being heard in Felixstowe instead of London? A hurried conference with his clerk assured him. But now, the justice discovered, the evidence nowhere disclosed the name of the lady with whom Ernest Simpson spent the night in the Hotel de Paris. Barrister

Birkett assured him that her name was in the original complaint; but he did not dare tell the justice that the real name of the woman with whom Ernest was supposed to have cohabited was Buttercup Kennedy. Only with great reluctance was the decree *nisi* granted; and as Wallis Simpson and her solicitor left the courthouse, police smashed the cameras of newspaper reporters attempting to get a story. They also saw to it that no reporter followed Mrs. Simpson back to London.

A gentleman's agreement arranged by press barons Beaverbrook and Rothermere was now in effect which permitted all major papers and magazines to completely ignore the fact that Wallis Warfield Spencer Simpson even existed, much less was involved with the King. It was an utterly incredible arrangement!

Prime Minister Baldwin called on the King again; and Edward, acting like a seller who immediately discloses his lowest selling price in advance of the bargaining process, told his chief minister bluntly that he intended to marry Mrs. Simpson, no matter what. He would marry her either on or off the throne; he had no intention of giving her up; it was simply a question of no marriage, no coronation.

In a situation that required tact and skillful diplomacy, Edward chose bluster and open defiance. Too late, much too late, he sought advice from Lord Beaverbrook and Winston Churchill. Both told him that he could win if he would but employ patience and time. Since Mrs. Simpson's divorce would not become absolute until the following April 27, there could not possibly be any constitutional issue between king and cabinet until then because she was in no position to consider marriage. Wait, be patient, there can be no real crisis unless *you* precipitate it *now!*

But Edward VIII elected to precipitate just such a crisis. Realizing that he had lost in his thrust to make Wallis Simpson his queen, he asked the Prime Minister to submit the question to the Cabinet and the Dominions of whether he could marry her morganatically: She would become his wife only and not his queen; and their offspring, if any, would not be in line to succeed to the throne.

Beaverbrook and Churchill pointed out to the King that

he had delivered himself into the Prime Minister's mercy: "You have put your neck on the chopping block," they said, knowing full well that Cabinet and Dominions would reject the morganatic marriage. Still Edward pushed on to his own destruction. His downfall was sealed December 5, 1936, a little over ten months after his reign began; but because of the gentleman's agreement with the press, his abdication had already been agreed upon before the British people even knew that it was threatened.

Tragically, his political defeat and demise almost pulled Winston Churchill down with him to eternal extinction. Although Beaverbrook told Churchill, "Our cock won't fight," Edward neglected to tell Churchill he was withdrawing. When Churchill rose to speak in the Commons on behalf of the King, he was hooted down and forced to retire in complete rout. It was the greatest embarrassment suffered by a member of Parliament in modern history, almost dealing his political career a death blow.

After his night flight to France aboard the destroyer *Fury* (Wallis had fled a week earlier), Edward turned to one of his friends and said, "I always thought I could get away with the morganatic marriage!"

Edward VIII had completely misjudged the temper and attitude of his British subjects. Qualities that made him popular, particularly with his World War I compatriots as Prince of Wales, would not do at all for a king; but he could never really appreciate the distinction between the two jobs. As Prince of Wales, he accomplished much; as a king of England, he was a total flop.

In July, 1943, with the impetuosity and petulance of a small boy, embittered by six years of tortured exile, Edward VIII, Duke of Windsor, Royal Governor of the Crown Colony of the Bahamas, gratuitously decided to give personal direction to the investigation of the murder of Sir Harry Oakes.

For at least one episode in his life, no man is without the need of a giant eraser.

3

"The Woman I Love"

Edward VIII's presence in the Bahamas that July morning was due entirely to the woman he married.

"What's she got?"

Almost every informed woman in the entire world asked that question about Wallis Warfield Spencer Simpson at some time or other during 1936. Like an unannounced comet she swirled brilliantly across the world's pages (except in the British Isles); and there was scarcely a dry feminine eye any place on the globe when Edward VIII, on the night following his formal abdication, in the most widely-listened-to radio message in all history explained: ". . . you must believe me when I tell you that I have found it impossible to carry the heavy burden of responsibility and to discharge my duties as King, as I would wish to do, without the help and support of the woman I love. . . ."

No one knew at the time, nor would it have mattered, that Winston Churchill penned in the Churchillian oratorical ruffles and flourishes of the speech. All that really mattered was that the king on the greatest throne in the world, in the years between the wars when kingship really counted, threw it all up for this unknown woman.

"What's she got?" The women of the world were haunted by the potentials!

The answer lies in the superficial generalization that while she might appear to have nothing, she actually possessed everything.

She began prosaically enough as Bessie Wallis Warfield, seemingly the only fresh offspring of two professionally southern families in Baltimore. Her mother worried that she inherited a dangerous abundance of hot French blood from her Montague ancestors who were described as magnetic Bohemian Virginians. They were now penniless, their assets consisting principally of a recital of family deeds of the distant past.

The Warfields considered themselves considerably more stable and pointed with pride to a family tree of business leaders, bankers, professional men, and statesmen. They too were upon bad economic times, except for Uncle Sol who paid for Wallis' education, her social debut, and various trips in and out of the country.

It was only thirty-two years away from Appomattox at the time of her birth, so she grew up in an anti-Yankee aura that honored Jefferson Davis but denigrated Abraham Lincoln.

Her father died of tuberculosis when she was only five months old. Since he left no estate, her mother labored as seamstress and boarding-house entrepreneur to supplement Uncle Sol's generosities. His money saw her through private elementary and high schools, and she entered Oldfields School just outside Baltimore for "finishing."

The finishing schools, which regrettably are no more, emphasized the decorous social graces. The two basketball teams at Oldfields, for example, were not the Lions and the Tigers but Gentleness and Courtesy; the entire posture stressed etiquette, comportment, manners, taste, and a reverence for God. The principal text was *consideration of others,* how to make them feel important; and Dale Carnegie's successful aphorisms in *How to Win Friends and Influence People* were culled directly from finishing-school philosophy:

> Become genuinely interested in other people.
> Smile.
> Remember that a man's name is to him the sweetest and most popular sound of any language.

Be a good listener. Encourage others to talk about themselves.

Talk in terms of the other man's interest.

Make the other person feel important—and do it sincerely.

The only way to get the best of an argument is to avoid it.

Show respect for the other man's opinion. Never tell a man
he is wrong.

If you are wrong, admit it quickly and emphatically.

Begin in a friendly way.

Let the other man do a good deal of the talking.

Be a good listener!

Try honestly to see things from the other person's point of
view.

Be sympathetic with the other person's desires and ideas.

Dramatize your ideas.

Throw down a challenge.

Although it was a concept not discussed openly, the real
raison d'être of the finishing schools was to convert their
girls into young ladies capable of snaring and retaining a
man. They were schools for prospective wives, and there can
be no doubt that society suffered a loss of graciousness when
the finishing schools departed.

No young lady could ever amount to anything socially in
Baltimore unless presented as a debutante in the Bachelors
Cotillion; and Uncle Sol footed the bill for Wallis' "coming
out" in the 1914 season. Being a deb was a full-time job as
she swirled to balls and dances and hops at the Naval
Academy and as far away as Princeton.

Her cousin was married to the commander of the Naval
Air Station at Pensacola, Florida; and during a premeditated
visit and introduction, Wallis Warfield met and subsequently
married Earl Winfield Spencer, Jr., a Naval Academy grad-
uate intrigued by the new field of aviation. It was 1916, and
Wallis was nineteen.

The marriage was rocky, doomed from its beginning: Win
Spencer never learned to understand his wife's insatiable
compulsions to flirt, tease, and attempt to please almost every
man she met. This was an emotional personality trait over

which she had no more control than any mortal possesses over the law of gravity.

They struggled through World War I in Massachusetts and North Island, just outside of San Diego, where Spencer organized and developed the Navy's first air installation. He perhaps never really understood why, but he developed into a heavy, surly drinker. The more his wife flirted, the more he drank; and both partners to the marriage welcomed his transfer to Washington as a needed respite as she elected to remain behind in California.

There were a great many men Friday in her life during her winter in Coronado, California. She had decided that the role of Navy wife was not for her, nor was her current husband, and she was already philosophizing about the type of man she would next like to marry.

She returned to Washington, D.C., and easily became the extra woman in what she referred to as "a special paradise for women," the sophisticated diplomatic corps of the Harding Administration, where there were at least three dashing, charming, unattached men for every woman. Many of them were separated from their husbands for one reason or another or divorced. There were special embassy parties, Sunday-night suppers, picnics in the Virginia countryside, and cruises on the Potomac seven days and seven nights a week. A special group of young men labeled themselves the "Soixante Gourmets" and were considered *the* final word in social arrival; she was constantly with them.

Wallis Warfield Spencer shared an apartment with a number of practically unattached women, although they remained encumbered legally with still viable spouses. She romped through several love affairs, some with foreigners and some with natives, but found no one to meet her now rather rigorous specifications for remarriage.

She jumped at an opportunity to join her cousin on a trip to Paris; and within a matter of hours they were in liaison with the naval attaché and the first secretary of the American Embassy; and as Wallis says, "We became a foursome." She thought it might also be an opportune time to divorce Win

Spencer, but after shopping about, concluded that lawyers' fees in Paris were higher than she could afford. When her cousin decided to return home Wallis elected to remain because "by this time, I had many friends, not to mention several beaux, in Paris, so the decision was easy enough to make." She shared an apartment with two other American expatriates.

Her Paris interlude rocked along until 1924 when, running desperately short of funds and temporarily bored with her rigorous social schedule on the Seine, she agreed to join Win Spencer in Hong Kong, where he commanded one of the American gunboats prominent in Far Eastern diplomacy of the era. The reunion lasted only a few weeks. She says that Win's "old jealousies" returned as he accused her of "carrying on" with Navy and other Hong Kong men. As she moved out, he agreed to pay her $225 a month, a handsome and comfortable sum for the life practiced by "the old China hands" in a nostalgic period before Chiang Kai-shek or Mao Tse-tung were even heard of beyond local provincial borders. Spencer's place was quickly taken by a dashing Englishman; she moved from Shanghai to Peking, which she found "an ideal place for a woman with time on her hands and a secret sorrow in her heart." It was a "point in time where every woman could be Cinderella and midnight never struck."

The ratio of unattached males to females of comparable status, legal or practical, was at least ten to one; so there was never any lack of male attention or companionship. She seriously considered marriage with a British military officer and an Italian navy officer who went on to become an admiral; but her grasp of Peking and China was characteristically shallow: She seldom saw or met a Chinese man or woman, learned nothing of the country's history, and studied its art only through the offerings of merchants and artisans in the shops and bazaars.

Still, by this time at age twenty-seven, she was the skilled, practical master of the finishing-school-Dale Carnegie techniques of winning and influencing people. A genuine interest in other people was second nature to her now; her intellect was quick though not deep; but when you listen to your conversational partner talking primarily about himself, with your sincere encouragement, intellectual depth is not a prerequisite to being good company. His station in life is not particularly material; the techniques work well at all levels.

She was 5 feet 4 inches tall, of slender build as if constantly on a diet, but she actually had difficulty maintaining an adequate weight. From time to time, her almost jet-black hair rolled in gentle waves held in place by permanents; at other times, she parted it in the middle, pulling it back in a bun behind her head to exaggerate her unusually high forehead and deep-set eyes, making her nose appear broad and flat in full-face views. Her face was disproportionately long with a sharp, determined jawline, square and firm.

By no stretch of the imagination was she beautiful; so her attributes lay in her wit, her gaiety, her spontaneity, her conversational ability, her body, and her hedonistic philosophy that life should be lived for the never-to-be-recaptured moment at hand rather than for the morrow which, if it came at all, was uncertain and precarious.

Soon, as she had in Paris, she became bored with China after only a year and returned to Warrenton, Virginia, to establish the one-year-residency requirement for her divorce action against Spencer. She lived alone at the Warren Green, a commercial hotel whose clientele was principally traveling salesmen, but she was soon caught up "in the social whirl of the local horsy set," which included activities of the Fauquier Hunt and all its attendant social rigmarole. She often journeyed into Washington to resume her activities with the gay diplomatic corps, which was only too glad to welcome back a participant of her abilities and reputation.

She visited an old school friend in New York, where she met Mr. and Mrs. Ernest Simpson. Ernest had been born in the United States, the son of an Englishman operating the family shipping business out of New York. His Harvard tour was interrupted by service as an officer of the Coldstream Guards, one of England's most historic regiments, during World War I; and he quickly elected to become a British subject. Like a convert to the Catholic Church, a reformed alcoholic, or an addict who has sloughed off the smoking habit, Ernest became more English than any native-born Englishman alive. His wife was an American; but Wallis' friend told her conveniently that the Simpson "marriage was in difficulties, and Ernest was turning to her circle of friends." Wallis Spencer was now genuinely worried about what she would do when her divorce became final; and she obviously saw in Ernest Simpson the opportunity for an ingredient up to now missing from her life: *security*.

Ernest Simpson was a classic Englishman: tall, handsome, with black wavy hair, adequate black moustache, and sparkling eyes; he was well-read, an excellent dancer, dapper dresser, a man who knew and enjoyed the theater, and a man with a quiet and piercing wit and a broad, cosmopolitan outlook. Further, the family shipping business prospered, his salary was excellent, and his future prospects even brighter; so Bessie Wallis Warfield, the product of two proud, economically distressed, professionally Southern families, would not need to concern herself about money ever again if she could become Mrs. Ernest Simpson.

Simpson became surprisingly easy to snare; and after both divorces came through, Bessie Wallis Warfield Spencer became the second Mrs. Ernest Simpson in a dingy marriage-registry office in London in July, 1928.

Her financial security was attested by the flat on Bryanston Court with its antique furnishings and four servants; but she was not accepted in the social circle in which Ernest and his sister moved. Wallis was not only a foreign American; she was an irreverent nonconformist. It was an era in which British women were relegated to a secondary, inferior status: They were asked to look well when displayed on a pedestal, to perform well in bed, to be seen but not heard. Wallis' gaiety and vivacity so far outsparkled her English contemporaries that they viewed her jealously and with undisguised contempt. She acted "differently," not only as the continuous flirt and tease of all the men, but as the dazzling conversational catalyst of the drawing room.

Ernest Simpson was an amateur scholar, particularly of British history, and he determined to introduce Wallis to "the real England." He took her on carefully planned excursions out into the provinces, where they used an inspection of a castle or a cathedral as a springboard for Ernest's lecture. He was a gourmet and lingered patiently over his food and ale. It was not for Wallis. She was not interested in British history, its castles or cathedrals, since this sort of background information did not fit into her hedonic approach of charging life moment by moment.

She soon became utterly bored with the drab routine of her ordered existence. Although Ernest could have dipped into bank accounts and other investments, he ordained them to a frugal budget which he supervised by balancing the household books of account once each week. His temperament was as even as a straight line across a graph, his habits as regular as the chiming of Big Ben; he went to work at seven in the morning and returned punctually at seven each evening. His idea of a riotous evening was dinner at a friend's home with a few rubbers of bridge. He did not like to be up past ten or eleven o'clock any night of the week. He considered this ordered regimen the good life.

Wallis and Ernest, accompanied by her aunt from Baltimore, were once on a trip when a fire broke out in their inn after all had retired. As she dashed madly out of her room in nightgown and robe, through the smoke, Wallis turned to see Ernest neatly folding his clothes and placing them in his suitcase. She did not delay, and when he shortly failed to join her in the lobby, she tried to return to their room, thinking that he might have suffered a heart attack; but she was stopped by a fireman. Some minutes later, Ernest appeared in bowler hat, Coldstream Guard tie, his suitcase in one hand and his cane in the other. Everything about him, even in the emergency of the fire, was perfectly structured and neatly in place.

This was a far cry from the life of the gay and vivacious Navy wife in Pensacola and San Diego, the party girl of

Washington and Paris, Shanghai and Peking, Warrenton and the Soixante Gourmets.

When hedonist David Windsor encountered hedonist Wallis Simpson, both were convinced that their destinies were inflexibly joined. This overwhelming feeling of an inviolate, superhuman union perhaps explains Edward's unbelievably inept strategy and tactics when the abdication crisis was upon him. Although Ernest Simpson was too scholarly and sophisticated to consider himself a hedonist, he became the hapless victim of his two active protagonists; and love of wife slid into subservience to love of king.

As her affair with the Prince of Wales, then with him as King, rocketed onward, Wallis came to relish her status as celebrity and king's favorite. It is doubtful that she had any real grasp of the precariousness of her situation until the constitutional crisis progressed far beyond the point of no return. The King continually reassured her: "Don't worry, darling! I can handle everything!" To the man who could delay trains and divert aircraft by the snap of his finger, who could command ocean-going liners to change course and destination, and whose beck and call was heeded by millions of loyal subjects, the possibility that he could be dethroned appeared unreal. He shielded her from the realities of his impotent negotiations with Prime Minister Baldwin. Certainly the King did not tell her of the Prime Minister's implication that the government would not object to his continuing with her as his mistress; it was marriage, morganatic or regular, that the government and the people would never accept.

When Mrs. Ernest Simpson finally fled England for southern France a week before the King formally abdicated, he was already inflexibly committed to this course of action. Her attempts to withdraw from his life and return to China, perhaps sincere enough at the moment, came much too late to alter the situation in any way whatsoever. All that her ill-advised renunciation of the King and her efforts to get him to remain on the throne did was to make the King appear, in the eyes of his subjects, the pawn of an unscrupulous woman who had led him down a primrose path to official damnation.

Through it all, ministers and subjects alike wanted Edward VIII to remain; but no one, literally no one, could conceive of Wallis Warfield Spencer Simpson as queen of England, or even Edward's morganatic wife. The morganatic proposal smacked of nefarious underhandedness which no one was prepared to stomach. To remain, Edward must give her up.

Off they went, just before Christmas of 1936, these two, traveling separate routes to France and Austria to await the final Simpson divorce decree so that they could be formally and officially married in June, after George VI's coronation. Although Parliament awarded the ex-King absolutely nothing by way of settlement or stipend, the British rule of primogeniture guaranteed him a substantial personal estate that included the castles of Balmoral and Sandringham. When the King's personal estate was laboriously separated from the royal estates, his net worth was estimated in excess of two million dollars. Although far from impoverished, he was reduced from one of the world's wealthiest men to a mere millionaire. Instead of being a leading statesman whose words were made important by his status alone, he was now considered an unstable oddity whose statements were ridiculed and denigrated. He was forty-two and "the woman I love" thirty-nine, their positions so rigidly caricatured that if they did not live out their lives together as man and wife, they would become the laughingstock of the world, particularly Edward VIII, whose sacrifices appeared more substantial.

The world survived the aftermath of the abdication crisis, which H. L. Mencken described as "The greatest story since the Resurrection!" Everyone still asked, Why did he do it? and, What's she got? The answers did not come easily because of the nearness of the story-book events.

4

The Bahamian Exile

The Windsors chose France for their self-imposed exile. Legally, nothing prevented their living in England; but practically, they thought it would develop into an embarrassing and uncomfortable arrangement.

Both were galled and humiliated, Edward apparently more than Wallis, by George VI's specification that created a dukedom for Edward. The title "Duke of Windsor" with all its hereditaments went to him alone; it could not pass to any children he might sire. As the wife of a royal duke, Wallis could not be prevented from using the title Duchess; but she was specifically excluded from royal status. A commoner she was born, and a commoner she would remain, a social "nothing" in the eyes of the Royal Family and those interested and awed by court protocol. She was not entitled to a place on the preferential lists such as was accorded the wives of Edward's brothers, the Duchesses of Gloucester and Kent.

It was all salt in the open wounds augmenting Edward's understandable agitations and frustrations. He and the woman for whom he gave up his throne attempted to work out something resembling an acceptable life pattern. The glamor and glitter of court life were no more, and their luster as world figures wore thin. Friends who would have jumped at the royal nod twelve months earlier now found the trip to France

to visit them highly inconvenient. The evenings grew longer
as the autumn of their discontent approached; neither enjoyed reading for pleasure and their most intellectual chal-
lenges focused around the assembling of a complicated jigsaw
puzzle. Edward liked to work with his hands, however, and
developed into a skilled and knowledgeable gardener, which
surprised many of his friends who knew his attention span
to be short and weak.

In October, 1937, the Windsors leaped at an opportunity
to escape their ennui through a trip to Nazi Germany arranged by the ill-fated French industrialist Charles Bedaux,
at whose Château de Candé they were married only the preceding June. (Bedaux would commit suicide after World
War II to avoid trial as a German collaborator.)

The moment Edward VIII's miniscule reign began in January, 1936, Hitler and his sub-Führers considered Edward
a fortuitous asset to the German cause: His pro-German loyal-
ties molded in his youth, before World War I, were well
advertised; as Prince of Wales he had defied British constitutional decorum to publicly urge a *rapprochement* with
Germany; he was thought to be anti-France and known to
be anti-League of Nations; and he could be used advan-
tageously to keep England from entering the war, or so Hitler
and his lieutenants believed.

It may well be one of the cruelest misunderstandings in
history, but Wallis Simpson was considered so pro-German
by Hitler and his clique that Baron Joachim von Ribbentrop
was named German ambassador to England in the late summer for the specific purpose of cultivating Mrs. Simpson
(whom he had previously met socially), and through her to
reach the King. It was another of Hitler's ridiculous ploys to
keep England out of the impending European war.

Vicious rumors about Mrs. Simpson's pro-Nazi attitudes
helped diminish any popular sympathy for her that developed among Edward's World War I contemporaries. Even if
she could have jumped the hurdle of two living husbands to
reach the position of queen, her rumored pro-German pro-

pensities would certainly have made the English masses think
two and three times before giving her their affection.

Under the dubious auspices of Charles Bedaux then, the
Windsors entered Nazi Germany in 1937 for the announced
purpose of permitting public-housing buff Edward, Duke of
Windsor, to inspect Germany's progress under Hitler in this
field. The British Foreign Office elected to take no official
cognizance of the visit and instructed the British ambassador to Germany, Sir Nevile Henderson, to be conveniently
absent when they arrived. Their official guide was Robert
Ley, leader of the Nazi National Labor Front which em-
braced the "Strength through Joy" movement. They visited
Dresden, Nuremberg, Stuttgart, and Munich; they thrilled at
an afternoon with Field Marshal and Frau Göring, Hitler's
number two in command, the roly-poly head of the Luft-
waffe, at their impressive home named Karinhalle; Heinrich
Himmler, chief of the vicious Gestapo, wined and dined
them; Rudolf Hess, who was then emerging as Hitler's heir
apparent, charmed them and hosted one of their train rides;
Paul Joseph Goebbels, the club-footed propaganda master,
impressed them; and Rudolf Hess personally escorted them
to Berchtesgaden to meet Hitler.

The Duke's personal audience with Hitler ran three times
its scheduled length of half an hour. Der Führer honored
them with a lengthy tea in front of his massive Bavarian
fireplace in a room that looked out over unsurpassed mountain beauty. Wallis Warfield Spencer Simpson Windsor, whose
charisma captivated almost every man she met, could not get
Adolf Hitler even to bat an eye in her direction. She attributed her total failure to the language barrier between
them. Hitler's line to the Duke was simple but effective:
Bolshevism was the common enemy of both Germany and
England. It contained epidemic seeds for the destruction of
both their countries that were really united culturally and
historically. If England could not see its way clear to join
Germany in this inevitable, defensive war against Bolshevism,
England could do no less than maintain a laissez-faire atti-

tude while Germany fought not only her own but also England's war of salvation.

All in all, the Windsors' German mission proved fateful and prophetic. After World War II, both the Duke and the Duchess went to extreme pains, almost to the point of protesting too much, to abuse their Nazi hosts and play down the '37 autumnal visit. The visit and its aftermath of episodes three years later prompted the Duke to deny vehemently again after World War II any breach of loyalty whatsoever; and even the British Foreign Office was constrained to announce, through a most unusual formal statement, that the Duke's loyalty to Great Britain during the war never wavered.

There matters rested at the time Germany invaded Poland, September 1, 1939, to launch World War II. The proud, restless, disillusioned, and bitter exiles struggled valiantly to work out a life routine together to keep their great love affair from degenerating into a regrettable item of derision before the world.

When England entered the war two days later, the British ambassador to Paris conveyed an urgent message to the Duke from his brother, George VI, to return to England immediately. Months and years were to pass before the Duke and Duchess of Windsor learned why they were ordered home in such drastic haste. The King offered to send a personal plane for the Windsors, but the Duchess refused to fly; so they drove to the Channel, where a destroyer commanded by the future Lord Louis Mountbatten, who would be the last viceroy of India, awaited them. Randolph Churchill as an army officer was there as an emissary from his father, now First Lord of the Admiralty. They were ordered to cross the Channel in the darkness of night, under total blackout conditions, zigzagging unrelentingly to avoid submarines; but first, it was necessary to load some thirty suitcases and boxes of the Duchess's clothes and the Duke's personal possessions. His valet confided to Mountbatten that they were traveling unusually light in deference to the emergencies of the moment: They had hoped to bring twice this much as the basic necessities of life.

Back in London, there was absolutely no thaw in the attitudes of the Royal Family toward the Duchess, who remained sequestered in a friend's home while the Duke bargained with King and Prime Minister—not on what he could do for his country but on the social status of his wife. His rationalizations ran wild for one brief, shining moment: He was cheered on several occasions when people recognized him on the street, and he reckoned with the possibility that some way, somehow he might be called back to his position as king, or at least with a title that would permit him to sit at George VI's favored right hand. But such are the unrealistic vagaries of rationalized perceptions!

He returned to France as a major general of the army, attached to the British military mission at Vincennes, not far from Paris, where the Duchess volunteered her services to the French Red Cross. They reopened their home in Paris with the help of a major of the Black Watch, Gray Phillips, who was assigned to the Duke as comptroller. There they rode out the Phony War until June, when the German Blitzkrieg doomed France. The Duke rushed his Duchess to the safety of a hotel in Biarritz only to have German agents send her correct room number at the Hotel du Palais so that it could be announced over the French radio. Within minutes she was besieged by the curious, the friendly, and the psychotic alike. As the military situation became hopeless, the Duke picked up the Duchess in Biarritz; and they drove to southern France, where they closed up their villa and turned it over to the American Consul General for protection. They joined a caravan of other escaping Britishers and reached Spain, this time the Duke's valet thoughtfully providing a trailer to accommodate their dozens of suitcases and boxes of personal effects.

They were without passports, but unbeknown to the Windsors, their secret "friends," the Nazis, made their border crossing not only possible but relatively easy.

Now began one of the most intriguing plots of the entire war. There is absolutely no doubt that it took place; the problem is to know just what the Duke and Duchess were aware of and knowingly involved in, and what to assign to their innocent gullibility.

We do know that some high Nazi functionary, with the personal approval of Hitler and Baron Joachim von Ribbentrop, who had become foreign minister, concocted the scheme to hold the Duke and Duchess in Spain, hopefully with their voluntary consent and acquiescence, but by kidnapping and false imprisonment if need be, in an effort to force England out of the war.

The Nazi leaders labored under the delusion that only a relatively small "Churchill clique" had captured control of the British government, to force England to remain in the war against the wishes of a substantial majority of the public. If, therefore, it was possible to inspire a "peace party" to rise up and express the unqualified wishes of the majority of the people of England, Hitler could forget about his western front entirely and concentrate on his holy war against Russia. For many reasons, the Germans thought King Edward VIII the tailor-made answer to their plans. He had made no attempt to conceal his dislike for the war; this led the Nazis to believe that there would not have been a war with Great Britain had Edward VIII remained on the throne. As late as August 31, 1939, the Duke received a telegram from Berlin:

I THANK YOU FOR YOUR TELEGRAM OF AUGUST 27. YOU MAY REST ASSURED THAT MY ATTITUDE TOWARD BRITAIN AND MY DESIRE TO AVOID ANOTHER WAR BETWEEN OUR PEOPLES REMAIN UNCHANGED. IT DEPENDS ON BRITAIN, HOWEVER, WHETHER MY WISHES FOR THE FUTURE DEVELOPMENT OF GERMAN–BRITISH RELATIONS CAN BE REALIZED.

ADOLF HITLER

So the comic tragedians proceeded to their roles in the bizarre melodrama!

On June 23, 1940, the German ambassador to Madrid cabled the Foreign Office in Berlin for advice on what Spain

should do with the Duke and Duchess of Windsor; the Spanish foreign minister assumed that the Germans would be interested in detaining and establishing contact with the Duke.
Von Ribbentrop immediately replied to ask Spain to hold
the Duke and Duchess for two weeks, but not to make it
appear that Germany was directly involved. The Spanish
foreign minister visited the Duke the following day and then
advised the German ambassador that the Duke would not
return to England until a suitable position was guaranteed
him, as well as the cloud removed from the Duchess's personal
and social status; he would be willing to remain in Spain in
a castle furnished by the Franco government and sustained
by fifty million Swiss francs, more if need be, to be supplied
by Hitler. It should be pointed out parenthetically that while
the Duke acknowledges the fact that he met with various
Germans, Spaniards, and Portuguese during this Iberian interlude, he denies that he ever agreed to any terms with the
Nazis.

When British Intelligence became aware of the plot, Winston Churchill ordered Sir Samuel Hoare, British ambassador
in Madrid, to explain to the Duke that he was to return to
England immediately via flying boat to be sent to Lisbon.
Even the details of his housing in England were worked out:
The Duke and Duchess would use Eaton Hall, the home of
the Duke of Westminster, near Chester. Ambassador Hoare
noted a delicate urgency in the cables involving the Duke
and Duchess.

But as the Duchess phrased it: "David had his back up.
Still resentful over the cool reception accorded him on his
last visit to London, he made up his mind, without taking
me fully into his confidence, that certain conditions would
have to be clearly spelled out in advance of his returning.
One was the kind of job that the Government had in mind
for him—and he was eager to be put to work. The other
was the question of whether or not I was to be accorded
equality with the wives of his brothers."

So far, the reports of the Duchess and of the Nazis mesh
perfectly.

The Duke and Duchess remained in Madrid, entertained lavishly by Falangists, Franco's own Fascist party members, the German Embassy and Spanish Foreign Office gloating in their success in carrying out their parts in the plot. At this point, the Duchess became alarmed over the Duke's "stubbornness." Churchill and Beaverbrook were trying desperately to patch up enough planes for the R.A.F. in the Battle of Britain; the bombing ordeal of London threatened to shatter the morale of the people; Churchill was extracting "blood, toil, sweat, and tears" in his valiant effort to save not only the British Isles but Western civilization; and the Duke of Windsor belted him with cables from Madrid demanding equal social and Royal Family status for his Duchess.

This was his characteristic stubbornness that worried the Duchess!

Ambassador Hoare was finally able to move them to Lisbon, closer to a point of departure to England, all hoped. The Germans maintained the chase. Ramon Serrano Suñer, Spanish Minister of the Interior and brother-in-law of Generalissimo Franco, informed the Duke that the British Secret Service was set to murder him to keep him from leading a peace party in England and to keep him off the throne after Hitler conquered the British Isles. The Duke and Duchess were put up in Portugal at a home of Senhor Espirito Santo e Silva, who was in liaison with the German foreign minister. He urged the Duke to return to Spain to hold himself in readiness: Either England would call him back for great and honorable service, or the Germans would ask him to step in and take over peace negotiations at the proper moment.

Finally, Winston Churchill could take no more. He offered the Duke the position of Governor General of the Bahamas. Since the Duke would not consent to return graciously to the safety of the home island, he must remove himself to safety beyond the seas, to seven hundred islands, cays, and rocks only fifty miles from the coast of Florida. When the Duke balked at this final insult to his position and title, Churchill sent Sir Walter Monckton, then director general of the

Ministry of Information, and Edward VIII's own personal counsel during the abdication crisis, to disclose the Nazi kidnap plot to the Duke and give him a final ultimatum: Return immediately in the flying boats that still sat in the Lisbon harbor to whatever awaited him in England, position and social rank of wife to be decided later, or leave immediately for the Bahamas. Winston Churchill felt that he could take no further chances with this unrealistic ex-King whose only concession to the fact of war was his voluntary attempt to do without a valet, a most inconvenient error insofar as his wife was concerned.

Churchill felt the situation so critical that the British ambassador to Portugal prevailed upon the captain of the *Excalibur*, an American Export Lines ship, to divert its route to New York for a stop by Bermuda so that the Windsors could be put off there to catch a Canadian National Steamship boat to Nassau. Generalissimo Franco's brother, who was Spain's ambassador to Lisbon, made one last appeal to the Duke to return to Spain, telling him he was moving into exile and captivity by Churchill if he accepted the assignment.

The Germans circulated rumors that a time bomb was planted aboard the *Excalibur*, and a search delayed its departure; the automobile carrying all the ducal luggage was sabotaged, which added further delay. But finally, the man who rationalized himself into thinking that his marriage to Mrs. Simpson involved following a path of duty as distinguished from one of love stood on the fan deck of the *Excalibur* as she steamed out of the Lisbon harbor under the cover of darkness, at last realizing that he was headed into his final exile, never again to appear in any active role on the world scene.

Sir Harry and Lady Oakes were among the Bahamians who personally and officially welcomed the Duke and Duchess to Nassau on a humid mid-August afternoon in 1940. The Duchess's most salient recollection was watching the Duke's khaki uniform of a major general gradually become saturated with sweat; the Duke's concern was the dilapidated Govern-

ment House, with jalousied windows and wide verandas, that
would serve as their home for what he now knew would be
the war's duration.

There were hundreds of thousands of dwellings all over
the United States far larger and richer in design and appoint-
ments than this structure to which he and his Duchess now
moved in their forced exile. They lasted only a week in the
house before announcing that it was too depressing for them
to remain longer; and as the House of Assembly had already
voted fifteen hundred pounds to modernize Government
House, the Duchess imported an interior decorator from New
York, an old friend, and gave her carte blanche. The decorator
stripped the house of all its Victorian and Edwardian testi-
monials; but the renovation bill soon reached five thousand
pounds, which the House of Assembly paid grudgingly, realizing that this was but part of the expense of a *royal* royal
governor.

While Government House was under reconstruction, the
Royal Governor and his wife first lived as guests of Sir
Frederick Sigrist, and then Sir Harry and Lady Oakes turned
Westbourne over to them. Here they occupied the same bedroom used at other times by the Oakes; and the Duke slept
many nights in the bed where Sir Harry's battered and burned
body was found. Moreover, Sir Harry and the Duke became
fast friends, the Duke a genuinely appreciative audience as
Sir Harry described the hardships and death-defying rigors
of his prospecting days.

The Duchess enjoyed Lady Oakes' company, a concession
that she gave few other women in the Islands. It was a thin,
fragile society in which a handful of "leaders" moved and
dominated. Small-townish, back-biting, rumormongered, and
gossip-decimated, this white social club that called itself
Bahamian Society was rich but without any structural basis
whatsoever. It lived from luncheon invitation to club acceptance to dinner-dance entree; slurs and cuts and character
assassination were its *modus operandi;* an opportunity to cap-
ture the royal governor's wife, particularly one married to the
former king of England, was worth fighting over. In an ex-

pensive game of one-upmanship, the bickering lionesses often spent several hundred dollars to import hairdressers from Miami, flying them over and lodging them in the British Colonial, just for one coiffure for a function at which the Duchess would appear. It was all part of the calculated gamble to move upward to the highest social plateau.

Lady Oakes, delicate, sensitive, tasteful, poised, and charming, reigned a notch above the other women on the Island; and she was the closest to friend and confidante that the Duchess encountered.

Both Duke and Duchess taxed themselves to the extreme to keep from showing their total contempt for the Duke's position and his inferior subjects. They spent as much time as possible on the mainland of the United States, since the Duke's functions were primarily perfunctory and could be easily delegated to the Executive Council in his absence. Palm Beach, Baltimore, New York, and Washington saw much of the Windsors during the war years; and any warmth of feeling the Duchess might have gained was eroded further when word leaked out that she openly called the Bahamas her "Elba" and "St. Helena."

Their frustrations and bitterness increased when in March, 1942, Winston Churchill, learning from British Intelligence that the Nazi plot to kidnap the Duke and return him to Europe via German submarine still fomented, dispatched a company of Cameron Highlanders to form a defensive posture around Government House, complete with barbed wire entanglements and twenty-four-hour-a-day command posts. The Duchess quickly added "Bastille" to her terms of endearment for her place and period of confinement.

Now, as the Fates would have it, their travail was darkened by the burden of Sir Harry's murder. The Duke vacillated and waited, hoping for an inspiration that would not come, maintaining reluctant telephone contact with Westbourne and the superintendent of police, fearful to intervene and assume responsibility for the investigation, yet more afraid of the results if he did not act.

5

The Governor's Domains

Time refused to stand still while the Duke paced his room at Government House, brooding over his next move. The news from Westbourne increased the pressures: The cursory examination made by two doctors of Sir Harry's charred body, which still lay on the bed, suggested extreme brutality. There were four distinct skull wounds above and about Sir Harry's left ear; and the "wet" and "dry" blisters on the head, chest, abdomen, arm, and legs indicated that the burning began before death and continued afterwards.

By this time, Harold Christie was in a calmer mood, but his direct telephone conversations with the Duke added greater confusion to the already perplexing situation. The Duke must have castigated his own earlier inaction which denied him the opportunity to keep Sir Harry's murder purely a local matter, and every further moment of delay only increased the hazards. As he looked north over the tropical city, through its deceptively peaceful harbor and on beyond the deep blue Atlantico-Caribbean waters, he may well have pondered the violent heritage of the Islands, Sir Harry's murder being merely another transient episode.

The island of New Providence, on which Nassau rests, is one of "29 islands, 661 cays (pronounced 'keys') and

2,387 rocks." * Only thirty of the islands and cays that stretch some 750 miles in a southeasterly direction from the coast of Florida were inhabited in 1943 and sustained less than seventy thousand people, over half of whom lived on New Providence.

The economy and social structure, and particularly the character of the people, have been battered for centuries by what Michael Craton calls "the poverty of their terrain." At no point do the islands exceed two hundred feet in elevation; and on most, there is no land higher than fifty or one hundred feet above the water line. These shallow elevations are not sufficient to support biotic communities that form soil; so much of the area resembles the pock-marked, crater-blemished surface of the moon. The soil that has developed, in open defiance of sea, storm, porous rock, and tropical sun, is tantalizingly fertile; but it nestles in synthetic synclines called "banana holes" scattered about on top of foreboding limestone formations.

The supply of fresh water is another teasing element in nature's paradox. It rests by some quirk of nature in shallow pools close to the top of the ground, atop pools that have direct communication with the ocean waters. If the fresh-water wells are drilled too deeply or pumped too aggressively, they turn brackish from the invading salt water.

The terrain of the Bahamas is not all that has ingrained itself unalterably into the character of its people: The languid air, so thick with humidity at times that it can be rubbed between the fingers, saps the ambitions of its captives while threatening them continuously with tropical storms and hurricanes in which winds rip at 150 miles per hour.

The winds and the sea and the air all work against the land in perpetual defiance to prevent the Islands from sustaining more than a mere handful of people. The one word imbued by genes and chromosomes into every native son is "survival," and the means by which or the persons against whom survival is attained are irrelevant.

* Michael Craton, *A History of the Bahamas* (London: William Collins Sons & Co., Ltd., 1968).

Nature deliberately baited a deceptive snare with the Bahamas. Their waters boast the most spectacular variety of color in all the oceans: deep purple from the reefs; the blues, greens, yellows, and grays of the thick and expansive strata of cobalt; the turquoise, emerald, gold, yellow, and silver from the shallower banks and layers of sand; the darker greens from the coral formations; and the grays from the beds of the brain sponges.

Columbus was understandably deceived when he made his first landfall in the New World on October 12, 1492, on what is now called the island of San Salvador (formerly Watling Island). He wrote about the natives to Queen Isabella:

> And they knew no sect nor idolatry; save that they all believed that power and goodness are in the sky, and they believed very firmly that I, with these ships and crews, came from the sky; and in such opinion, they received me at every place where I landed, after they had lost their terror. And this comes not because they are ignorant: on the contrary, they are men of very subtle wit, who navigate all these seas, and who give a marvelously good account of everything—but because they never saw men wearing clothes nor the like of our ships. And as soon as I arrived in the Indies, in the first island that I found, I took some of them by force, to the intent that they should learn [our speech] and give me information of what there was in those parts. And so it was, that very soon they understood [us] and we them, what by speech or what by signs; and those [Indians] have been of much service. To this day I carry them [with me] who are still of the opinion that I come from heaven. . . . And they were the first to proclaim it wherever I arrived; and the others went running from house to house into the neighboring villages, with loud cries of "Come! Come to see the people from heaven!"

Juan Ponce de León was also hoodwinked, believing that he had in truth found the Fountain of Youth in the Islands of the Biminis; * but he was killed at age sixty-one by an

* Florida also lays claim to Ponce de León's Fountain of Youth.

Indian before he could found his own colony to partake daily of the elixirs of the Fountain.

It is a violent and turbulent history, this inheritance of the Bahamas!

The Spaniards never really settled the Bahamas; they only ravished them. Carrying away the native Lucayans (a tribe of the Arawaks) to work them until they fell dead from exhaustion and malnutrition in the gold mines of Hispaniola (Haiti-Dominican Republic), fostering the natives' belief that the white men were gods from heaven, the pious Spaniards enticed away the entire population, leaving only eleven, less than a dozen, by telling them that they were being taken to join their departed ancestors in the perfect life beyond the sea.

For the next hundred years, more or less, the Spanish and English fought sporadically over these "prized" islands while such men as Sir John Hawkins, the first Englishman to traffic in African slaves, Sir Humphrey Gilbert, Sir Walter Raleigh, and John Rut advanced English colonization under the banner of Mercantilism. Sir Francis Drake was also a late swashbuckler, as were the English privateers—Newport, Middleton, Frost, Wood, King, and Roberts—who buzzed like bees around the honey tree of the Bahamas and Florida Straits to prey on Spanish galleons.

It was 1629 before England formally laid claim to the Bahamas and chartered a company of proprietors who were nothing more than licensed exploiters.

For the next hundred years, the pattern cut a monotonous sameness: neglect and total apathy at home, rogues and pirates in the Islands.

Modern-day Bay Street is still the site of Black Beard's Tavern, a colorful testimonial to the thirty-three-year period between 1684 and 1717, when the Bahamas were ruled in cruel totalitarianism by a mangy band of villains who literally took over the formal government. Because its harbor was open at two ends, New Providence Island rivaled Tortuga and Jamaica as a haven for the men who flew the skull and crossed bones on the black flag from the masts of stolen galleons. For a time, as England, France, and Spain bled themselves to exhaustion on the Continent, some two thousand pirates out of a total island population of 2,200 people tortured and pillaged, drank and whored through a synthetic prosperity that made the lot of the few honest men almost impossible to bear.

A statue of Governor Woodes Rogers stands in front of the British Colonial Hotel. It was Rogers who broke the rule of the pirates and re-established legitimate government in the Bahamas; but his efforts toward enforcing legal respectability won him only enemies, since the suppression of lawlessness threw the Islands into a devastating depression. Woodes Rogers, a former privateer himself, exhausted his own personal fortune in efforts to feed the starving and pay the salaries of government employees; but his thanks were years of confinement in a debtors' prison and an unknown place of burial following his death on New Providence from heartbreak and exhaustion.

The Bahamas seldom honor the good.

Ancient Fort Charlotte stood on the highest point of land in Nassau to attest the greed, arrogance, and amoral acquisitiveness of the royal governors during the rest of the eighteenth century.

The successors of Woodes Rogers are noted only for their personal cynicism, official corruption, and dishonest avarice. Listlessness and boredom, endemic throughout the Islands, were accompanied by ignorance and disease.

Economic salvation for a period occurred in 1756, when war again broke out between England and France, leading to the re-establishment of Nassau as a privateering base. It was a new generation of Blackbeards and their nefarious confederates all over again: theft, violence, official bribery, and collusion. The ending of the war between England and France produced the same tragedy: The Bahamas were hurled into a fierce, dehumanizing depression with discord and discontent at all levels; but redemption was another war, this time the War of American Independence. The years between 1776 and 1783 became the most profitable of all pri-

vateering times in the history of the Islands; but Cornwallis'
surrender at Yorktown forced not only the routine collapse
of the economy, but a phenomenon that would change its
history for all time to come.

A group of Loyalists to King George III poured into the
Bahamas, escaping the victorious colonies. Especially they
came from the Carolinas and Virginia, bringing their African
slaves, and attempted to establish a plantation economy on
the sparse, thin soil of the fragile Islands.

The years after the Loyalist invasion were characterized by
sulfurous acrimony. The Southern planters were arrogant
meddlers, looking with supercilious disdain upon the privateering community which offered no hospitality; but this
strange amalgam was the genesis of the intermixed population who call themselves Bahamians.

The economy was again rescued by war, this time the
French Revolution, which brought renewed prosperity by the
ageless means of privateering. Prosperity rose and fell mer-
curially during the Napoleonic years; so the roguish Bahamians devised a peacetime substitute for open privateering.
They lived for the most part by salvaging "wrecked" vessels
that theoretically ran aground on the treacherous coral reefs
of the passages among the Islands. Lloyds of London, however, was highly suspicious that the 257 boats "wrecked" in
1814 all met their fate by accident and poor navigation; they
rightly suspected official and unofficial assistance and
cooperation.

By this time, the religion of piracy, wrecking, salvage, and
parasitic preying on the property of others was so deeply
ingrained in the spirit of the people that it behaved like
malaria. (In times of general good health, the malaria or-
ganisms retreat from the blood stream to hide in the spleen;
but when the body's resistance is low, the microbes are in
ever-present threat to re-establish active illness.)

Nassau next became a thriving slave market which the
Royal African Company used as a sales station to supply
blacks to most of Spanish America; so the Bahamas were
deeply hurt by the Emancipation Act of 1834, especially the

Southern planters whose exhausted, paper-thin soil refused
to push up stalks of cotton. All the Islands were now on a
plane of actual starvation. Her Majesty's government in London continued the same apathetic approach that had measured Bahamian relations for the preceding two hundred
years.

Somehow though, for reasons which cannot be readily explained, the English Common Law courts became so firmly
established that writers of the day lauded the zealous fair-
ness of the British judges, all of whom came from England,
Ireland, or Scotland. It was a tribute to the mechanics of the
system itself that it could flourish in a totally hostile environment.

The American Civil War saved the Bahamas from complete starvation in 1861. Real-life Rhett Butlers made blockade running a thrilling, dramatic, profitable game. While
Queen Victoria looked the other way in her pious effort to
exhibit neutrality during the war, some two to three hundred swift, low-lying sloops, schooners, and clippers darted
between Yankee picket boats in two- and three-day runs to
Savannah, Charleston, or Wilmington. Using the Royal Victoria Hotel as their headquarters command post, these dashing Southern adventurers could carry $200,000 to $300,000
worth of cotton to the Bahamas, where they exchanged it for
ammunition, medical supplies, critical machine tools, and a
few items of luxury for the Scarlett O'Haras: silks, laces, per-
fumes, and jewelry.

The risks and losses of the blockade runners were astronomical; so were their profits. It was an unprecedented boom
time for the Bahamas, but then came the inevitable bust
following Lee's meeting with Grant at Appomattox. The sudden flood of money produced by the Civil War disappeared
as rapidly as it came; and there was an additional immigra-
tion of unreconstructed Southerners with their politically
liberated but still economically dependent slaves. The population ratio in the Bahamas reached approximately nine
blacks to each white.

For the next fifty years after the Civil War, the warehouses along Bay Street stood empty and rotting; the Royal Victoria Hotel deteriorated so rapidly that its owners could not even give it away, much less sell it. Sailors and non-sailors alike returned to "wreckage" and "salvaging" operations to survive. They fought and cursed like starved vultures over the sixty-three vessels that were mysteriously "wrecked" in Islands waters in 1866 alone.

Craton says that "during the last quarter of the nineteenth century, the Bahamian depression seemed too bad to be true." Everything failed: The conch-shell exports to be made into cameo brooches in France and Italy disappeared because brooches went out of style; an infant cigar industry perished because of the inferior quality of tobacco raisable on the Islands; the natives were so indolent that an ambitious shipbuilding program never turned out its second vessel; tomatoes looked like a promising agricultural crop, but they could not be shipped to the American mainland without rotting; the sisal (rope fiber) mills went into bankruptcy; even the sponge trade collapsed.

World War I more or less passed by the Bahamas with the parenthetical footnote that of the first seventy men who came forward to volunteer for overseas duty, only thirty were fit to go. The last years of the war placed the "Bandits of Bay Street" in their own milieu: World shortages of bread, meat, sugar, oil, butter, and kerosene precipitated a black-market trade which was just getting profitably under way when the Armistice was signed in 1918.

The ultimate restoration of the Bahamas proved to be the Eighteenth Amendment to the United States Constitution.

Suddenly, the quagmire of poverty became the paved street of endless wealth that paled the profits from the Civil War blockade runners into comparative insignificance. Overnight, twenty-eight huge liquor combines sprang up in Nassau; fleets of smaller motor launches commenced the fifty-to-seventy-mile run from the Biminis and Grand Bahama to the Florida coast; larger vessels made "Rum Row" bubble white in their wakes as they sped to thirsty Philadelphia, Manhattan, Long Island, Newport, and Boston.

"Re-exporting" Scotch from Scotland, gin from London, and rum by the cask from all over the West Indies was officially sanctioned by the Bahamian government through the imposition of an excise tax. In 1922, "re-exported" liquor valued at just under $10,000,000 was subject to tax, a 1,000 percent increase over 1921; whereas 486 ships of all classes with a combined tonnage of 81,129 tons left the Bahamas in 1919, 1,681 ships with 718,110 tons filed exit manifests in 1922.

The Civil War blockade runners had headquartered in the Royal Victoria Hotel, but the command posts for the rum-runners were the Lucerne Hotel on Frederick Street and the Bucket of Blood on George Street. The invading social types from the mainland included gangsters of all varieties: extortionists, strong-arm thugs, burglars, robbers, confidence men, the psychopaths with their assorted molls and hangers-on, amateurs and professionals, organized and unorganized. They paraded about Bay Street and its environs, flashing incredible rolls of thousand-dollar bills; they drank and whored and gambled; they carved up the bootlegging and rumrunning operations into cartels just as Capone, O'Banion, Moran, and O'Donnell were splitting Chicago. They even held an annual Bootleggers Ball where Guys and Dolls moved in real class.

Profits were astronomical. A load of Scotch whisky that cost $175,000 in Nassau brought $375,000 when transferred to waiting ships outside the three-mile limit of Boston and New York harbors. When the load was delivered to the waiting bootlegging mobs on shore, its price now approached $700,000; and the consuming "dry" American public ultimately paid between $2,000,000 and $2,500,000 for the prize.

The first families of Bay Street suddenly became liquor magnates. Harold Christie was one of them.

The economy sputtered and hit rock bottom when the Eighteenth Amendment to the United States Constitution was repealed by the Twenty-first. As before, when the Bahamas rode in the bottomless trough of Depression, no one could figure out where the monies of the preceding boom disappeared.

Harry Oakes' arrival in Nassau at the enticement of Harold Christie coincided almost exactly with the demise of the Prohibition-inspired prosperity from the States.

The social and economic structure of the Bahamas can only be described as parasitic. The Bahamas are like the birds who follow the crocodile to feed off the insects he attracts, or the stray dog whose fortunes depend upon uncertain handouts from a strange master's table. Not being able to sustain themselves internally, the Bahamas can exist only on the crises and internal unrest of other nations.

Now, the former king of England ruled these Islands, cays, and rocks as little more than a titular, ceremonial royal governor; and without training, knowledge, insight, or intuition into any facet of crime detection, he felt that he must inject himself into the Oakes matter for his own self-protection.

6

The Futile Attempt
at Concealment

At 10:50 A.M., the Duke's ordeal of indecision ended. He took what must have seemed to him a logical course of action. Reaching for the telephone, he placed an overseas call to Captain Edward Walter Melchen, chief of the homicide bureau of the Miami Police Department. Melchen, who claimed five hundred homicide investigations to his credit, later testified that he did not think the Royal Governor's request particularly unusual: A leading citizen of the Bahamas had apparently committed *suicide;* would Captain Melchen fly over to Nassau to confirm the details so that there would be no problems?

The Duke knew Melchen from prior visits to Miami when, for some reason, the captain of homicide detectives was assigned to protect him from the crowds as a sort of personal bodyguard. The Duke did not tell Melchen the name of the dead "leading citizen," nor did he volunteer any details of the death, leaving Melchen completely in the dark as to what exactly might be expected of him. Melchen elected to bring with him Captain James Otto Barker, Superintendent Detective of the Bureau of Criminal Investigation of the Miami Police Department, whose responsibilities included fingerprint records and criminal and technical investigations.

Within two hours these men were airborne; and by two o'clock that afternoon they were at Westbourne, where **Sir**

Harry's body still lay on the stained bed. No one dared order its removal until four o'clock in the afternoon, some nine hours after Christie first reported the death.

At this stage, it is impossible to know exactly what the Duke knew about Sir Harry's death as distinguished from what he only surmised. We know that he talked to Police Commissioner R. A. Erskine-Lindop by telephone several times before he placed his call to the American police. We know that he and Harold Christie engaged in a lengthy telephone conversation during which Christie had ample opportunity to brief the Duke on the night's horrifying events.

It is impossible to explain why the Duke thought that he could pass off Sir Harry's death as a suicide, even with the helpful complicity of the American police. Doctors Quackenbush and Fitzmaurice, who made the external examination of the body, plus an untold number of Bahamian police officers including Commissioner Erskine-Lindop, and even the rank amateurs who viewed the body, all recognized immediately that the death was *murder* in its grimmest form; it was physically impossible for the head wounds to have been self-inflicted, and there was no earthly way for Sir Harry to have burned himself in such a bizarre manner.

Within minutes after their arrival at Westbourne, Captains Melchen and Barker also concluded that it would be impossible to comply with the Duke's instructions "to confirm the details" of a *suicide*.

What Captains Melchen and Barker really knew of the case at the time they began their "investigations" evades realistic speculation. Both are dead, remaining close-mouthed about the Oakes case to the end.

What actually happened? Who killed Sir Harry Oakes?

Reliable confidential informants report that in the mid-afternoon of Wednesday, July 7, 1943, a sixty-seven-foot power cruiser, a speedy veteran of hundreds of rum runs during the Prohibition era to Philadelphia, Long Island, and Boston, cleared the eastern coast of Florida on a direct course to Nassau. Three of the five men aboard knew the

Nassau harbor and dock area well, for they too had played the rumrunning game during the Roaring Twenties and early Thirties. All were minions, faithful "soldiers," of Meyer Lansky, the financial genius of Organized Crime. Their unswerving loyalty to their leader stemmed from what intelligence officers at all levels—local, state, federal, and international—who make a career of Organized Crime watching know: Lansky is a unique pioneer whose phenomenal success rests upon his intellectual powers, the forcefulness of his personality, and his lack of hesitancy to resort to violence and murder when required—a man whose influence can never be replaced when he dies. One of the world's wealthiest men, he could rank ahead even of J. Paul Getty or Howard Hughes.

Organized Crime recognizably began in the United States in 1931, a year which saw the culmination of the Castellammarese War," a fifteen-month battle of blood between two well-defined groups. One was the legions of the "Moustache Petes," also called the "Old Moustaches," the Italian-born overlords who ran the Italian and Sicilian criminal gangs starting in the later years of the nineteenth century. Their formidable adversaries were the "new rebels," the ghetto-born, violence-oriented, first-generation Italians and their non-Italian *associates*, principally the ghettoized Irish and Jews. The young breed could not wait for power and profits.

The great power battle, starting in New York and soon spreading across the United States, resulted from death sentences passed by underworld czar Giuseppe ("Joe the Boss") Masseria upon a group of Sicilians who came originally to the United States from areas around the Gulf of Castellammare in northwestern Sicily. In one two-day period alone, forty members of the Old Moustaches generation and their younger rivals were slaughtered, the police standing by helplessly. An apathetic public felt no remorse as gangland's bosses killed each other off, including Masseria himself, who was betrayed by some of his own most trusted lieutenants.

Masseria's chief rival, Salvatore Maranzano, working with the leaders of the "young generation" rebels, initiated a peace meeting attended by an estimated five hundred Sicilians and Italians, and chose that opportunity to proclaim himself "The Boss of All Bosses," the self-assumed title that would cost him his life. There were enough aspiring leaders left who coveted their own cells and spheres of operations. They feared a Mr. Big who would hold the power of physical and economic life and death over his subservient fiefs; so they shot Maranzano to death on September 11, 1931, then cut his throat to instill fear in anyone who might think of proclaiming himself a *capo de tutti capi* in the future.

In an effort to prevent the rise of a single crime czar, Charles (Lucky) Luciano, nee Salvador Lucania, sat down with other top gang bosses and established a Council of Six to inaugurate policy, especially to arbitrate disputes among the self-contained "families" so that the internecine warfare would not decimate all of the criminal gangs. Within a year, Lucky Luciano's Council of Six was expanded into a National Commission, whose membership now alternates between nine and twelve men. Organized Crime became a flourishing reality. Depending on the area, it is also called the Syndicate, the Mob, the Outfit, and the Organization.

This Commission controls "Cosa Nostra," the Italian gangs of 5,000 to 7,500 *official* Italian members in twenty-four to twenty-six * "families" in twenty-four cities in the United States. There are an equal number of non-Italian *associate* members, not eligible for official membership because of their ethnic origin, but who are rigorously aligned with the Cosa

---

* The actual number of Organized Crime *families* in the United States remains a matter of subjective debate among intelligence officers at all levels of government. Most agree that there are twenty-four *families;* a few say twenty-six. Those who argue the figure "twenty-four" insist that the additional two *families* are only splinter groups who do not deserve separate status. The Nixon Administration is downgrading the "family" approach as well as the ethnic genesis, concentrating on prosecuting *all* persons engaged in criminal activity in a community, regardless of his exact rank within the Organized-Crime framework, be it *official* or *associate* member.

And there are still some who argue that no such entity as Organized Crime exists.

Nostra "families." All told, the official Cosa Nostra gangs and their intimate associates, a hard core of between 10,000 and 15,000 regulars, employ perhaps 150,000 to 250,000 people in illegal *and* legitimate operations and businesses that may gross sixty billion dollars annually.

Meyer Lansky was not eligible for membership in the Mafia since he was not Sicilian; he could not aspire to Cosa Nostra boss ("the Don") as he was not Italian. Historically, for reasons that still draw forth speculations from sociologists and psychologists, the membership of organized crime is predominantly Sicilian (Mafia), Italian (Cosa Nostra), and Irish and Jewish (associates of Cosa Nostra), although all races and nationalities are represented in varying numbers. Though not eligible for formal, official membership in either Mafia or Cosa Nostra, the Irish and the Jews have worked profitably with the Italians and Sicilians. One explanation for this heavy ethnic pattern in Organized Crime is that these groups were so brutalized by oppression in Europe that they could respond only with violence to survive. Their efforts in the New Country were seriously constricted, and their heritage of violence over the centuries caused a comparatively small number of the overall group to use Organized Crime as the vehicle for escaping the humiliations and dehumanizing shackles of the American ghettos.

Lansky's financial genius lay in his foresight, his ability to approach and corrupt public officials at all levels, and his incomparable ingenuity in moving great amounts of cash from one country to another.

He was the first to see the postwar potential of Las Vegas, became one of the pioneer owners of the Flamingo Hotel, and laid out the cartel divisions of territory in Las Vegas among rival Cosa Nostra "families" all across the country.

Lansky was already gambling czar in Florida when his international experience began just before World War II. He negotiated a contract with Cuban dictator Fulgencio Batista for the privilege, with a substantial fee to Batista, of operating Cuba's gaming casinos Sans Souci, Montmartre, and Tropicana, with seasonal operations at the Nacional. He is the man who arranged to export Las Vegas-style gambling to England after the war, and almost obtained a monopoly on gambling in Jamaica, but his bribed member of Parliament could not quite put it across.

Although a resident of Tel Aviv since August, 1970, Lansky is presently in the news. He and a number of associates were indicted by a federal grand jury in Washington for conspiring to channel $200,000 of Flamingo Hotel proceeds through the Albert Parvin Foundation to Lansky. This is the foundation of which Supreme Court Justice William O. Douglas served as the $12,000-a-year president until he resigned in 1969, although Douglas denies knowledge of the $200,000 payment to Lansky made during his tenure as president. (There are other federal indictments now outstanding against Lansky which make his return to the United States a matter of considerable doubt.)

Early in 1943, Lansky already anticipated the unlimited potentials of big-time gambling in the Bahamas, before even thinking of Las Vegas. Less than half an hour from Miami by air, two hours from New York, and within easy strike of the cruise ships, the Bahamas possessed enough "foreign" mystical flavor to draw eager gamblers from the United States, who would rush pell-mell to lose their money if properly wined, dined, entertained, and bedded.

Meyer Lansky and Harold Christie were acquaintances from the rumrunning days of Prohibition, although never formal business associates. It was easy, however, for Lansky to arrange a meeting with Christie, which took place in Palm Beach during one of Christie's many trips to the mainland. Lansky's proposition was spectacularly promising: He would build and operate a modern resort hotel with a plush casino if the Bahamian government would grant him a gambling monopoly. In exchange, he would pay either a lump sum of one million dollars or a percentage commission on gross receipts to Christie and whoever else was required to make the license possible.

Christie jumped at the opportunity. A promoter at heart, he could see his dream flourish of developing the Bahamas into a rival of Palm Beach, Biarritz, Rio, and the Riviera. The term "jet set" had not been coined, but Christie visualized the economic potentials of a postwar boom in travel and tourism which would exploit not only a jet-set class of idle rich but, even more important, the average working man who could not withstand the pull of the gambling casino in the lush and evil Bahamian setting.

Upon his return to Nassau, Christie's legal advisers assured him that the gambling monopoly could be legally conferred by the nine-member Executive Council; it would not need House of Assembly approval. The signature of the Royal Governor, of course, was required to implement the action of the Executive Council.

Christie correctly concluded that he needed the affirmative support of two other persons to insure the agreement with Lansky: the Duke of Windsor and Sir Harry Oakes, now the Island's number-one citizen.

Anticipating difficulty in obtaining Sir Harry's consent, Christie first presented his cause to the Royal Governor and received his enthusiastic endorsement. Christie's sales pitch was easy and accurate: The development of the gambling spa would attract an unprecedented tourism, which could save the Islands from the inevitable bust-following-boom of World War II that could be plotted in advance on the graph of Bahamian history as accurately as the course of the planets in their orbit about the sun.

At that time, more than a quarter of a century before the writing of *The Godfather*, no one outside the Italian community, Organized Crime participants, and a limited few intelligence officers in a small number of investigative agencies even recognized the words *Mafia* or *Cosa Nostra*. They simply were not in the vocabulary! The stealth and secrecy with which these criminal groups operate continue to mystify not only law-enforcement personnel but sociologists and psychologists as well.

The Duke probably did not know of Lansky's unique associations with the Mafia and Cosa Nostra, although Christie was well aware of the crime cartel with which he dealt. He may have known it only as the Syndicate, the Mob, the Organization, since he was never even an associate member. To the Duke, Lansky appeared a rather intriguing, dramatic businessman with a sound financial proposition that offered economic salvation for the Islands in the postwar years.

The informants are not in a position to know what, if any, financial terms were discussed between Harold Christie and the Royal Governor. Any guess on this point is nothing more than reckless speculation. The Duke would have been intrigued by any novel activity to break the monotony of his exile; and this alone would have been motive enough for his easy acquiescence.

Having sold the Duke on Lansky's innocent and financially promising business offer, Christie next broached the matter to Sir Harry. The informants cannot know what transpired during these conversations between Christie and Sir Harry, but they report that Christie advised Lansky of Sir Harry's approval. With the support of the three leading citizens in the Bahamas, each in his own critical zone of influence, Lansky assumed that his efforts would reach fruition and began to plan accordingly: By the end of the war, when building shortages of all types had passed, he would construct his plushest of all the plush resort hotels and gambling casinos. At this time, Las Vegas was little more than a desert shopping center, an old cow-and-mining town where stud poker could be played in a few greasy-spoon restaurants, and slot machines were flagrantly exhibited in the public rooms of most buildings. Only two minuscule casinos operated downtown; the Strip was still open, arid desert.

The informants do not know exactly why Sir Harry changed his mind and decided to oppose the gambling license to Lansky. He did not need the money that a financial arrangement with Lansky might bring him; as a matter of fact, he was busy giving away money in his own schemes of private philanthropy. The most plausible speculation is that upon second thought he envisioned Nassau trampled by thousands of tourists who would drastically ruin his tropical paradise on which he hoped to spend the remainder of his life

in comparative peace. Anyway, Lansky became furious upon
learning that Sir Harry had backed out of the arrangement.
Only a limited number of persons anywhere in the world
knew *at that time* that a man wrote his own death warrant
by reneging on a financial deal with the Mafia, the Cosa
Nostra, or an intimate *associate* like Meyer Lansky. No one
has ever accused Harold Christie of having detailed information about Lansky's plans for Sir Harry.

Lansky sent several blunt and positive warnings to Sir
Harry, admonitions that evolved into threats about which
there could be no misunderstanding: Sir Harry Oakes must
perform according to his original agreement with Lansky
or run the risk of death. Lansky might have settled for Sir
Harry's promise to take a passive, neutral role when the
matter of the license came before the Executive Council for
approval; but by this time the crotchety, vile-tempered, overbearing side of Oakes' personality had asserted itself. He
answered this Lansky—whoever he thought he was—that he
would not bend to his threats, would vigorously oppose the
contract, and wanted to hear nothing further on the matter.
It was High Noon between two rugged, forceful belligerents.

By this time, fully aware of the gang violence in the United
States during Prohibition, Harold Christie became genuinely
worried and futilely attempted the role of peacemaker. No
one accuses Christie of any actual knowledge that Oakes'
murder was specifically planned by Lansky; Christie's concern stemmed spontaneously from his general knowledge that
criminal gangs played rough and for keeps when their
wishes were thwarted. Lansky did agree to send one of his
chief lieutenants to Nassau for a face-to-face confrontation
with Sir Harry, and this man was one of the party of five
aboard the power cruiser that docked in the Nassau harbor
Wednesday evening, July 7. It tied up at the quay, only a
stone's throw from Rawson Square, the courthouse, the House
of Assembly, and the Executive Council Building.

Harold Christie was spending the night with Sir Harry at
Westbourne. Their unexpected dinner guests departed just
before eleven o'clock, and by prearrangement, Oakes and

Christie entered Christie's station wagon which had been parked near the golf club. They drove quickly to the quay and boarded the cabin cruiser for the fateful conference with Lansky's lieutenant. It lasted only a few minutes, as Sir Harry launched into a vindictive, profane tirade, telling the lieutenant what he could tell Lansky, what Lansky could do, and how Lansky should join the lieutenant in going to a well-adjectived hell.

The informants do not know exactly what the reply was, but the lieutenant decided there was no chance of changing Sir Harry's mind. With an almost imperceptible nod of his head, he signaled one of the three "button" men aboard the cruiser, who suddenly struck Sir Harry's head with a four-pronged winch lever. Each prong was triangularly shaped, the four arranged in two symmetrical rows so that the first two prongs were two inches apart, the second two one-and-a-half inches apart, and the second row two inches behind the first.

Sir Harry collapsed immediately while Harold Christie became paralyzed in terror, his worst general fears now particularized in this assault upon his great and good friend, the last person in the world next to his mother whom he would wish to be injured.

The lieutenant assured Christie that Sir Harry was not dead, only knocked unconscious to teach him a lesson. Two of the men now half-carried, half-dragged Sir Harry's limp body up onto the quay, through the mud of the street, and laid him face down in the station wagon. One returned to the boat and the other slipped into the driver's seat, ordering Harold Christie, still in a state of shock, to sit beside him in the front passenger seat and direct him to Westbourne.

For perhaps the next hundred hours, Harold Christie operated like a child's complicated mechanical toy whose remote control was only halfway knocked out. He is perhaps more to be pitied than censured since he too had drifted onto treacherous shoals which deprived him of anything resembling control. Round and round he swirled in his own eddies of half-truth and implication and insinuation until he deprived himself once and for all of any opportunity to grasp at the lifebelt of truth. Fear and the threats of fear are great inhibitors to the truth.

When they reached the house, Lansky's man ordered Christie to help remove the body from the wagon and take it up to Sir Harry's bedroom. They dragged the body up the hall stairway. (The following morning when the cook came to work, she called the attention of the police to the color of mud, sand, and debris on this stairway, different from any she had ever seen before from around Westbourne; but the police conveniently ignored her intelligence offer.)

By the time they reached the bedroom, both Christie and the "button" man realized Sir Harry was dead. Lansky's man had the presence of mind to give directions while Harold Christie oscillated between paralyzed shock and frantic panic. They laid the body on the floor, undressed it, and slipped on Sir Harry's pajamas. The man left the room.

Harold Christie was totally unprepared for what followed next.

As he remained in the bedroom on orders, he suddenly smelled fire, recognizing the pungent odor of petroleum. Then he saw the man reappear with a homemade torch on a pole that could have been a broomstick. The informants do not know where or with what this homemade torch was hastily assembled *downstairs*. It was used to smear the top of the staircase above the downstairs powder room, stain a trail *up* the carpeted risers, and smudge the wall of the hall and a wardrobe in the hall. The smear finally reached the bedroom.

Christie watched in a funk of fear as the man dabbed the torch at the carpeting, burned the head of Sir Harry's bed, stuck the torch underneath the mattress, and finally set the top of the mattress on fire. For some reason, it did not explode into a great flame, as the man may or may not have expected. He ordered Christie to help him lift Sir Harry's body onto the burned, but not burning, mattress.

He systematically played the torch over Sir Harry's body from head to foot, dabbing particularly at the eyes, the chest, and the abdomen, and apparently trying to burn off the pajamas. As the mattress and Sir Harry's body were burned separately, the mattress first, there was no *un*burned area of the mattress underneath Sir Harry's body. Finally, as if by afterthought, the "button" man lifted his torch to the mosquito net above the bed.

It was a classic mutilation, gangland killing, with its own special twist, designed to instill fear and foster discipline.

The man left, but not without ample warnings to Christie to convert him into a believer, if any doubt remained in his mind after witnessing the evening's episodes: If Christie did not want a similar "accident" to happen to him *or his mother,* if the Duke did not want to end up with a similar fate or have *his wife tortured or mutilated* before she was killed, they had better all turn to and force Executive Council approval of the gambling license for Lansky. Christie's knowledge from the days of Prohibition told him in no uncertain terms that these were not idle threats made in jest; they were the real McCoy.

The man was gone and Christie stood pondering his next move when suddenly, like an evil apparition, the man reappeared. He walked toward the bed, picked up a burned pillow, ripped open its blackened case, and emptied the feathers over Sir Harry's body. The informants do not know all of what he said to Christie at this time, but Christie was warned to sound no alarm under any circumstances until the usual rising time of seven in the morning. Presumably this was to give the power cruiser ample time to put Nassau in its wake.

That's the story the informants tell!

How reliable is this solution of Sir Harry's murder after a lapse of twenty-eight years, the death of several key participants, and the destruction of the physical evidence?

Any similar case presented to the FBI, Secret Service, CIA, Scotland Yard, the French Sûreté, Military Intelligence, or local police necessitates the use of *informants*. An informant is simply a person who *can* and *will* tell what happened. The "can" qualification per se makes the informant im-

mediately suspect in a great many situations. When the late
Governor Thomas E. Dewey was Special Rackets Prosecutor
in New York in the Thirties, the press chided him on the
unsavory reputation of his chief informants. Dewey replied:
"I can't find people singing in the church choir lofts every
Sunday morning who can tell me anything about pimps,
prostitutes, gamblers, blackmailers and racketeers!" This
philosophy did not originate with Dewey, but he stated it
accurately and dramatically.

The "will" capability of the informant depends upon complex motivations of human nature which are difficult to
gauge. Some informants perform for pay or to gain a personal
advantage from the agency seeking their knowledge: for example, a member or acquaintance of a safecracking gang
who "stools" to the police. Others become "involved" for
"patriotic" reasons: a housewife or university student who
penetrates a Maoist cell to gather espionage and subversive
information for the FBI. Some apparently achieve ego grati-
fication that lifts them above their peers in the criminal
world when they tell intelligence agents and police officers
what, when, and how their antisocial compatriots work. Still
others seem to use the informer role as a general catharsis to
the continuous churning of their conflicts and guilt complexes.

For the experienced investigator, establishing the informant's "can" function is relatively simple. A far graver task
is to evaluate and confirm the informant's report, to grade it
on something of a probability scale for safety and accuracy.
This means that the report of *any* informant standing alone
automatically rates low on the reliability scale, and its rise
to a position of acceptance and belief depends entirely on
whether it can be buttressed by other reports or, more sig-
nificantly, by physical evidence, or the recital of details that
only an actual witness to the event can know.

Informants seldom reach the courtroom. In the first place,
the appearance of an informant as a witness "blows" his
arrangement and bars his future use. Since reliable informants
are extremely hard to come by, most investigative agencies
use them in court only in extreme, desperate situations. Ad-

ditionally, the informant who comes into the courtroom may subject himself to considerable personal physical risk, and torture and death for his family. These possibilities are real, not imagined or conjured up for dramatic effect. This is especially true of the informant on Organized Crime, hundreds of whom have ended up with bullet holes in the back of the head, their throats slashed, or their feet weighted with cement blocks to take them to the bottom of a lake or river bed.

Exactly what transpired between Harold Christie and the Royal Governor between Major Phillips' rap on the bedroom door at seven o'clock and the Duke's overseas telephone call to Captain Melchen at ten minutes before eleven remains their secret. It is certainly reasonable to conclude that Christie communicated the threats on the lives of the Duke and Duchess, threats which included her torture and mutilation. From this point on, the Duke acted like a man pathetically terrorized until help finally arrived, or so the Duke believed, in the form of American police captains Melchen and Barker.

The Duke had no way of knowing then that some nine years later, the day after Christmas in 1952 to be exact, Miami Police Captain James Otto Barker would be killed by a .38 steel-jacketed bullet, fired from his own Police Special revolver by his son, in a death ruled "justifiable homicide" by the Dade County sheriff's office. By this time Barker had become a narcotics addict; it was well known that he had been on Meyer Lansky's payroll for a number of years; and just before his death, he actually led a faction that attempted to deliver control of the entire Miami Police Department into Lansky's hands.

Whether Barker was on Lansky's payroll or in his clutches in July, 1943, when he accompanied Melchen to Nassau to "confirm the suicide" of "a leading citizen of the Bahamas," is not known; and only the Duke and Christie know whether they separately or jointly knew of any connection between Barker and Lansky at the time of Sir Harry's murder. Many

of life's coincidences defy belief, and Barker's appearance in
Nassau may be one of them; however, it is not illogical to
surmise that he may have known even more of Sir Harry's
death than did the Duke of Windsor, who also has maintained a sphinxlike silence, officially and in private.

Of one fact we can be sure: By early Thursday afternoon,
the Duke, Harold Christie, Melchen, and Barker were in
desperate need of a murderer; but we have no way of knowing exactly how he was finally selected.

Lansky has maintained all along that he never actually
ordered Sir Harry's death. The lieutenant and "button" man
(the "soldier") got overly aggressive, but both were stringently disciplined for their unauthorized murder.

In retrospect, we know that Lansky possesses another
quality necessary for success—persistence. In 1963, exactly
twenty years after Sir Harry's murder, he obtained his gambling monopoly in the Bahamas for the payment of $1,100,-
000, according to some sources, or $1,800,000, according to
others. Neither represents a greatly inflated price over his
original offer to Harold Christie in view of the economic
spirals of those intervening decades. Lansky's arrival as gambling czar of the Bahamas precipitated the fall of the Conservative Party from power, but Lansky's ownership of the
profitable franchise remained.

He is also incredibly durable.

7

The Unpopular Accused

In theory, the Duke invited Captains Melchen and Barker to "assist" the Bahamian police in the investigation of Sir Harry's death; in actual practice, the two Americans took over the investigation immediately upon their arrival, directing and dominating its every detail. Their flurry of activity at Westbourne was tragically incompetent, unbelievably inept. It was a Keystone Cops performance that Hollywood could have used as a script with little alteration. How any experienced investigators could be guilty of so many violations of basic investigative techniques staggers belief. Clearly Barker played the dominating role with Melchen his obliging patsy.

They interviewed the usual witnesses, but their interrogations were shallow. Barker began a search for latent fingerprints shortly after his arrival but abandoned his inspection until the following day, on the ground that the air was too humid to permit the use of dusting powder to make any latent prints in the death room visible.

When he resumed his examination the following morning, he was forced to admit that he had not brought with him the special camera routinely used in all police departments for photographing latent fingerprints, a simple, fixed-focus, box affair with its own built-in lights. Virtually foolproof, it is a *sine qua non* to safe, effective, latent-fingerprint work.

They labored, of course, under two substantial impediments: They could not find the murder weapon; nor could they come close to explaining the source, direction, or mechanism of the fire which burned Sir Harry's body, the mattress on which he lay and the carpeting on the floor, and which left a trail out into the hallway and, they believed, *down* the stairs.

During most of Friday, Barker tinkered in the death room, presumably conducting a thorough search for latent fingerprints. Melchen interviewed at least two dozen witnesses in various rooms at Westbourne, where all the witnesses were assembled in the two downstairs living rooms to await their summons to appear before Melchen. From the time of Christie's first report the morning before, security precautions were unbelievably lax, a great number of official and lay witnesses entering and leaving the house at will. Certainly any physical evidence pointing to the murderer left on the lower floor, on the stairs, in the upstairs hallway, and even in some of the upstairs bedrooms, was vulnerable to alteration and destruction. The detectives held what amounted to an open house, welcoming anyone who walked into the act; and sensational murders the world over always attract dozens of thrill seekers who claim specialized knowledge that will permit the solution of the crime.

Police Commissioner Erskine-Lindop, his captains, lieutenants, sergeants, and officers, admittedly no world-renowned experts in homicide investigation, stood by in cowed silence while Barker, with Melchen's passive acquiescence, hopelessly bungled the case.

The pressures on Melchen and Barker for the identification of the murderer became as oppressive as the humid Bahamian air.

The Duke and Harold Christie maintained periodic contact throughout Thursday afternoon, Thursday evening, and until about three o'clock Friday afternoon. Melchen and Barker made periodic reports of their "progress" to the Duke. Colonel Erskine-Lindop and his colonial police were "quite out of it altogether," as he would explain years later. To them, it was a humiliating, embarrassing professional rebuff.

It may have been the purest of coincidences, but at around four o'clock on Friday afternoon, the Duke personally arrived at Westbourne and asked to see Barker, who was then working alone upstairs in Sir Harry's bedroom. His Royal Highness went up to him and remained for approximately twenty minutes. What they discussed is now the secret of only the Duke, but in less than two hours, the "murderer" was arrested.

As it happens all too often, once the police determine the guilt of their murderer, the investigation from that point on ceases to be objective. They concentrate only on evidence that confirms their predetermined conclusions of guilt; they ignore and sometimes even hide or destroy any evidence that points to anyone other than the "guilty" accused. Guilt, therefore, becomes the product of the subjective frame of mind of the police.

Major Herbert Pemberton, in khaki military uniform complete with Sam Browne belt, red lapels, and polished brass buttons, the Deputy Commissioner of Police, was dispatched to arrest Marie Alfred Fouquereaux de Marigny, Sir Harry Oakes' son-in-law.

Major Pemberton drove to de Marigny's house on Victoria Avenue around 6:15 P.M. on Friday, the ninth, and charged and cautioned him after placing him under arrest.

"Charged and cautioned" has been so routinely part and parcel of British police procedures for well over a century that all Englishmen know it means that the arresting officer has clearly and fairly told the accused that he need not make any statement whatsoever, and if he does make a statement, it can be used against him later in a court of law. De Marigny asked to make a voluntary statement which was reduced to writing, and later introduced at his trial:

> Marie Alfred Fouquereaux de Marigny, having been charged with the murder of Sir Harry Oakes and duly cautioned, makes the following voluntary statement:
>
> It is a ridiculous charge as I have no reason to do it. I had dinner at my house with my guests and the last ones were Mrs. Ainsley and Mrs. Clark, and I took them home

in my car in the morning, car No. 1383, between 1:00 A.M.
and 1:30 A.M. I returned home immediately. My servants
were still there as it was raining heavily. I entered the car
in the garage and went to bed.

My servants apparently left, they told me around 2:30.
Around 3:15, my friend Georges de Visdelou Guimbeau
took Miss Roberts home and the noise of the car passing
by woke me up.

He returned about fifteen minutes later, entered the
ground floor through the dining room door and went into
my room to get his cat who was making quite a noise
trying to get out. He left in a couple of minutes and I
went back to sleep.

I woke up early having some work to do with some
chickens and went to the farm. I returned to town and
went to the Post Office to see if there was any mail. I met
on the corner of Bank Lane and Bay Street, Basil McKinney
and Oswald Moseley. We discussed for about a few minutes the races of the previous afternoon. I left and returned
to the farm where I stayed until roughly 11:00 A.M.

I returned to town to purchase some cheesecloth to
make screens with. I met J. H. Anderson by the Pan
American, who told me that Sir Harry had been found
dead.

We both went home and we announced the news to
Mr. de Visdelou, and Mr. Anderson took me in his car to
the Westbourne house.

And I can say, swear, that I have not seen Sir Harry
Oakes to talk to since the 29th of March. I have not been
to Westbourne before, two years ago for a short visit. This
is all I have to say.

Everyone in Nassau knew something about the lean, lanky,
broad-shouldered man in his thirty-sixth year, whose arms
and legs dangled almost disconnectedly on his 6-foot-5-inch
frame. His hair was black, parted on the side, and slightly
wavy; and his clear skin was always tanned dark, the result
of constant exposure to sun and sea. He was a native of
the British island of Mauritius, a dot of land in the Indian
Ocean five hundred miles east of Madagascar, now the

Malagasy Republic. Indian laborers, descendants of African slaves, and a Chinese community far outnumbered the Europeans, mostly French, whose language was the dominant tongue. Its political allegiance went to Great Britain as a result of the Treaty of Paris in 1814 which marked the end of the Napoleonic Wars. Although physically larger than New Providence, Mauritius was also thin-soiled, barren, and rocky, suffering its own "poverty of terrain."

De Marigny's father, Alfred de Fouquereaux, owned a sugar factory; but even as one of Mauritius' wealthiest citizens, he could barely boast the average middle-class income found in most of the countries of Europe. Father and mother were divorced when the son was three; and at age eighteen he added his mother's name, de Marigny, to Fouquereaux. Later speculations about his motives implied that this was to permit him to assume the hereditary title of Count to which his mother's birth somehow entitled him. In an overaffectation of modesty, de Marigny claimed that love and honor for his mother alone caused him to take her name; he was never interested in the title Count; and he was embarrassed when his former wives insisted upon using it.

Alfred de Fouquereaux, now Alfred de Marigny, and a fellow islander, Georges de Visdelou Guimbeau, who was apparently authorized to use the title of Marquis, made several trips together to Europe. They were in and out of boarding schools after passing beyond the limited offerings of the educational system on their island; and in 1937, Alfred de Marigny married Lucie-Alice Cahen, the daughter of an Alsatian banker, who was classed as an heiress of sorts, although what she inherited was never clearly established. It may have been truth and it may have been subsequent fiction, but the banker-father is supposed to have charged that "Count" de Marigny was a confidence man whose only interest was his own bankroll.

De Marigny, his bride, and Georges the Marquis de Visdelou crossed the Atlantic to the United States as a merry threesome aboard the *Normandie*, in an era of cruise ships for the rich and idle.

"What a trip it was!" de Marigny later wrote. "I had been reading a play called *Design for Living* [by Noel Coward, about a husband, wife, and lover who lived in the same house] . . . and found the parallel most amusing."

The implications were clear: There was an easy and thrill-gratifying triangular co-option of bed partners, long before wife-swapping became popular in a later generation of swingers.

Almost exactly four months after the marriage was consummated, de Marigny was in the divorce courts in Miami with Lucie-Alice. As with all divorce actions, irreconcilable conflicts over the facts seep in, completely defying clarity. Lucie-Alice charged de Marigny with "desertion and lack of interest"; de Marigny rebutted that she was more interested in Georges de Visdelou Guimbeau's bed than his own.

It mattered not; the divorce soon became final.

In November of 1937, on the day that *she* received *her* divorce from A. Coster Schermerhorn, de Marigny married Ruth Fahnestock Schermerhorn, described usually as a "wealthy socialite" of a prominent Long Island family. Using Ruth's money, the de Marignys moved to the Bahamian island of Eleuthera, where they built a spacious beach home. They commuted in a Star Class sailing boat named *Concubine* to and from Nassau, where de Marigny, employing boyhood skills acquired in the Indian Ocean, developed a reputation as a leading sailor. He knew boats, how to crew and handle them, and how to win races. It was a playboy's life founded on Ruth's money. Her devotion to de Marigny continued, although within a year Georges, the Marquis de Visdelou Guimbeau, arrived to convert the latest de Marigny duo into a much-talked-about trio.

By 1940, de Marigny was once more in the divorce courts, but he continued to live with Ruth for nine months after his divorce decree became final. Many bizarre speculations grew from what was then considered a most unusual social, emotional, and moral arrangement, especially since Georges de Visdelou also remained. Later Ruth Fahnestock Schermerhorn would claim that her three-year marriage to de Marigny cost her approximately a quarter-million dollars.

Shadowed by the Marquis, de Marigny finally took up permanent residence in Nassau. He ran a grocery store near the British Colonial Hotel for a time and built a number of apartment buildings. When compelled to work by force of being between wealthy wives, de Marigny performed well as a laborer and manager, showing energy and sound business judgment. No one ever accused him of being lazy or even idle.

He spoke in a sort of throaty, Charles Boyer, French accent, punctuated by dapper manners that included back-slapping of men and hand-kissing of women. He could exude charm, grace, and poise; and he was considered an excellent conversationalist, his thickly accented English underscored by colorful phrases that conveyed descriptive imagery. His great captivator, enemy and friend both agreed, was his easy, fluid smile that wilted grandmothers, mothers, daughters, contemporaries, and granddaughters. There was about him a tantalizingly evil mystique.

He was, however, never accepted by the native Bahamians. His reaction was to look condescendingly at them and scorn even their few social invitations when they came. The natives never forgave him for being foreign, and they thought him supercilious, haughty, distant, boorish, and overbearing. He was called not only playboy, but fop and gigolo. He was reputed as immoral and amoral, the corrupter of womanhood, old, young, and in between, a lecher who lay in wait for gullible rich women; he was neither Bahamian nor British.

Few permanent residents of the Bahamas, particularly Nassau, were more unpopular in late 1941 than Alfred "Count" de Marigny, the exhibitor of his "phony" French title, who met Nancy Oakes, Sir Harry's eldest daughter, when she was but seventeen-and-a-half years old. Five months later, he followed her to boarding school in New York, the French School for Girls; and after accompanying her on a trip to California where the chaperone was a girl Nancy's own age, he married her two days after she reached her eighteenth birthday, when parental consent was no longer necessary.

Individual, family, and Island reverberations from the marriage were horrendous.

This was the man, disliked and unpopular, whom Major' Pemberton lodged in the vermin-infested Bahamian jail at a little after seven-thirty Friday evening. He was not a man to evoke sympathy within the community; and of all those in the crowded Islands in that midwar July, Alfred de Marigny was perhaps the easiest man to convict of Sir Harry's murder. This was undoubtedly a prime consideration of those who decided that he was the "guilty" murderer.

8

The Loyal Wife

Bahamian summers are thick and oppressive, and those who can afford it seek to escape them through flight. Lady Oakes and her four younger children were already in Bar Harbor, and Sir Harry was scheduled to join them on the very day of Alfred de Marigny's arrest.

Nancy Oakes de Marigny was in Florida, on her way to Vermont, where she planned to enroll in a private art school for the summer.

Within an hour after his arrival at Westbourne on Thursday morning, de Marigny cabled Nancy the news of her father's death and told her to fly to Bar Harbor to be with her mother. Stunned and shaken, Nancy complied.

Now nineteen, but considerably more mature than her chronological years, Nancy was redheaded—perhaps auburn would be more accurate—her 5-foot-5-inch height exaggerated by her thin build, although bust, hips, calves, and thighs were adequate enough to prevent her from appearing skinny. An innate physical frailty was beautifully concealed by natural grace and poise.

She carried her firm, almost belligerent chin high in the manner of a model, her mouth wide, her lips full, her nose long and straight. The intensity of her deep-set eyes was her most striking physical feature: she looked directly at the person speaking to her, confidently and with such animation that the other person invariably first broke the gaze.

From some angles, particularly head-on, her face was classically beautiful, radiant and sparkling; but from an oblique view, the Indianlike cheekbones became more exaggerated, the forehead lost its normal slope to become directly vertical, the wide-spaced eyes separated farther, and the jaw and mouth gave the illusion of being almost detached; her profile was excellent.

She dressed tastefully but conservatively and was not extravagant in her wardrobe. Her immaculate, every-hair-in-place coiffure emphasized neatness and cleanliness.

There was no doubt in Nancy's mind that her total break with the family came many months before her father's death. With mature introspection, she analyzed it as the result of a "generation gap," and this a full two decades before the term became popular.

"I know my mother always had my best interests at heart, from her point of view," Nancy explained without rancor or bitterness, always speaking gently of both father and mother with genuine affection and kindness. "But we had different points of view, about many things. She was Victorian and puritanical and really had not seen or done anything until she married my father when she was twenty-four. I was raised quite differently!"

And she was.

By the time she was ten, she was off to Polygala, an exclusive boarding school for girls in Gstaad, Switzerland. From there it was Heathfield and Torrington Park schools in London; skiing romps in St. Moritz; music and language tutors in London; Girl Guide summers in the English countryside; art school in Vermont; special tutors on trips with her parents all over the world.

"All this made me an individual," Nancy explained evenly and realistically. "I had to be me. I was not just an extension or a continuation of either my father or my mother, or both of them. I am probably more like my father than my mother; but the great advantage to a life in boarding schools is that

it lets you develop your own individuality without being
inhibited by the hang-ups of your parents."

There was no schooling for one full year, Nancy's fourteenth, when the family toured South America: Trinidad, the
east coast of Brazil, Rio de Janeiro, Montevideo, Buenos Aires,
Chile, and finally a long visit in Caracas. The summer of 1929
was devoted to Lady Oakes' relatives in Australia; but before
they sailed out of San Francisco, Harry Oakes nostalgically
retraced his steps over his fruitless wanderings around Death
Valley, the effort of a normal father to share experiences of
his younger days with his children, hopefully to develop
bonds of mutual interest and respect that lead on to genuine
friendship.

Nancy spent considerable time with her father, more than
the other children, not only because she occupied the special
position of the eldest, but because of that special bond
between father and daughter who were greatly alike. She
served as his genuinely appreciative audience while he re-
counted the eerie fights for survival during his lonely prospecting days; she considered him by far the most interesting
and unusual man in the entire world; she called him "a
strange person" and "the most extraordinary person I ever
knew." While Sir Harry was often close-mouthed and intro-
verted in the presence of most of his associates, he related
tale after tale, story after story to Nancy by the hour. She
dreamed of writing his biography, confidently believing that
his was a completely different life story which should be
preserved for posterity.

She respected her father, held him in awe, never really
feared his temper since she was confident it would not be
vented against her, loved him, but refused to be subservient
to him.

Always, she stood firmly on her rights as an individual,
not a rebel or revolutionary by any stretch of the imagination,
but as a separate and distinct personality who was inalienably
entitled to her own way of life.

From the time she was fourteen, she dated many boys,
mostly in the healthy groups that teenagers enjoy. As she

grew older, her parents permitted her to attend parties—which the British called frolics—and dances with escorts; she experienced crushes and puppy-love affairs similar to those of her contemporaries.

Her first total fall was for Alfred de Marigny, and it probably began before she actually met him in the flesh when she was seventeen and a half.

It was the day after Christmas, 1941, two days before Winston Churchill addressed the United States Congress to tell them that "the United States has at last drawn the sword for freedom and cast the scabbard aside!" Lady Oakes gave a lavish dinner-dance at the British Colonial Hotel to honor the popular Receiver General of the Bahamas, who was departing from Nassau for another assignment. The socially great and near great were all present. There was a vagueness about both the invitation and its acceptance by Alfred de Marigny. Regardless, early in the evening he sauntered over to Nancy and introduced himself in his most charming French manner. Lights flashed and bells rang, and Nancy now easily disclosed her great interest by detailing de Marigny's accomplishments as a sailor: She reeled off his victories and his awards.

There is conflict as to whether Sir Harry actually knew of Nancy's infatuation with de Marigny; but shortly after the first of the year, she was off for New York and the French School for Girls.

Nancy was incensed over the later insinuations about the trip to California. She and her roommate invited de Marigny to accompany them, which he did by plane from La Guardia to San Francisco. De Marigny was lodged at a hotel all the time while Nancy stayed with her girlfriend's parents. De Marigny became acutely ill and Nancy flew back to New York with him where he was operated on for an intestinal obstruction at St. Vincent's Hospital. She visited him every day, and from his hospital bed he asked her to marry him.

In May, two days after she reached her eighteenth birthday, Nancy Oakes—Sir Harry's pride and joy—and Alfred de Marigny were married by a New York City magistrate without notice of any kind to Sir Harry and Lady Oakes.

Both parents were crushed when Nancy and de Marigny arrived in Bar Harbor two weeks later to announce their news. Lady Oakes was able to separate Harry Oakes from the rest of the family for a cooling-off period, but it was only a transient lull before the inevitable complex storm.

De Marigny and Nancy began a protracted honeymoon in Mexico, financed by Lady Oakes. Nancy became sick and almost died, requiring seven blood transfusions. Sir Harry and Lady Oakes flew down to bring the bride and groom back to Palm Beach, where Nancy and de Marigny occupied adjoining rooms in a hospital suite, she to have a therapeutic abortion on the advice of her doctor and he a tonsillectomy. This arrangement was shattered by a boisterous telephone call from Sir Harry, accusing Alfred of ruining Nancy's health by getting her pregnant. De Marigny stalked from the hospital, taking with him all chances of peaceful relations with his in-laws.

At the time of her father's funeral in Bar Harbor, Nancy was a tragically torn woman: She professed to believe fervently in her husband's innocence (she had learned of his arrest on July 10), but the shock of her father's death still engulfed her.

Captains Melchen and Barker flew to Bar Harbor, where they talked to Lady Oakes, Nancy, and sundry assembled relatives after the funeral. Obviously, their mission was to poison all minds against de Marigny; and for the first time, even to Melchen's complete surprise, Barker announced that he had found "several" of de Marigny's fingerprints on a Chinese paneled screen that stood in Sir Harry's bedroom just south of his bed.

The ploy worked with Lady Oakes, who agreed to return to testify for the Crown against de Marigny if need be; but Nancy was highly suspicious of the American policemen. She announced to the assembled group that she believed firmly in her husband's innocence and would stand faithfully behind him.

Her decision, as might have been anticipated, produced a further rift with her mother, who would not speak to her during the long weeks of de Marigny's detention and trial.

Nancy carried herself with a confident poise that commanded respect from most who knew her, although a sizable number of jealous detractors alleged that her haughty pride rather than love of husband compelled her to stand steadfastly beside de Marigny in his ordeal. In many ways, she was the most poignant figure of all. She elected to cling to her husband like Ruth to Naomi: "Intreat me not to leave thee, or to return from following after thee: for whither thou goest, I will go; and where thou lodgest, I will lodge; thy people shall be my people, and thy God my God."

Brokenhearted, Nancy rushed to New York to consult with the father of a school friend who suggested that she contact Raymond Schindler of the Schindler Bureau of Investigation.

9

The Fact-Gatherer

Although at ease with celebrities, including movie stars, ambassadors, and heads of state, who were frequently guests of her parents, Nancy Oakes de Marigny was not quite prepared for the ebullient, flamboyant Raymond Schindler; nor he for her. Their first meeting was in Nancy's hotel suite, with Nancy performing ballet exercises the entire time.

Head of the Schindler Bureau of Investigation (SBI) in New York, Schindler went to a two-and-a-half-hour lunch each day at either "21" or the Stork Club, where fellow notables came to pay him court at his special table. By 1943, at age sixty-one, Schindler had followed this luncheon routine for two decades as regularly as the journey of a zealous communicant to daily Mass, and undoubtedly transacted more investigative business at these and similar spas than any investigator in history.

As with any successful private investigator, his tools in trade were the people, called "sources," on whom he could call for information; and Raymond Schindler was without peer in sources. There probably was not a single bank in all Manhattan without a Schindler source of information. By nothing more than a telephone call, he could obtain the details of any depositor's checking or savings account. Within minutes, he could find out whether a person was a registered member in any Catholic, Protestant, or Jewish congregation anywhere in Manhattan, and what the minister, priest, or rabbi knew of him. Personnel information considered confidential in the files of the largest companies and industries in the country were his for a telephone call. He treated and maintained these sources at "21" and the Stork, and became a celebrity in his own right after devoting many years himself to celebrity worship.

His rise to fame was meteoric.

After losing his last cent in a mining venture in northern California in 1906, Raymond Schindler arrived in San Francisco the day after the earthquake. For two weeks only, he worked as a historical researcher for the G. Franklin Mc-Macken Historical Society, then attempting to determine how much of San Francisco's damage was due to the earthquake itself and how much to the subsequent fire. Two weeks later, Schindler sold his "historical investigative" services to the insurance companies. A year later, he had used his famous "roper" technique to rid San Francisco of its grafters. (The roper is a decoy thrown into contact with a suspect to get him to incriminate himself.)

Schindler used the roping technique successfully in fighting official corruption in cities all over the United States. He also used it to solve sensational murder cases which up until his arrival on the scene were beyond solution. He supplemented his roper operations with the newfangled Dictograph which he developed into the most accurate mechanism in history for obtaining reliable facts. Practically the entire city council of Atlantic City was caught in a bribery swindle that would have replaced its famous Boardwalk with a prosaic cement walk. Corrupt union practices were detailed to Schindler's ropers and recorded for posterity by Dictograph. Pardons sold by governors in several states were similarly discovered. For Lever Brothers he saved Lifebuoy soap from competitors who profited unfairly from the company's formula and advertising campaigns. He recovered hundreds of thousands of dollars for clients swindled in the ingenious confidence schemes of the Twenties and Thirties, many perpetrated by international operators who plied the oceans on expensive cruise ships to find their gullible targets among the lonely. He decided early that scientific evidence offered the next great fact-gathering opportunity, so he formed a group of specialists to solve difficult and spectacular cases.

During his later years, he worked closely with Erle Stanley Gardner in "The Court of Last Resort," striving to interest the reading public in the problems of the overall administration of justice by espousing the cases of penniless, attorneyless, hopeless men who were serving life sentences for murders they claimed they did not commit.

One of Schindler's great clients was Anna Gould, the only surviving daughter of railroad financier Jay Gould. As did many of her wealthy compatriots before World War I, Anna went to France and married a title: the Duke de Talleyrand, the great-grandson of Napoleon's scheming foreign minister. Anna's home, The Castle, adjoined the Rockefeller estate in Westchester County, overlooking the Hudson. Schindler lived next door in The Cottage, a four-story, white-brick, twenty-three-room house, complete with its own basement nightclub, bowling alley, and indoor swimming pool, furnished with invaluable art pieces from Versailles. Twenty feet above the ground, in a huge four-hundred-year-old oak tree between The Cottage and the river, Schindler built a dance platform that could accommodate forty people. For his protection services and other investigative duties that he performed for Anna Gould, the Duchess de Talleyrand, Schindler lived at The Cottage free of charge; in addition, she paid him a retainer of $50,000 annually.

Schindler was striking and flamboyant, a *bon vivant* and gourmet, a connoisseur of fine wines, a dancer who could go every morning until the wee hours, a lady's man of unmatchable reputation and performance, and something of an egomaniac; but all in all, an ingenious fact-gatherer whose techniques were totally unpredictable, who pleased most of his clients by getting them what Schindler was hired to obtain.

Raymond Schindler either worked for exactly nothing, free of charge to a penniless client whose case interested him, or he was the highest-paid detective extant. In this case, Nancy Oakes de Marigny agreed to pay him three hundred dollars a day plus his expenses; and Schindler always expended with the best of them.

Schindler extracted a unique clause in his agreement with Nancy: If he uncovered evidence of de Marigny's guilt, he would be at liberty to divulge it to the Bahamian police or the Crown's Attorney, whichever Schindler deemed more appropriate. Nancy agreed without hesitation, so confident was she of her husband's innocence that she "knew from the beginning" that Schindler would have no reason to exercise this option.

Schindler found himself stymied by the Bahamian police upon his arrival in Nassau. When, with the help of Godfrey Higgs, de Marigny's attorney, he finally gained access to Westbourne approximately a week after the murder, Schindler found two Nassau police officers, in red-striped pants, white tunics, pointed helmets, and all, carefully scrubbing down the west wall of the upstairs hall, no more than twenty feet away from the door to Sir Harry's bedroom.

"Stop! Wait! What are you doing?" Schindler shouted, horrified at the sacrilegious rites taking place in front of his eyes.

"But these are our orders, sir," one of the constables replied nonchalantly, never once breaking the slow rhythm of his strokes.

"But those are hand prints! They're bloody hand prints, that's exactly what they are!" Schindler protested as he pushed away the constable who was attacking the wall with sponge and suds. "Stop it! We'll never get them back!"

Schindler looked in desperation from one black face to the other. Realization quickly dawned that he would not deter these men from their destructive mission, no matter what, unless he could reach their superior officer to have the order countermanded.

"Can't you wait until I telephone?" Schindler asked. "Why are you so determined to wash off those bloody hand prints?"

"Because, sir," the spokesman said evenly, "these prints

are not those of Count de Marigny; therefore, they'll only confuse the evidence."

Everywhere Schindler went on the Island, he was followed by the police. When he talked to witnesses, the witnesses were immediately questioned by the police who asked what Schindler said to them.

Schindler claimed that his telephone was tapped and proved it through the use of the Nassau telephone directory. He would call a number at random without checking the name. When the other person answered the phone, Schindler would say, "The same meeting place as last night. You know the road up to Fort Charlotte. The entrance to Fort Charlotte. Be sure and bring the stuff. We can't delay. We've got our work cut out for us. Hurry!"

He would hang up and try another column giving the operator another blind number.

"I'll wait for you at the entrance to Fort Charlotte, like last night. You know what to do. Don't tell a soul."

There would be another page and another number.

"Don't forget to bring the blood samples to the entrance to Fort Charlotte. This may be the last chance we get. Don't blow it! Be sure and be there."

Schindler rented a cab and drove out to a secret hiding place overlooking the road to Fort Charlotte; within minutes, police cars converged on it from all directions, gradually occupying strategic points of observation all the way up the hill to the entrance to the Fort.

Schindler labored in a hostile atmosphere that would have intimidated a less brash man to a point of surrender and defeat, but this type of official challenge was Schindler's elixir of life.

10

The Protectors of Society

The prime function of any government, whatever its form and whenever its existence, is to maintain public order. A breakdown of this basic obligation inevitably leads to some degree of anarchy; and man's greatest fear is anarchy. With anarchy, all productive pursuits necessary for survival become distorted; the frightening psychology of mob rule takes over; and the terrified citizens instinctively seek salvation by turning to an authoritarian protector. This pattern is as inflexible as the rigor of martial law which automatically follows.

Because of man's selfish, self-centered, acquisitive nature, no society can maintain order without enforcers, called police in the Common Law scheme of things [*police* = Fr.; from the Latin, *politia;* Gr. *politeia*, "government of a city" (*polis*)].

James Otto Barker was typical of all too many American policemen through the World War II era and beyond.

Unschooled, underpaid, and with no training except the bad habits accumulated over a career of some seventeen years, Barker's greatest deficiency lay in his inability to understand his professional role. If he had ever heard the words "Common Law system," his intellectual curiosity would not have been aroused to find out what they meant; he never dreamed that he was an inherent part of that system. No one ever bothered to explain to Barker the historical heritage of his job.

When the tuns (towns) were emerging, perhaps as early as seventh-century Anglo-Saxon England, the tithing system provided history's finest hour of community responsibility for keeping the peace and preventing crime.

The tithing consisted of a group of ten families who could not help but become involved: Every person in the tithing was accountable for the behavior of his neighbor, and the tithing as a whole vouched for the conduct of each of its members. Every freeman twelve years of age and above was enrolled in some tithing; no one was exempted from his call to duty.

Ten tithings made up a hundred, and all families, regardless of number, attached to the land of a single baron (a thane) constituted one tithing for which the earl or duke was responsible. The head man of a tithing was called a reeve; and as a group of hundreds formed a shire (roughly the geographical area of a county), the chief of the shire was designated *shire-reeve*, the source of the word "sheriff."

As the population increased and the towns evolved into cities, movement outside the established tithing became an economic necessity; so local group responsibility for policing crime and keeping the peace began its irretrievable decline with the breakup of the tithings.

By the time William the Conqueror, Duke of Normandy, won the Battle of Hastings in 1066, the collective force of the tithing system, hundred-courts, and shire-courts was greatly diminished. William's answer was the substitution of a military police and a martial-law concept 180 degrees removed from individual and community participation and responsibility. These agents of the king, organized in military units, maintained *his* peace; the interests of the individual citizen in a local community, far removed from Westminster and the royal trappings of the king's court, possessed no common bond with the "foreign" mercenary police agents of the king. What co-operation the citizens gave was tendered grudgingly; more often than not, paid or threatening informers with personal feuds to settle against their neighbors presented the "facts" to the king's police for arbitrary action.

As the Common Law courts developed during the next several centuries, the pendulum swung once again and the military police of the king gave way to a return to local responsibility; but it could never be the same type of group participation known in the tithings of a less populous day. The police, hated by the citizens but accepted as necessary for public order, became society's inevitable bastard children, required to perform the mundane, unpleasant chores of room and board but not entitled to merit the plaudits of personal respect and professional recognition.

In the thirteenth century, the watch-and-ward police sprang up, a rather drastic shift away from the king and back to the community. Heads of families in a geographical area within the city (a *ward*) were compelled to pool their services to maintain a *watch* at night to preserve the peace and deter crime. The duty was onerous and unpopular; soon, the householders sent paid substitutes to police the ward in their stead. Finally, because of the distasteful nature of the job, only cripples, the aged, the lame, thieves, sadists, and bungling idiots were available for hire. A special group of police evolved to regulate prostitution and push the whores into a section bounded by red lights. Some of these watch-and-ward "officers" served as pimps for the prostitutes.

Over the centuries, the watch-and-ward concept expanded to include the marching watch, the peace wardens, the merchant police (hired by the merchants of a section to protect their property), the parochial police (a modernization of the watch-and-ward in elite geographical areas called parishes), and the bellmen of Charles II (called "Charlies" and "shiver-and-shake watch"). By 1750, the Bow Street Runners (thief takers), perhaps the first detective unit in history, moved out of London's Bow Street police court to the scene of the crime to begin an immediate investigation after receiving its report.

The era of human slavery that grew from the Industrial Revolution from about 1760 onward produced crime that even Charles Dickens could not describe adequately in all its horror. It was a time of virtual anarchy, the police function fragmented into the merchant police, parish police, marine police, watch-and-ward, Bow Street Runners, and uncounted vigilante groups and private police units. Severity of punishment did not deter crime since crime was unattended by certainty of punishment. One hundred ninety-two crimes carried the death penalty; in one month alone, hangings in London ran as high as fifty per day, but pickpockets underneath the gallows thrived on the milling crowds who came to witness the hangings of other, less fortunate pickpockets, whose crime of robbery from the person carried the automatic death penalty.

Finally, in 1829, British Home Secretary Sir Robert Peel sensed that the decaying society described by Dickens could not endure much longer without new steps to combat crime. Under his auspices, Parliament passed the Metropolitan Police Act which combined all private, governmental, and quasi-governmental police agencies into one unit. These Peelian Reforms, as drastic and revolutionary as the times demanded, undoubtedly saved British society from either anarchy or totalitarianism, although the "Peelers," or "Bobbies," were never considered a part of the Common Law system. Like Topsy, they simply grew and rushed headlong to the task of maintaining order and suppressing crime.

The police situation in the United States also developed haphazardly, and without benefit of the Peelian Reforms. In New England, the watches-and-wards of Elizabethan England prevailed since the population clustered in towns and cities, dependent upon the sea for industry and commerce. In the plantation economy of the South, the sheriff-of-the-county system dominated. As the population flowed westward, the functions of town constable and county sheriff merged, but many communities utilized both officers, who sometimes became vicious proprietary rivals.

The great suspicion of strong, centralized government that dominated the thinking of the early settlers caused them to designate all law-enforcement offices as elective, with terms of from two to four years only. Under this limitation, policing and law enforcement could not develop as a profession, with technically trained people choosing it as a career. Rather, the policing function went to the indolent and the inept, even to prisoners serving sentences for misdemeanors. Local watches-and-wards were called "leatherheads" to emphasize their denseness.

Since the policing power always involves tremendous opportunities for graft and corruption, police appointment became little more than an official license to plunder, extort, solicit, blackmail, and steal. Discipline was unheard of; administrators and superior officers were frequently assaulted by the beat patrolmen; drunkenness while on duty was commonplace; guilt and innocence for real or trumped-up charges decided in drumhead police courts were bargained and sold like a side of beef in the marketplace. The police departments regulated licensing and performed inspections of all facets of business, so control of the police provided a corrupt political machine an unparalleled opportunity to extract political favors.

Just slightly over one hundred years ago, a policeman's uniform in the United States was looked upon as such a mark of moral degeneracy that no policeman would wear it. Rather, in lieu of the denigrating uniform, some wore official hats or caps and carried hidden badges for identification when called upon to perform official duties. As late as 1855, an effort to force police to wear badges outside their clothing met vigorous resistance by the police in Philadelphia; it was not until the beginning of the Civil War that officers in that city were compelled to wear full uniforms.

The citizens as a whole watched appalled and in ignorance, never realizing that these nefarious police were their own agents, nothing more than extensions of the citizens themselves, not some outside foreign group to be curtailed and eliminated if possible.

This was the heritage of the office in which James Otto Barker ignorantly began work as a policeman in 1925.

If the client's case in the Common Law courtroom depends upon a brilliant barrister to present it, the barrister depends upon the fact-gatherers for the evidence available for him to "lead": The barrister is no better than the evidence furnished him by the fact-gatherers; the work of the fact-gatherers may go for naught unless presented persuasively by a brilliant barrister. It is the vicious circle of causation.

But since the police were never told of their role in the Common Law system, it is only natural that their performances, at least a substantial number, would be outside its scope. The greatest mistake made by most policemen is the unshakable belief that they, *the police*, are charged with the duty of *deciding the guilt or innocence of a suspect!* The police, they are convinced, are the *only* protectors of society. It is up to them to find a suspect for the crime under investigation, and then to select and build the evidence that will lead to his conviction, all too often completely ignoring any evidence that inconveniently turns up to point to this hapless suspect's innocence.

Once having determined the suspect's guilt in this form of "trial by policeman," the Melchens and Barkers rationalize anything and everything that they need to do to guarantee the man's conviction as socially wholesome and good. If they overlook and suppress evidence, this is what the "guilty" suspect deserves; if they bend their testimony and encourage other witnesses to stretch theirs to help guarantee guilt, this is necessary because of the deficiencies of the court system; if they forge or fabricate evidence, well and good, if this is the only route to insure the "guilty" defendant's conviction in a court of law.

In the minds of the Melchens and Barkers, there are no "innocent" defendants, once the police exercise their inalienable right to pronounce them guilty.

Anyone and everyone, therefore, who looms as an obstacle to the conviction of the "guilty" defendant, as determined by this brand of policeman, becomes a mortal enemy of the police—this man whose self-assigned, saintly role is the protection of an unappreciative society. Judges are enemies of the police, because judges insist on fair trials by rules of legal technicality which allow the "guilty" to escape; defense lawyers are diabolical, blood-sucking monsters since their announced goal is to thwart the policeman's effort to convict his "guilty" accused; prosecutors who won't prosecute all the "guilty" defendants the police present are endemic enemies of the policeman; and stupid, dumb jurors who regularly turn loose "guilty" defendants are unworthy of the policeman's selfless attempts to protect them.

James Otto Barker, like far too many of his fellow police officers, suffered a chip-on-shoulder inferiority complex that warped both personality and perspective. He became a pathetically lonely and misguided man, an easy target for corruption by Meyer Lansky's agents. If he was not already tainted in 1943, his fall was but a brief moment away; the mental attitude for duplicity already existed.

Organized Crime cannot live without the insidious collaboration of the Barkers. Thankfully throughout the years, enough reasonably objective policemen of integrity have existed to counterbalance the Barkers, otherwise the system would have been overthrown long ago by public rebellion.

Although there would be no direct courtroom confrontation, the behind-the-scenes maneuvers of Schindler and Barker would control de Marigny's fate.

11

The Worst System
of Justice Ever

It was Monday, October 18, only thirteen short weeks since Sir Harry's murder.

The clock on the outside courthouse wall showed ten-thirty when the robed crier, thumping his crown-capped staff on the hardwood floor and shouting "Court! Court! Court!," moved slowly down the narrow stairs to enter the packed courtroom through the open doorway. Two carefully measured paces to the rear, the Lord Chief Justice, Sir Oscar Bedford Daly, followed in his scarlet robe and shoulder-length white wig, the personification of eight hundred years of British justice.

The preliminaries over, de Marigny's trial was beginning. Beyond doubt, it was the most sensational, newsworthy event in Bahamian history.

For the much-sought-after courtroom seats, favored ruling-class whites sent black servants to queue up at daybreak to claim a place for the master, who arrived shortly before court opened at ten-thirty. Others brought folding golf chairs for the center and side aisles and the back of the room. Standing was prohibited, but the Lord Chief Justice did not object to temporary seats lapping over every inch of floor space; and although the sky was marred by threatening dark clouds, an orderly overflow crowd of several hundred, mostly black, huddled around the building outside on the lawns to listen through the open windows.

Since the warring world welcomed a respite from head-
lines describing the Germans falling back along the Vol-
turno in Italy, new Russian blows at the German defenses
north of Kiev, the meeting in Russia of Secretary of State
Cordell Hull, Foreign Secretary Anthony Eden, and Deputy
Prime Minister V. M. Molotov to plan the "Grand Assault,"
the agitation by the British press for the return to Burma,
the Russian drive into the bend of the Dnieper River, and
the Japanese major air defeat over New Guinea, reporters
for leading papers and the major wire services sat at a
special table in the front row of the spectators' part of the
courtroom, their cables converting the de Marigny case into
one of the great murder trials of all history.

The Chief Justice ceremoniously ascended the mahogany
dais while the crier, his staff still thumping the floor, moved
to stand below and in front of the great bench that dominated the entire room.

The Oxford accent of the crier continued to command:
"All manner of persons having anything to do before His
Majesty's Supreme Court in the Bahama Islands, draw near
and give your attendance and you will be heard. God save
the King!"

The two prosecutors, standing stiffly at attention behind the
front narrow counsel table, and the two defenders behind
the second, all robed and wigged, bowed stiffly in symmetrical
unison to the Chief Justice, who returned his own Tudor bow.
It was a symbolic bow by all to Justice; and Sir Oscar's
ordered descent into the leather swivel chair was his unspoken
edict for all in the courtroom to sit. With it came the usual
shuffling of feet and clearing of throats.

The prisoner stood erect and motionless in the barred
dock—many call it the cage—across the well of the court
directly opposite the jury, flanked by two statuesque constables responsible for his custody. Centuries earlier in sim-
pler days, when pomp and circumstance prevailed, an inspired
artist painted their uniforms: dark-blue, red-striped woolen
trousers, immaculately starched white tunics, spiked black
helmets trimmed in gold, and sheathed bayonets hanging

from black belts. They were Constables of the Guard, His Majesty's Colonial Police.

The prisoner looked through and beyond the robed and wigged court registrar who read the indictment:

> Marie Alfred Fouquereaux de Marigny, you are charged with murder under Sec. 335 of the Penal Code (Chapter 60); particulars of the offense being that during the night of the 7th and 8th July, 1943, at New Providence, you did murder Sir Harry Oakes, Baronet. Are you guilty or not guilty.

Returning the registrar's glare, the prisoner responded firmly: "Not guilty!"

The ancient pageantry and procedures had emerged centuries earlier in the great halls at Westminster and the criminal courts of Old Bailey, within the shadow of the Tower of London, but they did not overwhelm this 105-seat courtroom in Nassau.

Attention shifted back to the court crier, who lifted a small wooden box from his table and shook it vigorously, the rattle of thirty-six miniature wooden balls creating the only sound in the courtroom. Cautiously, dramatically, he lifted the lid only high enough to admit his hand, removed a single pellet, and examined its number.

"Eighteen," he called crisply to the registrar, whose finger ran down his list of potential jurors.

"Donald Dealbinas," the registrar called out.

The selection of the jury was under way. Alfred de Marigny, more frequently called "the Count," was not to be exposed to the whims and prejudices of a single man whose personal moral standards might be either above or below the norm of the community. The prisoner would enjoy the inalienable right of every person charged with a crime against the Crown: To be judged by his peers, twelve independent citizens, representative subjects *of* the King, but in this performance of civic duty not subject *to* the King.

What is this Common Law system that functions with

equal vigor in Old Bailey in London and Nassau in the Bahamas, in a crown colony in Africa or Hong Kong, in New Government House in New Delhi or the Old Courthouse in Sydney, and, allowing for typical American contamination, in Boston and Berkeley, New York and Strawberry Plains?

Winston Churchill once told Parliament: "Democracy is the worst form of government, except all those other forms that have been tried from time to time." He might also have said of the Common Law system: "It is the worst format for justice, except all those other forms that have been tried from time to time." Despite the many justified assaults now made against it, it is the greatest gift by far of the mother country to all the English-speaking world; yet few can come close to understanding or explaining it.

The Common Law is usually said to have its *recorded* beginning in England during the reign of Henry II, "the Law Giver" (1154–1189), but much went on before then—some known but more unknown.

In the known beginning, if a man's property was stolen or his wife killed, all able-bodied men set up the hue and cry and pursued the offender until he was apprehended. When he was caught by this *posse comitatus,* he was hanged on the spot. There was no trial since any person found "in seisin [possession] of his crime" was presumed guilty; and nothing could be gained in listening to his explanations. Anyone accused of crime would naturally deny guilt!

But what of the offender who was not caught in possession of the fruits or the tools of his crime? A form of trial developed which was known as the "appeal." It was nothing more than an accusation of crime made somewhat informally in the local shire- or hundred-court, and if the accused failed to answer this appeal after it was announced once each month for four consecutive months, he was presumed guilty of the charge. He was outlawed, his lands and personal goods confiscated, and he was hanged as soon as he could be captured.

If he learned of the appeal against him and if he was courageous enough to put in an appearance, he was entitled to a trial. What a trial this was—the *judicium Dei,* "judgment of God," the ordeal! For persons of higher rank, the fire ordeal was used. The accused was forced to take pieces of red-hot iron ranging in weight from one to three pounds in his hands; or he was blindfolded and compelled to walk barefooted over nine red-hot plowshares arranged at staggered, uneven intervals. If he emerged unscathed, he was released on the theory that the Deity had interceded to attest his innocence. If he was burned, this confirmed his guilt; and he was punished.

The common people were subjected to the water ordeal—hot or cold. The naked arm was submerged as far as the elbow into a caldron of boiling water or oil; or the accused was thrown into a stream or lake to see if he could float without swimming. The end result was the same; if the man survived, he was innocent. If he did not, he was guilty! It is interesting to note that every system of law in recorded history has at one time or other employed a type of ordeal as a test of guilt; and some of the emerging countries still use it to this day.

With William the Conqueror and his Normans came a new mode of trial to supplement the ordeal—the wager of battle. The accused was forced to do mortal combat with his accuser. If he lost, he was guilty; if he won, he was innocent; and skilled gladiators often were hired by the accuser to augment the odds in favor of guilt.

These were crude methods of enforcing conformity to the moral and social standards of the community; but throughout them runs the common thread of contest, of one party pitted against an opponent, either human or supernatural. They are the beginnings of our present adversary system.

The wager of law eventually followed, which involved the use of compurgators—twelve friends and neighbors of the accused who would swear by the Deity that they knew him to be a good man who could be believed under oath and who could not be guilty. This was the rough beginning of trial by jury; and the magic number of twelve remains with us to this day.

The early judges, whether from the hundred-courts, courts of the shire, or royally appointed later on, went out to the locale of the crime. They saw what the accused looked like, observed his clothes, heard him speak, perhaps saw his wife and children in the courtyard; they were familiar with the manor and estate where he earned his bread and meat; they appreciated something of his aspirations and heartaches. Even more important, these judges knew the local rules of custom and usage which had been applied over hundreds of years to similar disputes. These rules of tradition, as distinguished from the royal edict of a king or an emperor, actually sprang upward from the soil and its people.

No one can explain for sure why particular royal judges during Henry II's reign began to write out their decisions in actual cases in the form of a written opinion. It could have begun as the fetish of a single visionary man. If a dispute arose between two individual trial judges out on the assize circuit over what the law of custom and usage was in a given situation of fact, an appeal might be taken to the *curia regis,* the king's court, at the Great Hall in Westminster. These justices also started to write out their decisions so that there could be a rule of *law common* for the entire realm. Here was the beginning of the Common Law concept, the promulgation of established rules of custom and usage in the *written opinions* of judges as they decided the fate of an individual accused who stood before them.

It was, for example, written out in an early opinion that if a man (1) broke and (2) entered (3) the dwelling house of another (4) in the nighttime (5) with an intent to commit a felony after getting in, he was guilty of the crime of *burglary;* and this definition has remained virtually unchanged throughout the centuries. If the house was not a private dwelling, or if the breaking and entering was in the daytime, the offender was not guilty of burglary but of some lesser offense. By custom and usage, night was more hazardous than day, a man's home more sacred than his shop.

In a real sense, the rules sprang from the people themselves to be enforced by the judges; and once announced in written opinions, they were precedent which all judges were bound to follow in all subsequent cases. Precedent became the bone and sinew of the Common Law system.

Through the early haze, it developed that a man could be prosecuted only for a crime already explicitly defined, so the principle of fair warning of the community standards of criminal responsibility expected of him emerged. This meant that a convenient definition of a new crime could not be conjured up *after* an unpopular man acted, just so the king's men could flog or jail him.

Other well-defined premises somehow evolved: The people began to fear the royal judges appointed by the king. They were the king's agents, no longer the community-oriented, local men of the hundred-courts and courts of the shire. The local leaders clamored for local representation in the process of justice; and by 1166, at the Clarendon assizes, Henry II gave in. The jury became a matter of right, not the jury we know today, but its crude yet important ancestor.

Still other concepts came along: the right to have witnesses examined publicly and on oath; the right to have the witnesses confront the accused; the right to cross-examination; the procedure of habeas corpus which guarantees release from illegal confinement and which Blackstone labeled "the most celebrated writ in English law."

By the time the great barons extracted the Magna Charta from King John at Runnymede on June 15, 1215, these basic principles were so well described that the clauses relating to the judiciary were in the main a restatement of the Common Law rules of the judges:

> Common pleas are to be held at a place certain; punishments are to be in accordance with the nature of the offense and are to be assessed only by the accused's honest neighbors who are not to deprive him of his means of earning a living; no justice, constable, sheriff, or bailiff is to be appointed who does not know the law or who is unwilling to observe it; no man can be sent to the Ordeal on the uncorroborated testimony of a bailiff; and [the basic description of due process of law] no freeman shall be taken or imprisoned or disseised or outlawed or exiled without judgment of his peers, or by the law of the land. . . .

It was these premises, first expressed in the written opinions of the judges, long before there was a Parliament or effective legislative assembly, or talk of constitutions, that became the foundation of individual liberty and human dignity. They became so deeply ingrained in the traditions and mores of the people that neither king nor Parliament could expunge them, although both tried hard at times.

"Twenty-seven," the crier continued after removing another wooden ball from his cloistered box.

"Leightbert Russell," the registrar responded after matching name to number on his list.

The professionals, black and white alike, moved easily in their robes and wigs that exemplified centuries of British justice in both the finite and the abstract.

The origin of the robes is no mystery, they being no more than the same academic gowns that identified scholars in the Age of Enlightenment during England's revival of learning as she broke out of the Middle Ages; but there was a personalized twist that distinguished the gowns of the barristers from those of the mere academicians.

A small, black pouch hung over the left shoulder, a nostalgic reminder of the early days when barristers could not accept a fixed fee for services in the king's courts. They could receive a voluntary honorarium from a client who slipped money into the black bag slung across the shoulder; but the barrister reserved the right to take or reject any case, contingent in part upon the amount of the honorarium dropped into the pouch by the accused as he passed behind the bar.

Although the pouch, like the anatomical appendix, serves no useful purpose today, its draw-cords which hang in front of the robe impart a sense of security to the nervous barrister who fingers them while examining a witness or addressing the jury.

The traditional wigs, on the other hand, are not as accurately explainable. The purists claim that they were merely a vain affectation which accompanied the robes when England's snuff-sniffing gentry adopted the fastidiously curled periwigs as a fashion of the moment. They gave no thought to creating a tradition for posterity, legal, academic, or otherwise.

The sentimentalists refuse this blasé explanation, insisting that the wigs were especially created for legal purposes. In the days of the sixteenth century or thereabouts, the secular courts, called the king's courts, were locked in deadly rivalry with the ecclesiastical courts. The men who performed the function of barristers in the Common Law courts, for the most part, were ecclesiastics with shaved heads. Jealous of their prerogatives and fearful of being overwhelmed, the king's justices ordered that no ecclesiastic would be permitted to appear in the king's courts; but there were not enough trained and competent nonclerical "barristers" to handle the pressing needs of the clients with business before His Majesty's courts. The deceptive expedient of the clerics, therefore, was the adoption of the wigs to cover their shaved heads; so the wig signifies that it is not the person before the bar who counts, but how he performs.

Perhaps the debate over the history of the wigs will never be settled conclusively—and what does it matter? For they are a part of the Common Law tradition.

"Challenge!" Hon. Eric Hallinan, Attorney General for the Crown, said crisply, shattering the silence of the room, when name "Number eleven" was announced by the registrar. There was no other word of explanation, but prospective juror eleven was excused.

There was an expectant air in the courtroom, but it was relaxed and assured. Right and justice would prevail because safe precedents were firmly established to protect both king and citizen. Tradition dictated that this trial, although potentially sensational, would be nothing more than the *orderly* search for the truth. Regardless of the deep-seated emotions of the participants, courtroom decorum would prevail since this ingredient is as essential to the determination of truth as cleanliness is to the safety of the patient in an operating room.

❋   ❋   ❋

The jury was finally selected: three accountants, a bakery owner, a sponge merchant, a liquor dealer, a general-insurance agent, a grocery clerk, two general merchants, an icehouse manager, and the owner of Nassau's largest grocery store, who was elected foreman. One by one, each man placed his right hand on the Holy Bible and repeated the oath of the centuries: "I swear by Almighty God that I will well and truly try and true deliberance make between our sovereign lord the King and the prisoner at the Bar, whom I shall have in charge and a true verdict give according to the evidence. So help me God!"

Now, Hon. A. F. Adderley, with black skin and African features, rose automatically, made his Tudor bow toward the bench, and began: "May it please Your Honor. . . ." He swung gracefully to his right to face the twelve white men seated in individual chairs in the jury box: "Mr. Foreman and gentlemen of the jury. . . ."

With those opening words from the mouth of counsel for the Crown, His Majesty the King "joined issue" with Marie Alfred Fouquereaux de Marigny, citizen. Under this Common Law system, if their roles could be reversed, the king would hold no greater rights than Alfred de Marigny, for each man's rights are tantamount to those of all others, and no man suffers any dilution of his fundamental rights because of his station in life.

Two personages were missing not only from the courtroom but from Government House and the Island of New Providence as well: the Royal Governor and his Duchess who had fled to Baltimore, Washington, and New York to escape the threat of involvement and embarrassment.

12

The Crown's Thrust

The jurors, whose selection and swearing required only fifty-five minutes, waited like a first-night audience at a well publicized play for Alfred Adderley to reach his pace. Although the jury box was elevated a good three feet, he towered over them in an attitude of command. His massive shoulders, bursting to escape the confines of his robe, were permanently slouched as though the man deliberately sought to minimize his overwhelming physical bulk; and the slight hump of his back added depth to his chest dimension.

"All individuals within the jurisdiction of any British territory are subject to the king's peace; and every life is entitled to full protection by the strong arm of law and justice"—this most eloquent member of the Bahamian bar warmed to his task—"but the details of this murder, the torture of a fellow creature, surpasses by far the records in the annals of this colony and the history of crime in our fair land. Murder is murder and a life is a life, but this murder is as Shakespeare says in one of his sonnets, 'as black as hell, as dark as night' in its foul conception, a deed which could only originate in a depraved, strange, and sadistic mind, a mind indeed which is foreign to the usual mind which comes before this court, with a complete disregard for humanity in so vile a murder which besmirches the name and peace of this tranquil land."

Adderley's audience, in the jury box, within the confines

of the courtroom, and outside, the overflow crowds on the lawns surrounding the yellow stucco building who could hear through the open windows, was now mesmerized by the rhythmic roll of his words. Extraneous sounds, the occasional nervous cough, the rustle of a cardboard fan moving through the humid atmosphere, the shuffle of a foot, and the squeak of a chair, were all ignored in the far reaches of the single hypnotized mind of the jelled congregation.

"Sir Harry Oakes, a baronet of Great Britain, came to the Bahama Islands about eight years ago. He loved this colony and became a resident and indeed a Bahamian citizen, beloved and respected by all. Sir Harry was married and the father of five children, the eldest of whom is Nancy de Marigny, the wife of the accused, now nineteen years and five months of age."

Adderley captivated his audience for over an hour before reaching his final act:

"If in the end after you have considered the nature of the crime and the evidence dealing with:
(1) The compelling motive of hatred, humiliation, and gain which the Crown alleges influenced the accused to end the life of Sir Harry Oakes;
(2) the desperate financial condition of the accused;
(3) his presence alone outside the gates of Westbourne on this night of all nights;
(4) his wakefulness on his return home;
(5) his curious visit, yet significant, to the police station;
(6) his anxiety to remove all traces of gasoline from his premises after the discovery of Sir Harry's burned body;
(7) the discovery of burned hairs on his hands, arms, beard, moustache, eyebrows, and head;
(8) his excuses for burned hairs;
(9) his failure to produce the shirt and tie worn by him on the fatal night;
(10) the discovery of his fingerprint, that sign manual of all human beings;
(11) his expressions of hatred;

(12) his callous references to Sir Harry Oakes after death;

(13) his most important inquiry relative to a conviction on the failure of a prosecution to discover the deadly weapon;

(14) his inquiry into the value of circumstantial evidence in convicting a person. . . .

If a case built upon such a foundation fails in satisfying you of his guilt, then in the name of all we hold good and sacred in the administration of British justice, do not let the innocent suffer."

Skillfully used by a master like Adderley, the English language is one of the most potent tools known to man. It can quell antagonists and start wars, give solace to the weak and doom the mighty.

Even now as he stood in the well of the court, Alfred Adderley shared that eerie bond of coincidence attaching him to Harry Oakes. He was the youthful black barrister who had relinquished his seat in the House of Assembly years earlier so that Harry Oakes could be elected a member.

Now with the wheel come full circle, Adderley not only enjoyed the reputation as the most eloquent member of the Bahamian bar, he was also its most successful. Regardless of the side on which he appeared, for the Crown or defense, he had never lost a murder case; and it was not surprising that Eric Hallinan, the Attorney General for the Crown in the Bahamas, immediately briefed Adderley on the de Marigny case to assure Adderley's timely presence at his side at the prosecution table, and to deny him to the defendant.

"On the other hand:

(1) If the evidence satisfies you beyond all reasonable doubt of the guilt of the accused;

(2) and if the evidence based upon circumstances which are so convincing that the facts considered by a reasonable man lead you to the conclusion that the accused is guilty, then I say to you let no extraneous consideration interpose itself between you and your duty to your country, through the oaths which you

have taken, but rather return a verdict of guilty without fear or favor, knowing that you will be doing the
thing which will satisfy your God, your consciences,
and the demands of British justice."

Adderley was finished. He bowed easily to the jury, turned
to his left, and bowed once again to the Lord Chief Justice;
and the only sound in the entire room was the swish of his
robe and the thudding of his feet as he made his way back
to his position behind the prosecution's table.

None of the active participants in the courtroom—Sir
Oscar, the barristers, the jurors, or the witnesses (except
Harold Christie)—knew what went on aboard Meyer Lansky's motor cruiser at the quay, only a stone's throw from
the courthouse, and subsequently at Westbourne, the night
and early morning hours of July 7–8; but if the Common
Law formula was sound, and if each of the major actors
played out his role skillfully and with integrity, the truth of
de Marigny's guilt or innocence would emerge from the
caldron of the contest: de Marigny would be found not guilty.
If, on the other hand, the formula was faulty or if the per-
formers muffed their lines with lackadaisical performances,
Marie Alfred Fouquereaux de Marigny would hang by the
neck until dead.

The Common Law trial was not designed to solve the case
finally by ferreting out Lansky's involvement; rather, it was to
test the guilt of a particular accused, de Marigny, by forcing
the Crown to prove this guilt beyond a reasonable doubt.
If the Crown could not meet this burden with all the wealth,
personnel and physical facilities at its command, the accused,
guilty or innocent, was entitled to go free. Any other arrangement is fraught with too great a danger to the liberty
of any and all individuals.

13

The View at Westbourne

As the weary bus transporting the jurors to Westbourne for their view of the scene pulled away from Rawson Square to turn west on Bay Street, the crowds reluctantly gave way for the passage of this elite band which now enjoyed celebrity status. The sights were all familiar: the Prince George Hotel, the Savoy Theatre, the Produce Exchange where their servants shopped daily, Sir Harry's British Colonial, the public beach of the Western Esplanade, and then the open road that led past Fort Charlotte, out around Brown's Point, and finally to the golf course that supplied Westbourne's backdrop of ease and opulence.

All the jurors had passed Westbourne dozens of times; some had been inside for one chore or another. American actress Maxine Elliott once lived there. Oakes paid $250,000 for it in 1934. Now, as they alighted from the bus, all held back, shuffling forward slowly and with uncertain pace, reflecting man's innate fear of death, especially violent death.

Westbourne was not particularly overwhelming, being an architect's veritable nightmare. Its longest dimension ran east and west, paralleling the long axis of the Island of New Providence itself. There was always confusion as to whether the north or south of the house was front or back, since the north faced the water and the south the road. The golf course was on the east. Westbourne's outside appearance was

plain, like that of a Missouri River house, or even a western
hacienda. A covered walkway around the ground story was
fenced in by irregular and sporadic latticework of no particular design that supported heavy clusters of bougainvillea.
The covering for this walkway was formed by the floor of
the balcony around the second story, which was enclosed by
a simple balustrade of vertical two-by-fours. Outside stair-
ways climbed the north and east walls of the ground floor
to emerge through the balcony floors. Without their own
protective balustrades, these rectangular openings would
have created dangerous hazards.

The second level was also reached by an inside L-shaped
stairway which opened from the entrance hall on the west
side of the house, accessible to main entrance doors in the
front and back (north and south sides).

As the jurors hesitantly climbed this flight of stairs, they
noticed sooty smudges on the wood paneling that encased
them, although the varnish and paint were not blistered.
These smudges increased in size and random pattern on the
wardrobe doors in the second-story hallway; the jurors anticipated that the fire would be explained to them during the
trial. There were irregular rust-colored stains on the hall
carpeting, as well as on the covering on the treads of the
stairs.

At the urging of the Attorney General, the foreman of the
jury, Sands, hesitantly led his compatriots into the master
bedroom, which lay just east of the hallway. It was a nonconformist double-L-shaped room with part of its southeast
corner truncated to permit the balcony to become symmetrical, an illogical sacrifice of usable interior space. There
were two twin beds in the room, the head of each abutting
the west wall, which meant that the beds were set east-west,
the same as the main axis of the house. The light-beige carpeting was heavily stained by a brownish liquid, and an irreg-
ularly shaped rectangle from its center was missing near the
beds. The north bed was rumpled but still covered with
a set of sheets, smudged and sliding to the floor.

The south bed was in total disarray, stained, odorous, and heavily sprinkled with feathers from a pillow.

Four doors permitted ingress to and egress from this master bedroom: One opened onto the north balcony, just west of the outside stairway; a second passed into what was known as the middle bedroom; another opened back into the main hall on the south side; and the fourth led to the northwest room, a bedroom-sitting room combination that also contained a bath in its south portion which Sir Harry used part of the time. This northwest room was also reached by a door off the hall, just north of the L-shaped staircase.

The middle room was initially designed as a dressing room but was now an inept architectural inconsistency, since anyone using Sir Harry's master bedroom either had to pass through the middle bedroom or go outside and walk along the north balcony to enter the main upstairs bathroom, which was immediately east of the middle room. A door from this middle room also opened onto the north balcony.

There was a further bedroom just east of the bathroom with one bed placed north-south. It also contained doors that opened onto the north balcony and the south balcony; and in addition to the door opening into the bathroom to the west, its two windows looked out over the east-balcony stairway.

The jurors all watched Alfred de Marigny, slyly out of the corners of their eyes, as he accompanied them between the two constables of the guard. All labored under the firm edict of the Lord Chief Justice not to speak to de Marigny, nor he to them, nor they among themselves, during this "view of the scene." Their mission was simply to familiarize themselves with the physical contour of the house so that the evidence, as it unfolded in subsequent days in the courtroom, would be more understandable.

Although he peered into it from the hall door, de Marigny did not actually enter the death room, stopping as though deterred by some invisible barrier.

It was a strained, subdued, almost silent inspection; and

without audible instruction, the jurors congealed behind Foreman Sands to head for their bus with steps far quicker than those used to enter Westbourne twenty minutes earlier. The sun was halfway through its sudden plunge below the horizon as the bus hurried back toward Rawson Square so that the jurors could make their pensive ways to the Rozelda Hotel, where they would be sequestered under custodial guard until they voted the fate of Alfred de Marigny.

14

The Paradoxical Witness

Harold Christie's knuckles blanched as he clutched the rail around the witness box where he stood in British style to give his evidence, nervously swaying his body from one leg to the other in a vain attempt to gain composure.

The Crown called him with considerable reservation, although Attorney Eric Hallinan really had no alternative: As everyone officially connected with the case then believed, Harold Christie was the last person to see Harry Oakes alive and the first to discover him dead—at least this was Christie's story from the beginning. This conclusion was accurate enough, but the in-between details were badly flawed.

Then forty-seven years old, Christie was a native Bahamian whose white family proudly traced its arrival to the mid-eighteenth century, not too long after Woodes Rogers' first efforts to clean out the pirates. Long a leading "Bay Street Merchant," "Bay Street Boy," or "Bay Street Bandit," the label depending upon the prejudice of the describer, he was considered the Bahamas' number-two citizen, topped only by the dead baronet, whom Christie gladly called number-one.

In physical appearance Christie was average and undistinguished in every respect. His receding dark hair exposed a great, curved, symmetrical dome which was now naked for several inches back of where the hairline had run years earlier. The hairs thinned at this new boundary, exposing

bare skin behind them to give the illusion of a canted halo.
The eyes were nondescript as was the nose and, for that
matter, the entire round face. He stood some forty pounds
heavier than he was when he served in the Royal Canadian
Air Force during World War I, although he did not appear
particularly puffy or grotesquely overweight.

In response to Hallinan's preliminary questions to permit
Christie to become more familiar with his forum of the
witness box, Christie explained that his occupation was "real
estate and a member of the Executive Council."

Christie was a bachelor whose loyalty and devotion to his
mother dominated his every activity. Lansky's men obviously
knew of this character trait when they included Mrs. Christie in their death-and-mutilation threats; but the jurors had
no way of knowing of this pressure on Christie as he gave
his evidence.

He cautiously released the rail with his right hand, like an
invalid testing his ability to walk, and reached into his rear
pants pocket to pull out a folded, starched white handkerchief, which he used to dab his face erratically. Great beads
of sweat popped out uncontrollably over all his exposed
skin, and his spastic blotting with the handkerchief was
palliative only. Soon his white linen suit, complemented by
a solid-black four-in-hand tie, was wet under the armpits and
across the shoulders.

"Well, in June, and I believe also in the latter part of
May," Christie replied nervously, "while Lady Oakes and
the children were in the States, I spent considerable time at
Westbourne. She was at Bar Harbor, you know, and I believe
the younger children were out of their private schools; and
Nancy was in Miami on her way to a school in Vermont, an
art school, I believe; so Sir Harry was living alone at Westbourne and I had stayed with him on many occasions."

Hallinan made no effort to halt Christie's nervous ram-
blings, hoping that he would soon find the witness box more
to his comfort.

We are without an *official* court transcript of the verbatim questions and answers of the trial testimony, for British court procedure in the Bahamas did not include the services of an official court reporter. The Lord Chief Justice, at the end of each witness's testimony, using a nib pen which he dipped into an ancient and stained inkwell, laboriously wrote a longhand summation into a bound black ledger. This slowed the pace appreciably and dulled some of the dramatic effect. Fortunately, several of the news reporters and wire-service representatives, seated at a special press table directly behind the bar of the court, in front of the spectators' mahogany benches, made their own verbatim shorthand notes which were subsequently transcribed and printed.

For orienting purposes, it is well to remember that July 7, 1943, fell on a Wednesday which means that the eighth was Thursday, the preceding Sunday was July 4.

Christie's voice was now settled and his responses came in more natural, loud tones. He spent at least 50 percent of his time with Sir Harry, he continued, and slept at Westbourne on Sunday and Tuesday nights of the critical week. According to accidental custom, he and Sir Harry usually woke each morning at about the same time, somewhere between seven and seven-thirty. Each came out from his own room onto the north balcony where they said good-morning, inhaled the bracing sea air, and admired the spacious views. Within minutes, the maid, undoubtedly hearing them moving about, came up to take their breakfast orders. Most often, they would re-enter their respective bedrooms to dress and prepare for the hot breakfast which they ate at a table on the north balcony. Sometimes they would breakfast in their pajamas, depending upon the day's schedule; but they were men of action and were usually ready to sally forth as soon as breakfast was finished.

This standard routine was followed on Wednesday morning, July 7, when Christie, alone, left Westbourne to attend a meeting of the Executive Council. At around noon, he met Sir Harry at the security office in the Royal Victoria Hotel, where Sir Harry obtained an exit permit, since he expected to leave for Bar Harbor on Friday, the ninth, to join Lady Oakes and the children in an escape from the humid, sultry Bahamian summer.

Christie and Sir Harry got into the Oakes car with Oakes driving (Sir Harry considered a personal chauffeur an extravagant expense and a supercilious affectation) and stopped by Seagate, Christie's residence toward the center of Nassau, to pick up his tennis racket and shoes. He and Sir Harry then relaxed for perhaps an hour on the north balcony of Westbourne before going to play tennis. He did not remember whether the maid offered drinks on the porch, but he was positive that he took nothing to drink. By five, he and Sir Harry were playing tennis with Christie's niece, Sally Sawyer, and her friend, a Miss McMahon, until the arrival of Mrs. Heneage, a neighbor, and Charles Hubbard, a retired dime-store millionaire from London who lived two doors west of Westbourne. This broke up the tennis match, and all six people retired to the north balcony, which Sir Harry preferred to any room of the house because the ocean view reminded him of the coasts of his native Maine.

Christie was now much more relaxed, almost at ease with himself and his surroundings, as he recited noncontroversial events that required a minimum of explanation. His profuse sweating had slackened, although it had not stopped altogether, and he continued to dab reflexively at his forehead, now working the wet white handkerchief in and out of the breast pocket of his jacket.

The two girls left about dusk, he explained, and it was perhaps eight-thirty when Sir Harry, Mrs. Heneage, Charles Hubbard, and Christie went downstairs. Hubbard wanted to take the party to the Prince George Hotel for dinner, but Sir Harry persuaded them to remain at Westbourne. Dinner was finished by nine-thirty, and afterward the four of them played Chinese checkers.

Christie began to sweat again, shifting his weight uncomfortably, when the Attorney General brought up the subject of his car. When he joined Sir Harry in the Oakes car in the afternoon, Christie replied, his own car was left at his

office on Bay Street. At about nine in the evening, his driver
telephoned; and Christie told him to bring the car and park
it in the area around the Bahamas Country Club, not immediately adjacent to Westbourne. He did not see the car until
the next morning.

He was eager to volunteer that since he did not go outside
the main entrance of Westbourne, he could not see his own
car parked near the club. Sophisticated courtroom observers
realized immediately that Christie's eager gratuitous remark
about not leaving the main entrance of Westbourne was anticipatory and of critical importance to both Christie and the
Crown.

At about eleven o'clock—it could have been a few minutes
either way—Hubbard and Mrs. Heneage said good-night and
left. Sir Harry offered to drive Mrs. Heneage home in his
car, but Hubbard would not permit it. Christie and Sir
Harry walked the guests to Hubbard's car, which was parked
about three hundred feet away, west of the tennis court.

After seeing the guests off, Christie and Sir Harry went
up to Sir Harry's room. He watched Sir Harry undress and
get into his pajamas, raise one side of the mosquito netting
which was carefully tucked under the mattress, and crawl
into bed. He thought Sir Harry turned on the radio before
crawling under the mosquito net.

Christie sat down in a chair, and the two of them talked for
perhaps fifteen or twenty minutes before he borrowed a pair
of Sir Harry's spectacles, took an earlier issue of *Time*, and
went to the easternmost bedroom, where he put on a pair
of Sir Harry's pajamas that he had also used the preceding
night.

Having been on the second floor at Westbourne, the jury
could better understand Christie's next description as he explained that his east bedroom was the third room away from
Sir Harry's master bedroom, there being a bath and middle
bedroom between them.

Christie could not remember whether he closed any of the
doors between the two bedrooms, although he remembered
closing the door between his room and the bath the night

before because of swarms of mosquitoes that entered the house through the windows, which Sir Harry always insisted on keeping open.

Now, Harold Christie read *Time* for half or three-quarters of an hour, until he became drowsy; he turned out his light, tucked in his mosquito netting, and went to sleep. Sometime later—there was no way for him to fix the time either precisely or remotely—he awoke itching uncomfortably from mosquito bites. He got out of bed grumpily, turned on the lights, and discovered that several mosquitoes were inside his bed net; he killed them, once more extinguished the light, and returned to bed.

Some time later—again there was no way to even estimate the hour—a violent summer storm woke him. The lightning flashes invading his room lit it and the entire island bright as day; the thunder of countless megatons of bombs pounded and exploded; the hurricanelike winds drove the rain in solid, horizontal sheets against roof and walls. Although the storm woke him, it did not keep him awake, as violent Caribbean outbursts were as commonplace to his experience as sun and humidity.

He guessed that he might have remained awake ten minutes during both the mosquito and thunderstorm episodes; but he perceived no other sounds or stimuli to cause him concern or wonder.

The Attorney General respectfully requested the languid luncheon adjournment of Sir Oscar, anticipating that his witness now approached the most vulnerable part of his entire stay in the witness box; but it proved a mistake, since Christie's afternoon testimony required another ten to fifteen minutes before he regained anything resembling ease and composure.

He never remembered any doors at Westbourne being locked at any time, Christie continued, Sir Harry not thinking it necessary. Christie knew that he himself did not lock any doors that night. None of the servants were live-in. They were day help only, the cook, Mabel Ellis, leaving Westbourne around ten o'clock after dinner was finished and the

dishes and kitchen cleaned up. There was a guard or care-
taker of sorts who patrolled the Bahamas Country Club and
presumably looked in on Westbourne occasionally. It was a
loose arrangement, his security duties never being specifically
spelled out. One of the great attractions of the Bahamas to
Sir Harry was its informal openness: No burglar ever dared
to enter the homes of the wealthy and privileged. Sir Harry
had often spoken of this delightful contrast to the States,
Canada, England, and other parts of the world where cautious security arrangements afforded the only safe way of
life.

The Attorney General next shifted his interest to the
critical events of Thursday morning.

Christie awoke shortly after daybreak and lolled in bed
for a time before going out on the north balcony to meet Sir
Harry. It was now after seven o'clock, but Harry was not
there. He walked the few paces to the screen door that covered the opening into the master bedroom and called, "Hi,
Harry!" He waited for a short time, probably seconds, and
upon receiving no response he opened the unlocked door and
entered Oakes' bedroom.

Christie was again sweating profusely; and while his voice
remained loud and clear, it was obvious that he forced his
painful description, calling up all his resources.

Even before he noticed the charred mosquito-net bars
eerily suspended over the bed, his stomach sank and his
legs became weak as he intuitively sensed something dread-
fully amiss. He saw Sir Harry's body, and as far as he could
now remember, the head was nearer the south side of the
bed than the north. Christie was greatly shocked. He lifted
up his friend's head and shook his warm body. Since the body
was not cold, Christie poured some water from a vacuum
flask on the table into a glass. He got another pillow from
the adjoining bed and placed it under Sir Harry's head.

Now his descriptions of his reactions, stark and reflexive,
dramatically detailed his panic. When he first saw the body,
the head was on a pillow; but to the best of his recollection,
there was no covering on the pillow. Christie rushed out on

the west side of the north balcony in the direction of the
servants' house and yelled for help, although he does not
remember the exact words used.

He re-entered Sir Harry's bedroom and called the watchman from the south window out over the south balcony. He
remembered going down the main staircase inside the house;
and it was possible that he went outside as he was looking
for help, but he could not say for sure, because he did not
remember.

Christie described himself as being in a funk of terror, as
consuming as the earlier tropical blast that had wakened
him before the daylight hours; but his cries awakened Mrs.
Madeleine Kelly, the wife of Sir Harry's Nassau business
manager, who lived in a house on the grounds. What he
meant was, Christie corrected himself through strenuous
breathing, that he telephoned Mrs. Kelly; he then called his
brother, Frank Christie; he called Colonel Erskine-Lindop's
house, but he was not at home, so Christie was forced to
explain to the police commissioner's wife that something had
happened to Sir Harry. As a result of this telephone call the
police commissioner was alerted and soon arrived at
Westbourne. Christie did not mention his calls to the Duke
at Government House.

At about this same time, Mrs. Kelly appeared in Sir Harry's
room to report that she had called a doctor. Christie thought
that he had wiped Sir Harry's face with a wet towel from
the bathroom before he called Mrs. Kelly; and now, heart-
ened by her actual presence on the scene, he wet the towel
again with water from the bathroom and wiped Sir Harry's
head.

When he first entered the bedroom, he noticed that the
carpet was burned. There was smoke in the room but he did
not see any fire. He went through the entire east end of the
second floor, his bedroom, the bathroom, the middle bedroom, to see if there was any sign of fire; but he saw none.
He likely went out onto the south veranda from his room
but he could not be sure. When he went down the inside
stairs, he saw burn marks on the wood paneling.

He remembered seeing an electric fan on the floor in the northeast corner of Sir Harry's room, just at the edge of the north twin bed, turned on and blowing air toward Sir Harry's body.

He saw the six-paneled Chinese screen standing in the usual zigzag way, paralleling Sir Harry's bed on the south.

He thought he called Charles Hubbard on the telephone after Mrs. Kelly's arrival; and he was still wearing Sir Harry's borrowed, "sort of bottle-brown" pajamas when Dr. Quackenbush arrived. As a matter of fact, Christie did not get dressed until around nine-thirty because of the excitement.

He and Sir Harry had planned a trip that morning with Raymond Moss and Étienne Dupuch, Nassau's leading news-papermen, to a pasture of new sheep that Sir Harry had imported from Australia in the hope that they might thrive on the thin grasses of the Islands, to give the Bahamas a fledgling wool-growing industry to ease the inevitable depression which everyone knew would follow the end of World War II. They also planned to inspect the waterworks that Sir Harry had built at Satellite, another philanthropic attempt to elevate the standard of living on the main island of New Providence.

Christie noticeably winced when the Attorney General once more brought up the matter of his car, admitting that they planned to use it as the vehicle of transportation for the inspection tours. He was usually elected the driver on this type of outing with Sir Harry.

He could think of no one who would have known that he was spending the night at Westbourne except his man, Gibson; or Mrs. Heneage and Charles Hubbard might have learned it during the course of the evening, although he had no independent recollection of the subject having been discussed.

Yes, he remembered turning Sir Harry around in the bed so that his head was at the north instead of the south end. Christie did this before wiping Sir Harry's head with the damp towel the first time.

Christie's personal turmoil appeared genuine, and his direct evidence came through effectively enough. It set the stage for the Crown's theory that Alfred de Marigny, intimately familiar with the physical layout at Westbourne, treacherously stole in under the cover of night to bludgeon his father-in-law to death as he lay in his bed.

Eric Hallinan scored well with this first witness. The jurors quite properly attributed his extreme nervousness only to his ordeal in reliving the trauma of discovering his great friend's battered and cruelly burned body. There was no reason to suspect Christie of any other involvement.

No one had any reason to think it strange that Harold Christie failed to describe any telephone calls to the Royal Governor at Government House after discovering the body. After all, he did telephone the superintendent of police, which was all that could be expected of him.

15

The Meddlesome
Cross-examiner

"My lord, that is all!" The Attorney General's words reverberated around the courtroom while Harold Christie remained uncertainly in the witness box.

And in the Civil Law system, also called the Roman Law
system, used in the countries of Europe, throughout the ex-
panse of South America, in Japan, in both the Chinas, and
with modification in the Communist-bloc nations, *that would
have been all*, even in those countries where the accused is
entitled to be confronted personally with the witnesses
against him.

Cross-examination is the distinctive contribution of the
Common Law system to the fact-finding process.

In those Civil Law countries where a trial in open court
does take place, if the opposing lawyer wishes to ask more
of a witness called by the other side, he cannot put his questions to the witness directly. Rather, he must ask the presiding judge to ask the question of the witness; and the judge
may or may not grant his request. Even if he does, the stilted
questions which result, worse than an effort to communicate
through an inadequate and biased interpreter, in no way
serve to test the truthfulness of the witness. They may be
used for some slight elaboration and clarification, but there
are seldom more than three or four or half-a-dozen questions

asked through this priggish, indirect procedure which is hardly worth the title of "cross-examination."

In those Civil Law countries where there is *no* face-to-face confrontation in open trial, the evidence of all witnesses is presented to the judge in the form of sworn affidavits before functionaries who resemble notaries public. If the opposing lawyers and their respective clients are not satisfied with the initial written affirmations of the witnesses, they may submit additional written interrogatories to the notary public, who passes them along perfunctorily; but the answers are worked out leisurely, in consultation, even collusion, to advance the witness's side of the case. There may be several exchanges of written interrogatories; but at no time and in no place can the witness be personally challenged by the opposing attorney in a spontaneous test of truthfulness.

For reasons that are totally incomprehensible to Common Law lawyers, the Civil Law procedures assume, in effect, that every witness is honest, open, and above board, without bias or prejudice; he perceives perfectly like an automaton, arranges and checks his perceptions like a computer, so that his reports are the inviolable truth in every case.

The Common Law concept denies the belief that angels in the form of unimpeachable witnesses exist on this earth. The report of *every* witness, therefore, must be subject to challenge by direct confrontation in the courtroom, no matter how lofty his status, exalted his intellect, or hallowed his reputation for honesty and integrity.

Godfrey Higgs rose immediately from his station at the defense table, bowed to the Lord Chief Justice, and said, "May it please Your Honor!"

In his mid-forties, Higgs was white, with the usual British background in the Inns of Court, his apprenticeship through the Outer Bar, and his professional arrival in the Inner Bar. His fine, straight black hair, parted high on the right in the vogue of the Twenties, was perpetually slicked down, rimming a tanned face which exaggerated sky-blue pupils. His broad shoulders set off a trim, athletic waist, making him appear a professional cricketer or baseball player.

He spoke in quick, clear sentences, always grammatically correct, with precise, measured syntax. He was the logician and careful tactician, making no effort to match Adderley in oratorical eloquence.

He was actually de Marigny's second choice as chief counsel for the defense. Two days after his arrest on July 9, when de Marigny decided that the authorities meant business and intended to put him away for his father-in-law's murder, he requested the superintendent of police to ask Alfred Adderley to visit him in jail so that he could engage Adderley to defend him. When he heard nothing from Adderley for a week, he employed Higgs to represent him at the preliminary hearing on July 19, when the Crown was forced to present enough evidence to convince the magistrate that de Marigny should be put through the expense and humiliation of a full-dress Supreme Court trial.

De Marigny learned at the preliminary hearing for the first time that Adderley was appearing for the Crown; and after being bound over to stand trial in the Supreme Court, de Marigny passed Adderley in the corridor.

"At least you could have had the courtesy of sending me a refusal," de Marigny addressed Adderley hostilely.

"I don't know what you mean," Adderley responded in surprise.

"Ha!" de Marigny blustered in dramatic French huff. "I had the police superintendent contact you to see if you would represent me. You could have had the personal and professional courtesy to acknowledge my request and turn me down!"

"This is the first time I have heard of it," Adderley said in a subdued manner. "Had I received your request for consultation, professional protocol would have demanded that I come to see you in person. I assure you that this is the first time that I have heard of any such request."

Although de Marigny obtained the man he considered the next best barrister to Adderley in the Bahamas when Higgs became his lawyer, he was badly shaken that the police superintendent had not even delivered his message to Ad-

derley; and because of Adderley's reputation and the requirements of his professional ethics, de Marigny was certain that
Adderley told him the truth when he denied receiving the
message.

It is not possible to know what happened to de Marigny's
message to Adderley. Under British law, the police are clearly
required to transmit a prisoner's request to see a solicitor or
barrister of his own choosing. It could have fallen innocently and accidentally by the wayside; or someone interested in strengthening the Crown's strategic position at the
time of trial may have assumed responsibility for stifling it.
We can be sure that Attorney General Hallinan would never
have stooped to such a shenanigan. Melchen and Barker were
back in Miami. Of all those with deep personal interest in
the outcome of the case, only the Duke and Christie remained
in Nassau.

Higgs opened his cross-examination with a relatively col-
lateral matter. It is usually a mistake for the cross-examiner
to launch a frontal attack directly on the crucial issues without considerable preliminary sparring.

No, he did not know, Christie responded, that Sir Harry
had offered de Marigny the managership of the Bahamas General Trust Company in Frederick Street, which Sir Harry
planned to purchase. Yes, Sir Harry had contemplated acquiring "the Jones property" which comprised between four
and seven acres with a frontage of three hundred feet. Sir
Harry told him he had offered this to de Marigny as a gift; and
there was an adjoining tract of a little more than a thousand
acres, valued at approximately $150,000, which Oakes offered
to de Marigny to develop and use. Sir Harry told him about
it after the de Marignys returned to Palm Beach from Mexico, within the year, possibly somewhere around February
of this year. As far as he knew, de Marigny refused to accept the Jones property as a gift, or to make any arrangements
for the use and development of the thousand-acre tract.

Higgs's thrust with these preliminary questions was two-
fold: He must negate, where possible, the Crown's theory
of complete and open hostility between Oakes and de Mar-

igny; and he wanted to lull the witness into a feeling of false security before hitting him with his main punches. Able cross-examiners throughout the Common Law world employ this format as sound psychological technique, tested for hundreds of years in thousands of courtrooms.

Now Higgs darted into something else, this time to test Christie's memory generally, and also to startle him with the unpleasant subject of the car.

Mr. Higgs: "You know Mabel Ellis, Sir Harry's housemaid?"

"Yes."

Mr. Higgs: "You know that she says that you always left your car outside Westbourne when you came there. Is that correct?"

"No, I did not always leave my car outside the main entrance."

Mr. Higgs: "Did you leave your car there on Tuesday night?"

"Yes. On the northern end of the tennis court, a little east of Westbourne, nearer to Westbourne than to the country club."

Mr. Higgs: "You know that Mabel Ellis says that on Tuesday night, July 6, you left your car immediately outside the entrance to the southern court?"

"Mabel Ellis is incorrect. It was to the east of the main entrance. The courts are about three hundred feet away."

Mr. Higgs: "You know that Mabel Ellis says that on Tuesday morning you drove up to town with Sir Harry Oakes?"

"I do not remember that. I am sure that I went alone and went to the Executive Council. If Mabel Ellis says I went with Sir Harry in his car, she is saying what is not true. I am positive of this because I was in a hurry; I had to be there at ten o'clock."

Christie was sweating again, and he experienced difficulty getting the white handkerchief out of his breast pocket. It was almost as heavy as a towel. He realized now that his statements would be disputed by other witnesses, his personal integrity laid bare for all the world to measure.

Higgs decided to pursue the comparison tactic a bit further.

Mr. Higgs: "Do you remember if you got there on time?"

"I believe so. It meets at ten o'clock. To the best of my recollection, it met at ten o'clock that day."

Mr. Higgs: "And yet you say you left Westbourne between nine-fifteen and nine-thirty?"

"I said I did not remember exactly. I remember that I was in a hurry because I was late."

Mr. Higgs: "If you did not have a watch, how did you know what time it was?"

"I may have seen a clock some time before."

Mr. Higgs: "Do you think your recollection is better than Mabel Ellis'?"

"I could not say that."

Mr. Higgs: "Have you a good memory sometimes?"

"Sometimes."

Mr. Higgs: "Did you not stop at your house on the way?"

"I may have. I usually stop to pick up papers for Council."

Higgs's ploy was routine at this point. His goal was to imply to the jury that if Christie's memory was not razor sharp on these relatively insignificant matters, it might also be unreliable on points of critical relevancy.

Higgs now shifted to a conversation between Christie and de Marigny which Christie acknowledged, saying it was possible that de Marigny spoke to him over the telephone around nine-thirty Wednesday morning about a permit to work a chicken farm; but if the accused said that he invited him to his home for dinner Wednesday night, he was not speaking the truth. He had been invited once for dinner at the accused's home after his marriage to Nancy Oakes, and once for lunch; but he did not remember telling de Marigny he could not come to dinner Wednesday night because he was spending the night with Sir Harry.

Higgs was admittedly groping somewhat blindly at this point. His barrister's intuition told him that Christie's story did not resound with the ring of truth; but not knowing exactly what had happened at Westbourne or outside it, he probed delicately for the key to Christie's tortured reporting.

Mr. Higgs: "Would you say that the accused was lying again if he said you told him that you were staying with Sir Harry Oakes that night?"

"Yes."

Mr. Higgs: "Why are you so positive of these two facts?"

"I should hate to do an injustice to the accused but I did not tell him that. I did not know myself that I was going to dine with Sir Harry."

Higgs was using a roundabout route to press Christie further on his activities at Westbourne the critical night.

Mr. Higgs: "When did Sir Harry invite you to dine that night?"

"About eight o'clock."

Mr. Higgs: "When did Sir Harry invite you to sleep there?"

"He did not invite me. I had slept there on Sunday and Tuesday night."

Mr. Higgs: "When did you decide to sleep there?"

"After dinner. There was nothing that I had to do in town and I had an appointment in the morning."

Mr. Higgs: "I put it to you that you had planned to stay at Westbourne on Wednesday night?"

"Had we dined at the Prince George, I probably would have slept at home."

Higgs sensed that something was amiss about Christie's "spontaneous" decision to sleep at Westbourne, but without exact knowledge of the prearranged date to meet Lansky's lieutenant, he was unable to score on this subject.

By custom and usage, "I put it to you" is the supreme "on guard" thrust of cross-examining British barristers to opposing witnesses. It is defiant charge, belligerent challenge, courageous indictment, and unbridled attack all in one. "I put it to you" is the barrister's request for undivided attention, his siren alert to all that he has reached the point where he hopes to obtain an inculpatory admission from the witness.

Mr. Higgs: "You phoned your man Gibson during dinner?"

"Gibson phoned me while I was at dinner, and it was then that I told Gibson to bring my car down."

Mr. Higgs: "Why did you want your car?"

"I always want my car with me and have it brought to me. I particularly wanted it that night because I was going on a trip the next morning."

The real thrust of Higgs's persistent questions about the car would not be apparent for several minutes.

Mr. Higgs: "So it was during dinner that you decided to stay at Westbourne?"

"Yes."

Mr. Higgs: "Did you instruct your man Gibson to leave your car at the country club?"

"I did."

Mr. Higgs: "Why?"

"Because I wanted to conserve my gasoline, and if it had been brought over to Westbourne there was a good chance of my car being used."

So it was that the number-two citizen of the Bahamas wanted his car surreptitiously hidden out near the country club, so that he would not be compelled to burn his own gasoline; rather, he would force the Island's number-one citizen to expend his rationed gas.

Higgs was not finished with the subject of Christie's car.

Mr. Higgs: "When was there a good chance of it [Christie's car] being used?"

"There were guests at Westbourne and there were suggestions of going to the Prince George, or possibly some other place."

Mr. Higgs: "Was it not the suggestion that *dinner* be had at the Prince George?"

"We could have gone afterwards."

Mr. Higgs: "Wasn't Mr. Hubbard's car there as well as two of Sir Harry's?"

"Yes."

Mr. Higgs: "Why were you then fearful that your car would have been used?"

"In the circumstances, there would have been every possibility of my car being used if it had been there."

Mr. Higgs: "All would have been handy? Is that your best reason?"

"Yes. I was going on a trip the next day, and might not have had enough gasoline to use the next day. Gasoline is rationed."

Mr. Higgs: "Did you know how much gasoline you had in your car?"

"No."

Mr. Higgs: "If you did not know, you were not in a position to say whether you would have had enough for the next day in any event?"

"That is correct."

Mr. Higgs: "Did Sir Harry have anyone to dinner on Tuesday night?"

"I do not remember anyone being there. I do not remember if we went out that night; that is a long time ago."

Mr. Higgs: "Gibson did not bring the keys to your car into Westbourne, did he?"

"No. Gibson used my car frequently, and they were put in a place in the car."

Christie now released the rail and attempted to stand upright, but it was not a position of comfort. After wiping his brow again, he replaced the handkerchief and leaned forward on the rail, his two hands clutching it tensely.

Mr. Higgs: "Did only you and Gibson know your car was there?"

"Gibson, his wife, and another boy knew it was there."

Mr. Higgs: "No one at Westbourne knew your car was there?"

"Not that I know of."

Higgs then produced the official record of the preliminary hearing at which Christie testified. If the witness has made a prior statement, orally or in writing, which is in any way inconsistent with the evidence he gives in the courtroom, he can be confronted with that prior inconsistent statement and asked to explain the discrepancy between it and his present

testimony. This is one of the most effective grounds for im-
peaching (discrediting) a witness's testimony.

Higgs now read Christie's testimony from the official record
at the magistrate's court in which he said that he left his car
at the country club, as he did before many times, because
he wanted to use it the next day, and he wanted to conserve
gasoline; and ". . . the country club was the logical place to
leave the car."

Mr. Higgs: "What do you mean that the country club is
the logical place to leave the car?"

"It was the logical place to leave it because there was a
watchman there, and none at Westbourne."

Mr. Higgs: "Then you left it there for security?"

"I did not think of that at the time."

Mr. Higgs: "Why are you so especially careful to say you
did not want to use the car that night?"

"I said I wanted to conserve my gasoline, and if my car
was brought to Westbourne, there was a possibility that it
might be used."

For a man who did not know what happened, Higgs was
amazingly close to pay dirt as he pursued Christie's reason
for having his car deposited outside Westbourne so that it
would be available for the rush to the quay just as soon as
the unanticipated guests departed. Christie reacted by appearing especially upset by any reference to his car having
been available at the country club, not at Westbourne, but
still only a matter of a few hundred feet away.

Higgs now shifted to another subject. Christie explained
that he knew he had not turned out any lights downstairs
before he and Sir Harry went up to bed, and he did not
remember Sir Harry doing so; he believed the lights were
turned off after the guests departed. He always understood
that the small light was left burning on the south downstairs
porch, and as far as he knew, the other lights were out.

Higgs read again from the official record of the Preliminary
Hearing in the Magistrate's Court, this time from Charles
Hubbard's testimony, in which he said that when he returned

to his house at eleven-thirty, after driving Mrs. Heneage
home, he noticed Westbourne "well lighted up."

Christie dabbed again at his sweating face and did not
reply for twenty seconds. In the courtroom, a five-second
pause between question and answer seems an eon; twenty
seconds are an eternity. During this pause, Christie also
closed his eyes as in deep concentration, letting his head tilt
back so that his neck rested on his wilted collar. It was a
pose of virtual despair.

He would not deny that Westbourne was lighted up,
Christie finally said. Hubbard might well have seen the one
light on the porch, or more. The light to his bedroom upstairs would have been on, as he was still reading.

Christie again repeated his direct testimony about being
awakened by the mosquitoes and the storm; it seemed to
him that he had been asleep longer the second time than
the first. Whatever he might suspect, Higgs could not get
Christie's admission that both he and Sir Harry were gone
from Westbourne by the time Hubbard returned.

Mr. Higgs: "Were they the only two occasions when you
awoke that night?"

"They were the only two occasions I woke that night."

Mr. Higgs. "Did you leave Westbourne any time that
night?"

"I did not leave Westbourne any time during the night of
July 7, or until the next night of July 8."

This was the ground which Christie obviously feared. Grip-
ping the rail firmly with his left hand, he took his right index
finger and drew a straight line across the top of the rail. His
eyes blinked several times, again his head rolled back, and
he twisted his neck from left to right uncontrollably as if to
shake out the tensions and kinks of a decade. Then Higgs
let him have it.

Mr. Higgs: "Do you know Captain Sears, Assistant Superintendent of Police?"

"I do."

Mr. Higgs: "You are friendly with him?"

"I am not friendly or unfriendly; I see very little of him."

Mr. Higgs: "Have you known him since boyhood?"

"Yes."

Mr. Higgs: "He has no ill will against you that you know of?"

"No."

Mr. Higgs: "If Captain Sears were to say that he had seen you in town the night of July 7, what would you say?"

"I would say that Captain Sears is very seriously mistaken and should be more careful in his observations."

Mr. Higgs: "I put it to you that Captain Sears saw you at about midnight in a station wagon in George Street."

Christie knew this blow was coming, the Attorney General having alerted him, but he refused to accept it.

Mr. Christie: "Was he certain?"

The witness's own question was plaintive.

Mr. Higgs: "*I put it to you.*"

Mr. Christie: "Captain Sears was mistaken. I did not leave Westbourne after retiring to my room that night until the next night, and any statement to the effect that I was in town is a very grave mistake."

Mr. Higgs: "Would you say that Captain Sears was a reputable person?"

"I would say so. Nevertheless, reputable people can be mistaken."

It was time for the five o'clock adjournment. Christie's total discomfort permeated the entire courtroom. Even Alfred de Marigny was so intent on the Higgs-Christie riposte that his face pressed forward between two bars, and his long arms dangled grotesquely over the front of his cage. Between his right thumb and forefinger he rolled a battered toothpick which he had played with most of the day, its angle now pointing downward toward the floor in a salute of surrender.

Effective cross-examinations require time; they are not accomplished in half-a-dozen brilliant questions which force the witness to cave in with an humble admission that he testified inaccurately in his direct evidence. The cross-examiner often undresses the witness's soul for the jury so that they can better decide whether he is to be believed.

Christie returned to the witness box the following morning in an identical white linen suit, white shirt, and black four-in-hand tie. All were immaculately starched and pressed, as he stepped into the box, but within minutes, all were saturated and Christie dabbed helplessly at his sweating brow.

Higgs now proceeded to the events of the critical morning of Thursday, July 8.

Mr. Higgs: "You know that Mabel Ellis, the housemaid at Westbourne, says that usually you and Sir Harry were dressed before you had breakfast?"

"If we were going out early we dressed; if not, we probably would not."

Mr. Higgs: "Why did you not dress for breakfast on Thursday morning?"

"After I had discovered the body?"

Mr. Higgs: "Before you discovered it. Were you going out to have breakfast?"

Christie acted as though instructed to take deliberately long pauses before he answered. Erle Stanley Gardner, covering the trial with the pen of Perry Mason for the Hearst newspapers, observed the second hand on his watch tick off thirty-seven seconds, an interminable time in the courtroom, before the answer finally came.

Mr. Christie: "Sir Harry rose at daybreak and he usually could be found looking out over the water."

Mr. Higgs: "You were planning to go out that morning?"

"At ten-thirty."

To the best of his recollection, Christie reported he went directly out to the north porch from his room. He usually brushed his teeth when he got up, but he did not have a toothbrush with him that morning. Usually, he went to the bathroom, but he did not remember whether he went that morning.

Mr. Higgs: "If you had, you would have seen signs of the disturbance?"

"I do not think so. Sir Harry's bed was quite a bit to the south of the doorway."

Mr. Higgs: "If you had smelled the smoke, would you have gone directly to Sir Harry's room?"

"I don't remember if I went to the bathroom or not. I knew nothing until I entered Sir Harry's room that morning."

Mr. Higgs: "When you went in, was the smell of burning intense or not?"

"Not particularly. I would not say extremely intense. I did not smell it when I went by on the porch."

Through labored replies, Christie said that he did not notice that the wooden mosquito bars over the bed were upside down; he did not remember the position of the bars, or whether they were hanging down instead of parallel to the floor. When he lifted up Sir Harry's head, it was approximately one foot from the south side of the bed. His face was almost straight up, and his head was a little to the right side. His feet were almost to the south side of the bed; and he was slightly diagonal, but not much. His feet were more to the south than his head.

It is doubtful that Christie or anyone else in the courtroom realized the significance of these basic questions to a crucial point Higgs would discuss shortly.

Mr. Higgs: "If his head was a foot from the south edge of the bed, then his right shoulder would be practically hanging off of the bed?"

"My impression was that the right shoulder was six to eight inches from the south of the bed."

Mr. Higgs: "Was he lying more on his right side?"

"A little."

Higgs then read again from the record of the magistrate's court during the preliminary hearing where Christie said that the body was not exactly flat on its back; it was slightly inclined to the right. It was lying slightly diagonally across the bed.

Mr. Higgs: "You lifted his head and shook him. Which arm did you use?"

"I used my right arm and lifted his head and shoulder."

Mr. Higgs: "Did you notice any blood coming from him?"

"No."

Mr. Higgs: "You then got some water out of the carafe?"

"Yes. I do not remember whether it had a stopper."

Again testing the witness's recollection of the crucial details, Higgs forced the admission that Christie did not remember exactly how he got the water from the carafe to pour it into the glass; his impression was that he used both hands.

Mr. Higgs: "What happened to the water when you put it into Sir Harry's mouth?"

"It appeared to go down his throat. It went into his mouth."

To the jurors, Christie's report of his terrified actions sounded logical enough. They too might have responded similarly. Was there anything at this point to cause reasonable men to suspect the witness of misrepresentation?

Mr. Higgs: "What shoes were you wearing that morning?"

"I was barefoot."

Mr. Higgs: "The porch was soaking wet that morning, wasn't it?"

"The porch was damp but not to my recollection soaking wet."

Mr. Higgs: "Was there a bad rainstorm after you went to bed the night before?"

"Yes."

Mr. Higgs: "Do you usually get up and go out on the porch barefoot?"

"Usually. Sir Harry always wakened first and we would usually meet and have a chat before we dressed. Sometimes I wakened first and our meeting place was on the northern porch, outside Sir Harry's room, where there were always chairs and a table, and where we nearly always had breakfast."

Mr. Higgs: "Why did you touch the body?"

"Why did I? Well, if you walked into a room and found

your best friend in that condition, what would you do? I thought he might still be alive. The body was not cold, it was warmish and Dr. Quackenbush will confirm that."

Higgs now walked slowly to the registrar's table and picked up a photograph taken the critical morning by the official R.A.F. photographer. Slowly, dramatically turning the photograph in his hand, eyeing it pensively as he approached the witness box, Higgs finally handed up the picture to Christie who received it in shaking hands. It was the grisly, full-length view of Sir Harry's body lying grotesquely on his bed.

Mr. Higgs: "Does that look like the body of a man alive?"

"No, it does not, but the body was warm. I did everything I could, hoping there might be life. I asked Mrs. Kelly and my brother to get a doctor."

Mr. Higgs: "Yet, you called for the servants?"

"I called for the most immediate help which would be the servants."

Mr. Higgs took back the photograph which Christie gladly surrendered; he turned to his right and passed the picture to Foreman Sands. It was the jury's first look at the murdered baronet.

Mr. Higgs: "You then went to the south window and called for the watchman?"

"Yes."

Mr. Higgs: "You say you had some hope?"

"I had some hope, yes. I was panicky and I called for the nearest assistance."

Mr. Higgs: "What help did you hope to get from housemaids and watchman?"

"I called them because they were nearest. I then called Mrs. Kelly."

Mr. Higgs: "You never did phone a doctor, did you?"

"No. I asked Mrs. Kelly and my brother to get one."

Mr. Higgs: "Would you not have got more immediate help if you had phoned a doctor?"

Christie first relaxed his grip on the witness-box rail and straightened up, arching his back; then he leaned forward again, shouting his answer at Higgs with such force that the audience clustered outside under the windows of the building had no difficulty whatsoever in hearing his response.

Mr. Christie: "I had two people calling for a doctor. I might have called one myself."

Mr. Higgs: "Was not Sir Harry's mouth clenched tight when you gave him that water?"

"No. I was able to get the glass between his lips."

Christie trembled noticeably as he relived this most trying episode in his forty-seven years; but there was no need for the jury to conclude that his emotional reactions were due to his untruthfulness.

Mr. Higgs: "And the water went into his mouth?"

"It appeared to."

Mr. Higgs: "Did you notice any burning spots on the bed?"

"No."

Up to this point, little had been reported by anyone about the fire itself. The residue of the fire—burn marks on the wood paneling, the destroyed mosquito netting over the bed, the sooty staining of parts of the carpeting—had been described; but beyond any doubt, the character of the fire itself was the most baffling mystery in the case.

Mr. Higgs: "Yet you went through other rooms to see if there was any sign of fire?"

"There was smoke in the room and burned spots on the floor."

Mr. Higgs: "In searching for signs of fire, I believe you went into the adjoining room to the east, into your bathroom, and into your bedroom?"

"Yes."

Mr. Higgs: "Why did you go into your own bedroom?"

"To see if there were any sparks, or if there was anybody in there."

Mr. Higgs: "But you had been in your bedroom all night, Mr. Christie?"

There was a biting sarcasm in Higgs's voice, not enough to be offensive, but no one within earshot missed the barbed insinuation. Moving uncomfortably in the box, shifting his

weight from foot to foot, Christie literally yelled, "Yes!" It
was an overly aggressive implied denial once more of Captain Sears's accusation that Christie had not spent the entire
night at Westbourne.

Mr. Higgs: "Did you then expect to find fire or someone
lurking in your room?"

"It was logical to look there, which I did."

Mr. Higgs: "In a room in which you had slept all night?"

"Yes."

Mr. Higgs: "Did you go into the western bedroom?"

"I went as far as the hallway where there were some signs
of burning, but I do not remember going downstairs."

Mr. Higgs: "But although there were signs of burning in
the hallway, you did not look in the western bedroom?"

"No."

Mr. Higgs: "Was Sir Harry's bed still hot?"

"It was warm."

Mr. Higgs: "You got a towel and wiped Sir Harry's face?"

"I did."

Mr. Higgs: "You think you wet that towel in your bathroom?"

"I think I did, but I am not positive. But that is my
impression."

Mr. Higgs: "Did you soak it?"

"I would not say I soaked it. I wet the side of it."

Mr. Higgs: "Which side of it?"

A Hollywood scriptwriter would be accused of being unrealistic if he conjured up the next line.

Mr. Christie: "For God's sake, Higgs, be reasonable. I
don't remember which side of the towel."

Christie's shout, which reverberated all around the courthouse outside, was more of surrender than challenge, like that
of a cornered fox who turns for one last stand against his
pursuers.

Mr. Higgs: "And then later you wet that towel again?"

"I am not positive whether I got another towel, but I
thought I used the same one."

Mr. Higgs: "You did this in order to try to revive Sir
Harry?"

"Yes."

Slowly, realizing that every eye burned into him, Higgs walked once more to the registrar's table, thumbed through a stack of photographs, and selected another, this time a portrait view of the left side of the dead baronet's face. He studied it for a moment, then with a twist of his head he looked up at Christie, who retreated a step to the rear of the box. With dramatic flourish, Higgs thrust up the photograph so that Christie had no alternative but to accept it.

Mr. Higgs: "Would you say that that face has been wiped?"

"I say that this face had been wiped. I would say that water had been put on the forehead and on the face."

It was the only answer Christie could give, but it still served Higgs' purpose, because the jury would see from the photograph that if any wiping of the face with a wet towel was attempted it had not disturbed the drops and spatters and lines of crusted blood which remained clearly visible.

Mr. Higgs: "That picture shows blood flowing from the ear across the face and over the nose?"

"It does."

It was impossible for anyone in the courtroom to tell from the inflection of Christie's voice whether the "it does" was an affirmative response or a countering question of his own.

Godfrey Higgs' measured questions now injected an item of physical evidence into the trial far more reliable than the potentially inaccurate and conflicting reports of eyewitnesses. When the medical evidence came in later on, it would show that Sir Harry's skull was fractured by four heavy blows above his left ear. In a great many skull-fracture cases, blood flows in varying amounts from the ear; and it does not require the knowledge of an expert to deduce that the flowing liquid follows the law of gravity.

The picture that Higgs and Christie now discussed showed a clear, almost straight line of dried blood, perhaps one-quarter of an inch wide, that ran from the left ear across the upper face, just below the bottom edge of Sir Harry's sideburn, to pass below the left eye and follow the contour of the orbit, finally to run up and over the bridge of the nose. It was simply not possible for Sir Harry's head to have been in other than a *nose-down* position for this line of crusted blood to flow and coagulate. If the head had been in the position that Christie described when he first discovered it with Sir Harry lying on his back, the blood flow from the left ear would have been toward the bed, *down and around the back of the head.*

Mr. Higgs: "Would that suggest to you that Sir Harry had been lying face down on the bed?"

"Yes."

Christie could not answer otherwise; the jurors would have the photograph shortly and be able to judge for themselves. Any answer other than his "Yes" would have completely discredited Christie.

Mr. Higgs: "But you did not find Sir Harry that way?"

"No. I did not find Sir Harry that way. When I first saw him, his face was straight up, not completely but partially."

Now the Lord Chief Justice, the three military medals which he wore on the left front of his robe dangling as he bent downward over his bench, took up the questioning himself.

His Honor: "After you lifted it, did it get into this position?"

"It might have fallen into that position shown in the photograph after I had raised his head and put a pillow under it."

The Lord Chief Justice shook his head slowly from side to side; he was not pleased with the implications.

Higgs took the photograph from Christie and passed it quickly to Foreman Sands who studied it at considerable length. It was apparent that the other jurors eagerly awaited their turns to view this spectacular disclosure.

Godfrey Higgs maintained his relentless attack, the professional boxer driving his opponent backward against the ropes. It was time though to shift to a new but intimately related subject.

Christie was obviously near the point of exhaustion, this the late afternoon of his second day front and center. In the British way of doing things, only the crippled or infirm are excused from standing in the box for all to see and measure the witness's truthfulness and ability to relate accurately.

After an interminable, thoughtful pause of forty-two seconds, as timed by Erle Stanley Gardner, Christie said that he did not see any blood flowing from Sir Harry's head wound; he did not know whether water was good or bad for burns; he telephoned Charles Hubbard to come to Westbourne because he was desperate for help; he remembered Hubbard in Sir Harry's bedroom, as were Mrs. Madeleine Kelly and his brother, Frank Christie.

Although the elevated witness box permitted Christie to tower a good two feet above Higgs, who stood at floor level behind the counsel table, Higgs continued as the dominant figure in the room.

Higgs now shifted to another critical element.

Mr. Higgs: "Did Mrs. Kelly's mother, Mrs. Gale, come over also?"

"I did not see her at first. Mrs. Kelly came alone into the room. I do not know if Mrs. Gale entered the room later."

Mr. Higgs: "You don't remember going onto the southern veranda?"

"I very likely did, but I don't remember."

Mr. Higgs: "Do you recall using the southern door to your bedroom?"

"I don't recall it, but it is quite likely that I may have done so."

Higgs knew that the police search of the second floor had disclosed bloody smears both inside and outside Christie's door; presumably, they were hand prints of some person who had physical contact with Sir Harry after his wounding, for one reason or another.

At Higgs' urging, Christie described a glass door and a screen door within the same door frame leading from his bedroom out onto the south veranda.

Mr. Higgs: "You knew that hand marks were found on both the inner and outer surfaces of these doors?"

"Yes. Very likely they were made by my hands, but I am not going to say that I went anywhere that I do not remember. I can only say that it would be the logical thing to have gone out that door onto the veranda."

Once more the Lord Chief Justice interposed his own question. Christie, turning almost gratefully toward the bench, away from Higgs, insisted that he did remember going out of his bedroom by the north door the first time he left the room that morning.

Sir Oscar Daly stopped his next question in midclause by a reluctant wave of his left hand, the dripping nib pen thrust skyward in his right. An airplane flew low over the courthouse, its unmuffled engine momentarily drowning out all other sounds.

Mr. Higgs: "You have not heard of any bloodstains being found on the door leading from Sir Harry's room to the *north* balcony?"

"No."

After thinking over Higgs' question, Christie finally responded that the center door into the middle bedroom was the first one he used after lifting Sir Harry's head; but a moment later, Christie turned to the Chief Justice asking permission to correct himself. It was, he believed, the north door through which he exited; and later when the Chief Justice read his summation of that portion of the evidence which he wrote into the black ledger book, Christie reiterated that the north door *was* the first door he went through.

Higgs then questioned Christie at some length about de Marigny's appearance at Westbourne later in the morning, and about many of the details of the police investigation that day. It was nearing the adjournment hour when Higgs announced that his cross-examination was finished.

Christie's body and spirit visibly sagged in relief as he turned prematurely to step down from the box. There could be no doubt but that force of will alone kept him from coming completely apart during his day-and-a-half ordeal of public display.

But his time for dismissal was not quite at hand. Since Higgs' cross-examination impeached at least parts of Christie's testimony, the Attorney General was entitled to rehabilitate his own witness. Responding slowly to the Chief

Justice's order, Christie climbed back into the witness box like a beaten dog.

Mr. Hallinan: "Do you recollect on entering that room whether the feathers were scattered about the bed, or whether they were scattered after you had moved Sir Harry's head?"

"I think the feathers were scattered when I first saw them, but I cannot say with any certainty."

The feathers piqued the Chief Justice's interest. He asked whether a wind was blowing in through the open windows and screen door, and Christie replied that there was "only a little wind" that morning. His impression was that the feathers were scattered on the body when he first entered.

The jurors now huddled around Foreman Sands: this was their inning, their right to interpose questions which neither Higgs nor Hallinan nor the Chief Justice put to the witness, to satisfy their curiosities.

Foreman Sands: "When you first saw Sir Harry, were his eyes open or closed?"

"I do not remember for sure, but I am inclined to think that they were closed."

Foreman Sands: "Was the electric fan in a position to blow the feathers over the room?"

"The fan was on, but the feathers were not being blown about the room by the fan. I am sure I would have noticed if this was going on."

Mention of the feathers prompted one further question from the Chief Justice, and Christie replied that the feathers were at the side of the body, on the south side rather than on the top of the body; and they were definitely not being disturbed by the electric fan.

This time Christie received his release, and it was with considerable physical effort that he lowered himself from the box.

The jurors quite properly pondered the great paradox of Harold Christie's evidence: Why did he vehemently elect to place himself throughout the night within twenty-five feet of Sir Harry's dead body, and then just as vigorously insist that he neither heard, smelled, nor perceived any physical stimuli of any kind to alert him to anything amiss in Sir Harry's room?

The jurors also knew that Harold Christie, through his business operations and his open manner, probably dealt personally with more people on the Islands than any other man. In effect, he maintained a highly effective intelligence rete. Accurate and reliable information about any person or any activity throughout the Bahamas was as close to Harold Christie as his telephone. How could he fail, they reasoned, to know exactly who killed Sir Harry, why and under what circumstances? His appearance alone on behalf of the Crown was enough to argue strongly the guilt of Alfred de Marigny.

But the jurors could not help remembering the picture of Sir Harry's head and the trail of blood that, according to the Crown's theory, flowed *upward* in defiance of the law of gravity. It was a physical impossibility for Sir Harry to have lain on his back on his bed while that line of blood trickled and dried.

Erle Stanley Gardner, an outstanding trial lawyer in California for twenty-five years before devoting himself to a full-time writing career, thought that Christie stood up reasonably well under Higgs' attack. Christie's obvious discomfiture in the witness box could easily be assigned to his trauma in retelling this emotionally charged event, the brutal killing of his close friend and business associate.

Higgs' most effective stratagem was to use Christie as the vehicle for getting the picture of Sir Harry's head with the blood flowing uphill in defiance of gravity in front of the jury immediately. The jurors could well accept Christie's account as gospel, which they did, but they could not help but question the Crown's theory that Sir Harry was bludgeoned as he slept peacefully on his back in his own bed.

Alfred de Marigny, totally wrapped up in his own life-and-death struggle, could not fully appreciate Higgs' tactics. He did not sleep that night at all, nor did his wife.

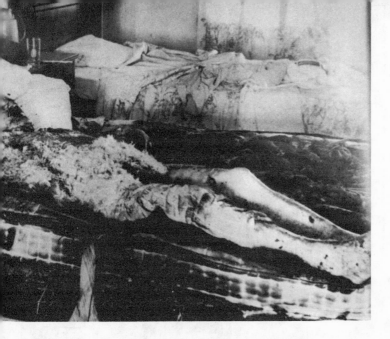

ABOVE Sir Harry's burned and charred body on the bed in Westbourne when first seen by the police on Thursday, July 8, 1943.

BELOW The line of blood that flowed uphill, in defiance of the law of gravity, from Sir Harry's left ear, across the cheek and over the bridge of the nose.

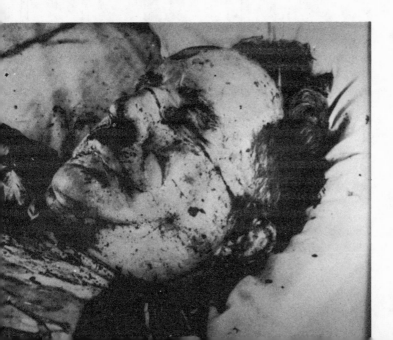

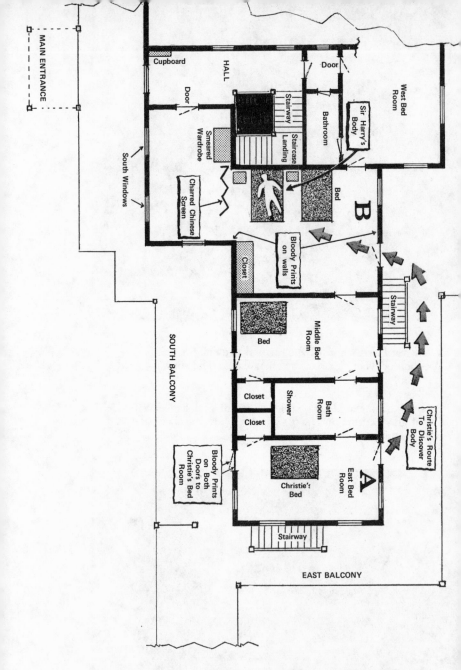

Floor plan of the second story of Westbourne (after official sketch prepared by RAF personnel for courtroom use).

NORTH BALCONY

Truncated, partial view of the north (seaward) side of Westbourne. Harold Christie swore that although he spent the entire night in bedroom *A*, he perceived nothing to indicate anything amiss in bedroom *B* (some 30 feet away) where Sir Harry's battered and charred body was discovered the following morning a little after seven o'clock.

ABOVE The charred Chinese screen at the south side of Sir Harry's bed, the alleged site of Exhibit J.

BELOW Area "5" on the Chinese screen (left) from which Captain James Otto Barker swore he lifted Exhibit J. Exhibit J (right), the clear, pristine fingerprint of de Marigny's little finger which shows no background markings whatsoever, although a pattern of circles was actually on the surface of the screen.

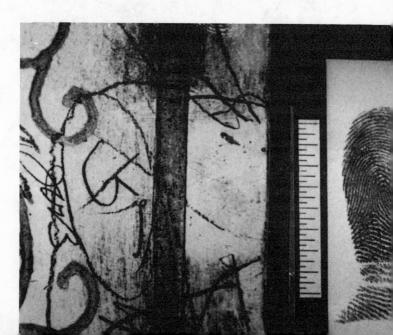

16

The Ponderables of Death

In any case of sudden and violent death, there are always three ponderables: cause of death, manner of death, and time of death. The correct answer to each of these separate enigmas produces the ultimate solution of the case as a whole.

The first of these, cause of death, is purely and simply a medical question: Was it pneumonia or meningitis, thrombosis or stroke, bullet through the brain stem or stab wound into the spinal cord, cardiac contusion or blow to the head, asphyxia or carbon monoxide poisoning?

Manner of death is the means by which cause of death is brought about and is described within the confines of the generic N-A-S-H classification (natural-accident-suicide-homicide): Was the ruptured aneurysm in the circle of Willis at the base of the brain caused by the blow to the head, or did it break spontaneously before any blow was received? Was the bullet through the brain suicidal and self-inflicted, or fired by the defendant's hand? Did the deceased's fractured skull result from his own careless fall, or a crushing blow rained by the accused? Did the blood clot in the coronary artery occur first to cause the deceased's fall from the scaffold, or did the fall precede and cause the occluded artery?

Because of the imprecise state of medical knowledge, manner of death can seldom be determined by medical evidence alone; other facets of proof must be consulted. The same is true with time of death. There has been absolutely no sophistication in the last hundred years of the trite and ancient rites of *rigor mortis*, body temperature, and analyses of stomach contents as medical clues for determining time of death. In most cases, these are so vague and variable that the most that can be said with any degree of medical safety is that the death *could* have occurred within a broad interval of perhaps eight to twelve hours. Using medical evidence alone, any doctor who claims that he can determine time of death within a narrower timetable of events speaks as a charlatan and faker, regardless of his motivation.

Time of death can be determined accurately only by non-medical evidence.

Attorney General Eric Hallinan called the only two doctors at his disposal with medical and nonmedical knowledge on the three ponderables of Sir Harry's death. By coincidence, both were trained at Montreal's prestigious McGill University School of Medicine; but neither was a forensic pathologist (*forensic:* as used in the courtroom or in some step in the administration of justice; *pathology:* the study of the cause and nature of disease and death). Although competent in their fields of general medicine and surgery, both were without backgrounds in forensic medicine (medicine used to help solve the dilemmas of the courtroom such as cause of death, manner of death, and time of death).

Actually, Dr. Hugh Arnley Quackenbush's nonmedical descriptions of Sir Harry's bedroom were more valuable than his purely medical evidence.

Trim and relaxed, and speaking in the same confident tones he used with patients in his examining room, Dr. Quackenbush told the jurors that he received Mrs. Kelly's telephone call at exactly seven-thirty Thursday morning, and he was at Westbourne by seven-forty. When he entered Sir Harry's bedroom, he was immediately struck by the signs of a fire. Walking around the screen that paralleled the south side of the south bed, he saw Sir Harry's body lying on the bed; he examined it and concluded that it was badly burned.

There was a perforated wound in front of the left ear large enough to admit the end of his left index finger; and he could feel the fractured bones of the skull.

It was now seven forty-five and he estimated that Sir Harry had been dead between two-and-a-half and five hours. This would place time of death between 2:45 and 5:15 A.M.; but he did not give the factors on which his opinion as to time of death was reasoned.

There was nothing dramatic about Quackenbush's court-room performance except the subject matter of his testimony, which captivated the jurors.

It was possible to ascertain the time of death, he continued relentlessly in his relaxed way, but this case was difficult because of the burned body; and it would be most difficult for even an expert to tell within an hour when death occurred.

Sir Harry was wearing pajamas but most of the cloth was burned off, with the exception of a little scrap remaining under the left armpit. A portion of the pajamas also remained on the right side of the body.

He noticed a small piece of "something glowing," and instinctively he took a glass of water from the night table and put it out.

There were several marks on the north and east walls which could have been made by hands or fingers, but they did not look like bloodstains.

An electric fan was running so that it blew across the middle of the bed, but the feathers from the pillow were not disturbed by it.

He immediately observed several blisters on Sir Harry's body, on the neck and upper part of the chest, on the left shin, right toes, and right hand. In his opinion, these particular blisters occurred *ante mortem* (before death), although the greater portion of the burns were post-mortem.

Quackenbush's evidence misled both Sir Oscar and the jury. Both "dry" and "wet" blisters *can* form for several hours after the circulation stops. Fluid in the blisters depends upon the liquid sources in the tissues, not in the flowing blood. This was a far more distracting error than his unwarranted preciseness in fixing the time of death. We can presume that Quackenbush's misrepresentations resulted from his own ignorance since he was not a forensic pathologist; still, he had talked at considerable length to Captain Barker at Westbourne, who could subtly have suggested exactly what he thought the Crown would need on time of death. This is the way of all too many investigators and *expert* witnesses: The investigator suggests and the witness adopts the suggestion, a mechanism perilously close to fabrication.

Dr. Quackenbush left the room at eight-twenty, he explained, returned to Westbourne at two-fifteen again to view the body which had not been moved, and examined Sir Harry's skull at the hospital morgue after the body arrived there late in the afternoon.

Quackenbush was not to be the Crown's chief medical witness, although his testimony adequately established the *corpus delicti* (*body of the crime* = elements of the offense). Obviously, the doctor described a dead human body; and his statement that the four wounds to the head could not have been self-inflicted detailed an extraneous criminal agency as the manner of death.

With his instinctive bow to the Lord Chief Justice, Godfrey Higgs rose to see what he could obtain from the witness that might benefit the defense.

Mr. Higgs: "Was Sir Harry's body warm?"

"The body was still warm on the undersurface where the back contacted the mattress. It was cooler but not cold on top. The head was toward the north and the feet toward the southeast. *Rigor mortis* had begun. There was an odor of burnt ash and feathers, not, however, particularly strong or offensive."

Mr. Higgs: "Have you any idea what caused those hand marks on the wall?"

"My impression was that they were caused by hands or fingers, and could not be caused by anyone standing up as they were three-and-a-half to four feet above the level of the floor. There were some on the north wall and some on the east wall, but I do not remember noticing any on the south wall. Some of the marks might have been made by a hand, and some by finger tips. There was no clear imprint of a hand, and the marks were not consistent in size or shape."

Mr. Higgs: "You could not tell if they were made by a large or small hand?"

"No. I looked specially as I wanted to see if there were any blood marks. All marks might have been caused by the hands of the same person."

These tantalizing and peculiar markings on the north and east walls were as baffling as the character of the fire itself.

Godfrey Higgs, pleased with the quizzical postures of the jurors, shifted back to a medical consideration.

Mr. Higgs: "If a man gets a burn and dies instantly, does it blister?"

"No. If he lived five minutes, there might be a blister. Blisters would occur as long as there was any circulation of the blood."

Mr. Higgs: "In this particular case, how long did Sir Harry live?"

"I don't think Sir Harry lived very long, not more than five minutes from the time he received the burns."

Mr. Higgs: "How long would you say Sir Harry lived after receiving the blows to the head?"

"I cannot say for certain, but I would not expect him to live very long. My examination was only of the surface of the body."

These were at best pure guesses on his part; but the witness was clothed in the mantle of infallibility which many laymen accord to doctors, particularly those under oath in the courtroom, and he spoke certainly and convincingly. There was not the slightest modicum of doubt that his every word was gospel.

De Marigny sat stunned in his cage as Hallinan's witness mesmerized the entire courtroom.

Higgs now walked dramatically to the registrar's desk and located the full-length picture of Sir Harry's body on the bed, the same one which had confronted Harold Christie the day before. He flashed the picture in front of the jury box to be certain they understood what it was before passing it up to Dr. Quackenbush.

Mr. Higgs: "Why would those feathers adhere to the deceased's body?"

"I cannot say for sure. There would probably be enough blood serum to make them stick. The body was fairly well burned except around the face. There was no actual blood, but where blisters break, blood serum cakes. It is a very sticky substance."

Higgs now retrieved the photograph from the witness without showing it to the jury. He walked back to the registrar's table, changed it for the large profile view of the left side of Sir Harry's head, and repeated the technique of flashing the picture in front of the jurors before handing it up to the witness. Dr. Quackenbush reiterated that the blood on Sir Harry's head was not flowing when he first examined him; there was only a little blood on the pillow, and he saw none on the drinking glass or thermos. There was a clot of dried blood on the nostril and on the upper tip of the nose. He remembered being struck by the fact that the head appeared relatively free from burns.

He examined the body as little as possible as he realized the serious nature of the matter, his only goals to find out for sure that Sir Harry was dead, and next to try to estimate when he died.

Certainly, the blood did *not* flow when he moved the head; and the line of blood shown in the photograph, across the face between the ear and the nose, was obviously caused much earlier by blood flowing from the ear. This proved that the body had been moved, as the blood could not have flowed in that direction had the body been in the position in which he found it. It was possible that the blood might have been swept across the face by someone wiping the face with a towel; the blood line was straight and did not look like a trickle.

Higgs stiffened and immediately challenged this last gratuitous suggestion of the doctor. Mr. Higgs: "If the face had been wiped with a towel, would it not be more smeared?"

"If the towel had been swished across from left to right, it is possible that the line of blood might be caused as on the photo. If the face was wiped with the towel, I would expect a smudge rather than the fine line shown in the photograph."

Together, Higgs and Quackenbush examined the photograph for the benefit of the jury, Sir Oscar rising unrestrained from his chair to rest his weight on his hands on top of the bench to have a better view of the picture.

Yes, Dr. Quackenbush agreed, the photograph also showed other spots of foreign matter on the face. There was a mark on the right forehead of bruised skin, and there was dried blood, bits of soot, and burned feathers on the face.

Mr. Higgs: "Would you expect a face wiped twice with a wet towel to look like that?"

"It is possible."

Like most expert witnesses, once Quackenbush committed himself to a position, he defended it tenaciously, regardless of its patent improbability.

The Lord Chief Justice resumed his seat, shaking his head pensively, as did several of the jurors. The photograph clearly passed doubt on the vigor with which Harold Christie claimed to have wiped Sir Harry's face, not once but twice; and the jurors were not particularly pleased with what they interpreted as a somewhat illogical attempt by Quackenbush to buttress Christie.

Higgs returned to a nonmedical point as Quackenbush identified the white, paneled Chinese screen standing in court, just to the right of the Lord Chief Justice's bench. It was the same one he saw standing parallel to Sir Harry's bed, probably two feet to the south, when he entered the room Thursday morning. The clean side of the screen was toward the bed, and the smoked and smudged side faced south, away from the bed; and this caused the jurors the same problems. The fire loomed more mysterious than ever.

He had been present later in the afternoon when Captain

Melchen found a soaked and crushed newspaper under the lower portion of Sir Harry's body. It was wet, probably from urine.

Foreman Sands now placed several questions from the jurors.

Foreman Sands: "Would the *ante mortem* burns have made Sir Harry unconscious?"

"In my opinion, they would not have been sufficient to render him unconscious or to prevent him from moving from his bed or crying out."

The foreman's question clearly showed that the jury believed the doctor's expert fantasy that some of the burns were administered *before* death.

Foreman Sands: "If a man is unconscious when he dies, does he die with his eyes open or closed?"

"If a man becomes unconscious as the result of an injury, his eyes may remain open or may close; and if he dies, they may remain either open or closed, until closed by someone after death."

Foreman Sands: "In your opinion, did Sir Harry move after receiving the blows?"

Dr. Quackenbush: "In my opinion, Sir Harry never moved after the blows were struck."

Such an arbitrary statement is totally without medical basis. It can only be made by a charlatan, the witness with some ax to grind, or the careless novice who enjoys playing God from the witness box; but laymen must helplessly accept most doctors' fiats as the naked truth.

Sir Oscar Daly, shifting forward in his chair, asked Dr. Quackenbush how long it would take a normal, healthy person to die. The tenseness of the courtroom broke into great peals of laughter when the witness replied that a normal, healthy person couldn't die! The guards shouted "Order! Order!" in an effort to conceal Sir Oscar's embarrassment; but as frequently happens, their overreaction merely emphasized it.

Godfrey Higgs was showing himself a superior cross-examiner. The unexplained markings on the north and east walls, at the awkward height of three-and-a-half to four feet, loomed large in the jurors' minds, as did the enigma of the feathers, the blowing electric fan, and the smudges burned onto the south side of the screen, the side *away* from Sir Harry's burned body. Even more important, as Quackenbush's evidence now stood, Sir Harry would not have been able to move after the blows to his head; but how could he have lain supine while the blood from his left ear defied the law of gravity to flow upward over the cheek, under the eye, and over the bridge of the nose?

Higgs' cross-examination took much of the sting out of Quackenbush's effectiveness as a Crown witness; his harm to the defense was neutralized. Erle Stanley Gardner thought that Higgs accomplished the supreme goal of any cross-examiner—he actually converted Quackenbush into a witness for the defense.

Eric Hallinan immediately called Lawrence Wylie Fitzmaurice, who described himself as the acting chief medical officer of the Bahamas; and within a few preliminary questions, he began detailing the autopsy he had performed on Sir Harry's body the following morning, Friday, July 9. The macabre subject matter captivated jury attention; and Fitzmaurice's professorial demeanor made him helpfully spell out and interpret into lay language the technical jargon he felt compelled to use to be medically accurate.

Dr. Fitzmaurice made an external examination of the body upon its arrival at the morgue of the Bahamas General Hospital around four o'clock on Thursday. He was especially interested in the burns on the forehead above both eyes, one being 2 by 1 inch over the right eye. There were slight burns on both upper eyelids, both cheeks, the nose, the corners of the mouth, and the left upper lip. There were slight burns with blisters on the front part of the neck, beneath the chin; in his opinion, all these were *ante mortem* (before death).

There were burns on the chest, the sides, and the back, all the way down to the abdomen. The fingers on the left hand were contracted severely, and the left arm was burned from hand almost to shoulder. The right hand and forearm were only slightly burned, and the fingers slightly contracted and burned, these burns stopping just below the elbow. He described burns on both legs and feet as also being *ante mortem.*

Everyone in the courtroom tensed at the first mention of Sir Harry's head wounds since it was common knowledge that these were the real cause of death, the fire being at this stage only a perplexing distraction. There were four separate wounds, Dr. Fitzmaurice explained patiently, speaking directly to the jurors, whom he considered equals and to whom he was not talking down condescendingly. All were triangular in shape; they were made by an unknown blunt instrument; their course and direction were all downward and slightly toward the front. Wound 1 was in front of the upper lobe of the left ear, about .8 by .5 inches in size; there was a second wound directly above the first about .7 by .3 inches; a third wound .7 by .5 inches in size was just behind the upper lobe of the left ear; and a fourth wound registered one-and-a-half inches above the third, .7 by .2 inches in size.

Blood had flowed from all wounds; there had been bleeding from the nose and the left ear. He observed a slight abrasion around the edge of the upper lobe of the left ear.

The jurors sat in pensive silence in their attempt to imagine the unidentified blunt instrument wielded by the murderer to leave these *four* triangularly shaped wounds, all less than one inch in length, in a square perimeter 2 by 2 inches in front, above and behind—actually crowning—Sir Harry's left ear. Quackenbush had claimed that Sir Harry would not have been able to move after taking these blows; but as the jurors now reasoned, unless the murderer stood directly above Sir Harry as he lay supine in his bed, his face looking upward at the ceiling, it would be virtually impossible to strike four blows so that all wounds indicated a forward and downward thrust. And where was the mosquito netting that enclosed the bed at the time the four blows were struck?

All the jurors accepted without doubt the Crown's theory that *four separate* blows from a blunt instrument hit Sir Harry's skull. No one then in the courtroom had any way of knowing about the real four-pronged weapon that required only one vicious swing.

Shrewdly, Eric Hallinan waited for thirty seconds while the jury pondered the physical mechanics of the head wounds before moving his witness into other paths.

Dr. Fitzmaurice continued after receiving a glass of water from the crier, the only witness thus far with enough courtroom experience to be unafraid of making this simple request.

He performed his internal examination of the body the following morning, Friday, June 9. He opened the skull cap and found considerable blood inside the brain capsule, most of which poured out when the capsule was pierced, and there was some clotted blood around the base of the brain. After removing the brain, he could observe the fracture area of the skull in the region of the left ear. One fracture line ran as far as the upper front part of the middle portion of the skull, while another ran all the way around to the back. One fragment of skull bone about 1½ by 3 inches in dimension was broken completely off; this attested to powerful blows by the assailant. There was a slight contusion of the brain opposite the fractured area; but he could not see any hemorrhage into the brain substance itself. There was no blood in the internal base of the brain, nor did he find any foreign substance within the skull.

The heart showed some fat in its muscle, but it otherwise appeared normal, as did the lungs. The apron inside the abdomen contained a considerable layer of fat, just what he would expect to find in a 180-pound body on a 5-feet-6-inch frame.

The stomach was normal and contained about four ounces of a black viscous substance. All other organs appeared normal. Death, in his opinion, occurred approximately four to six hours after completion of the last meal.

This would place death between 1:30 and 3:30 A.M., since

the Wednesday dinner Sir Harry ate with Harold Christie, Mrs. Heneage, and Charles Hubbard was finished at nine-thirty. Like Dr. Quackenbush before him, Dr. Fitzmaurice failed to detail the physical facts on which his ultimate opinion as to time of death was based; but the jury could not be expected to know that both doctors, for whatever reason, exceeded the bounds of medical knowledge to give opinions on time of death that confined it to these precisely limited schedules.

Death was caused, Dr. Fitzmaurice continued, by a heavy blunt instrument with a well-defined edge.

Sir Oscar Daly could not restrain himself and await further questioning by either Eric Hallinan or defense counsel.

His Honor: "Do you have any opinion as to the material with which this instrument was made?"

"No, I do not."

Fitzmaurice deserves credit for shunning the temptation to answer this question definitively, as would have too many "experts."

Mr. Hallinan: "And what, in your opinion, was the cause of death?"

"The cause of death was shock, hemorrhage around the brain, and fracture of the skull."

Mr. Hallinan: "Please tell us what you mean by shock?"

"I mean surgical shock, which is a medical term describing a fall in blood pressure, as distinguished from fright."

Ernest Callender, Godfrey Higgs' assistant, rose to cross-examine. He was a native of Nassau, getting his mulatto coloring from his English mother who married his British Guianan father in Georgetown before the family moved to the Bahamas. Callender spent twelve years in England, the last four at the Middle Temple where he completed his law training, before being called to the bar in Nassau in 1936 on his twenty-seventh birthday. He had been strongly torn between law and a career on the stage that would have exploited his exceptional speaking and singing voice; but he decided that law would be a safer and less mercurial career,

even though he served as a newscaster for the British Broad-
casting Corporation in London during the early Thirties when
radio was just breaking into a position of international importance.

Callender was a little more than average in height, at thirty-
four years just beginning to take on weight, round-faced
with greatly modified Negroid features, a young, mulatto
Charles Laughton, but more handsome.

Callender opened routinely on several relatively incon-
sequential matters. He rested somewhere between Adderley
and Higgs on the rating scale of eloquence, his voice con-
taining a biting tone which he fought to overcome, although
he found it effective to let himself go at times.

Dr. Fitzmaurice said that *rigor mortis* could set in while
the body was still warm. When he first saw Sir Harry's body,
the eyes were closed. He examined the eyeballs later at the
hospital and was sure he would recall it if they had been
badly burned. As far as he recalled, the eyelashes were
burned off considerably, but he did not remember the eyebrows.

After looking at the photos in the courtroom, he believed
the eyebrows were plainly visible; but he could not say
whether the lashes could be seen in the pictures.

At Westbourne, he had pondered over the feathers on the
right side of the body but did not notice whether they
adhered directly to the skin. The feathers were removed in
his presence at the morgue by hosing off with water; he did
not notice any foreign substance on the body other than
feathers; they may have adhered to the body because of
moisture; he was not sure whether a portion of the pajamas
remained on the body, but he did remember the feathers
adhering to it.

The exchange between Callender and Fitzmaurice was
conversational, relaxed, even pleasant. In his opinion, the
burns with blisters were *ante mortem* burns; but most of
the burns were post-mortem because post-mortem burns
could not form blisters since there would be no liquid avail-

able to fill in underneath the top layers of skin, to insulate it from the trauma of the fire, which is the physical function of blisters.

For whatever reason, Fitzmaurice also spouted medical nonsense. Beyond doubt, he and Quackenbush discussed their testimony before reaching the courtroom so that it would be consistent. Fitzmaurice spoke in a firm, convincing manner that left no room for doubt.

Mr. Callender: "If a person is burned when alive, how long must he live after sustaining a burn for a blister to form?"

"I cannot set a definite time on it."

Mr. Callender: "You have no idea whether it would be five minutes or an hour?"

"I would say clearly five minutes, as long as there is circulation of the blood, I believe it is possible to get blisters, but not after the circulation stops."

Mr. Callender: "Having examined the body and burns on the body, do you think the burns could have been caused by some inflammable liquid sprayed on the body?"

"Not necessarily, in my opinion."

Mr. Callender: "Do you think the burns on the face could have been caused by somebody spraying inflammable liquid with a Flit gun?"

"I cannot say this would not be possible."

Mr. Callender: "Could you say whether the positions of the burns on the body indicated how it might have been sprayed with inflammable material?"

"No, I cannot say. Much would depend upon the size of the nozzle, and of the gun, and the number of squirts."

Both Higgs and Callender were considerably relieved at this response. The maid, Mabel Ellis, told the police of a half-filled spray can of Fly-Ded which was used at Westbourne for mosquitoes; the police suggested that this petroleum-based liquid could have been used to create the mysterious fire. This meant that the accused, acting impulsively, could have sprayed the body and room with material within easy reach *after* smashing Sir Harry's skull. In other words, he need not have carried with him in planned, premeditated manner the tools of his arson. Higgs and Callender both concluded from Fitzmaurice's response that the Crown still did not possess a workable theory for the physical mechanics of the fire.

Callender now asked a question intended to impeach not this witness but Harold Christie.

Mr. Callender: "If water is put into the mouth of a deceased person, would any of it get to the stomach?"

"Some of it might; the rest would remain in the mouth."

This was all that Callender and Higgs could reasonably hope to get from the Crown's chief medical witness, so Callender let him go; but the jurors were not completely satisfied. The first question submitted by Foreman Sands clearly showed that they already wrestled with the most perplexing item of evidence to this point.

Foreman Sands: "Were there any marks on the body that would indicate that the body had been completely lifted before it was discovered in the morning?"

"There was nothing that I saw to suggest that the whole body had been lifted before I saw it."

There was no particular logic in the sequence of the remaining questions; but they showed that the jury already grasped full well the magnitude of the problems presented to them for solution.

Foreman Sands: "Were there sufficient *ante mortem* burns on the body to render Sir Harry unconscious?"

"No, I don't think so."

Foreman Sands: "Would any of the blows have rendered Sir Harry unconscious and unable to move and cry out?"

"That is a rather difficult question. I know of cases where people have been sandbagged and fallen dead instantly, and other cases extreme enough where a crowbar was put through the head and the patient came to the hospital to have us take it out. These two extremes show the difficulty in providing an answer to the question."

For once, Fitzmaurice spoke the medical truth of a cautious witness.

Foreman Sands: "Would four blows, one after the other, have rendered him unconscious?"

"I do not believe that after four wounds such as I saw, if delivered by blows rapidly one after another, he could either have got up or cried out."

Foreman Sands: "What in your opinion came first, the blows or the burns?"

"Particularly the *ante mortem* burns I saw would not, in my opinion, have prevented Sir Harry from jumping up or shouting if he had not first had the blows."

Foreman Sands: "Were the fractures of the skull caused by the blows?"

"The combined effect of the blows caused fracture of the skull."

Foreman Sands: "What would cause contraction of the fingers?"

"There are two possibilities: one, that *ante mortem* burns could cause the contraction; or two, they might have been contracted naturally when he was asleep."

Obviously, Dr. Fitzmaurice accepted the theory that Sir Harry was bludgeoned while sleeping peaceably in his bed.

Foreman Sands: "Would the worst of these blows have left him conscious?"

"The blow behind the ear, number three, might have rendered him unconscious."

Foreman Sands: "Was the hair of his head burnt?"

"I do not recall that it was."

Foreman Sands: "Was there sufficient heat up there near his head to burn it if his head remained there?"

"I don't know how much heat there was about the head."

Foreman Sands: "If Sir Harry's body was burned shortly before death, would the formation of blisters continue while Sir Harry was unconscious and not dead?"

"I believe to a certain point, yes."

The first phase of the Crown's case was complete: proof of cause of death and manner of death, the killing of a human being by an unlawful, criminal agency. Erle Stanley Gardner wondered why Eric Hallinan did not call his medical witnesses before he put Harold Christie in the witness box. This simple shift in order of witnesses might have improved Christie's image appreciably, although the Crown felt reasonably confident in the physical evidence of both cause and manner of death.

From Eric Hallinan's point of view, the big cloud on the horizon favorable to the defense, of course, was the crusted line of blood that flowed *uphill* in defiance of the law of gravity. Would he be compelled to shift his theory of the case at this late stage to admit that Sir Harry was *not* lying supine in his bed, staring upward at the ceiling, when his murderer rained the *four* crushing blows against his skull?

At this stage, Higgs and Callender were forced to the waiting game. Since all four barristers operated in the dark, without accurate knowledge of the facts, the defense could not do otherwise.

Before adjourning court, the Lord Chief Justice announced that special arrangements for the afternoon had been made so that the business men on the jury could meet with their business representatives, in the presence of police officers, to sign checks and other necessary orders; but there must be no written communication whatsoever about the case or any oral comment on it. Sir Oscar would hold each man personally accountable for his own actions and those of his subordinates; and if it should develop that improper conduct on the part of anyone necessitated a new trial, Sir Oscar would not look favorably upon the culprit.

Hallinan and Adderley conferred far into the night upon phase two of their case: converting the abstract "criminal agency" into the specific of Alfred de Marigny; and de Marigny contemplated seriously for the first time what it might be like to hang by the neck until dead.

17

The Innocent Interludes

Great chunks of life are but innocent interludes, and Dorothy
Clark stood in the midst of her most dramatic role. Petite,
doll-like, doe-eyed, her black hair and dark eyes glistened
against the backdrop of her white linen suit and broad-
brimmed white straw hat. White linen obviously was in
vogue in the Bahamas in October, 1943.

Like thousands of her fellow countrymen, Dorothy Clark
was a war transplant from the tight little island of Great
Britain to the tighter, littler island of New Providence. They
came generally in two groups: the military, primarily the
R.A.F. pilots and their supporting crews who operated the
ferry command from airfields all across the United States to
the besieged mother island; and the privileged and wealthy
who could buy their way out of the Battle of Britain, wartime shortages and rationing, and other personal discomforts,
including the real threat of death.

The invaders who could not completely integrate with
the natives were looked upon as a caste apart, forced to live
in a special, unstable war subculture which itself became
parasitical.

The war's disruption created a ratio of approximately
fifteen women to every male among the invaders with all
the attendant social, emotional, and financial maladjustments

and imbalances. People grasped their spur-of-the-moment diversions which passed for pleasantries when and where the opportunity presented itself, staid modes and customs steeped in British formality falling by the wayside. The most pressing question of the moment was "What are you doing tonight?" and with whom.

Dorothy Clark differed from most of her compatriots in that her husband was in Nassau; but as a ferry-command pilot, he was away frequently on lengthy trips to the United States and to England. Suddenly, Dorothy Clark became a chief witness for the Crown, the Attorney General requiring her testimony to place Alfred de Marigny near Westbourne at a highly incriminating hour, the hour of opportunity.

It all began quite innocently enough during cocktail time Tuesday, July 6. Dorothy's husband was in England, she restless and at loose ends; so she walked next door for a cigarette with Jean Ainsley, whose husband was also an R.A.F. flyer. The Clarks and the Ainsleys, along with a dozen other British couples, were lodged in the Hubbard Cottages, a housing development just west of Westbourne. It was Captain Ainsley's last night in Nassau; and within the hour, all three were at the bar in the Prince George Hotel on Bay Street. The habitués were carefree and lighthearted, convivial and open—wartime qualities that assured the Prince George its charm and clientele. A mutual acquaintance introduced the Ainsleys and Dorothy Clark to Alfred de Marigny; and during their first round of drinks together, de Marigny explained that his wife was in Miami on her way to Vermont, he was giving an informal dinner at his home the following evening, and he would be honored if the Ainsleys and Mrs. Clark could join him. Eagerly, the two women accepted the invitation with Captain Ainsley's approval, and de Marigny agreed to call for them the next night.

Dorothy Clark now found that Attorney General Eric Hallinan spoke the truth when he assured her that her testimony would go easily. She was almost relaxed as she stood erect in the witness box, looking down directly at Hallinan, and occasionally casting a furtive glance toward the prisoner's cage where de Marigny lounged in a feigned attitude of disinterest in his own white linen suit and colorful paisley-print tie.

The next evening, Wednesday, the seventh, Alfred de Marigny arrived promptly at eight o'clock at her cottage where Jean Ainsley also waited. He was in his Lincoln, and since neither of them were familiar with the Yacht Club, he drove there first before taking them to his home on Victoria Avenue, just east of the center of Nassau and some four miles and ten minutes away from Westbourne.

She hurried through her story for her captive audience, but painted only the most generalized conclusions and omitted the details.

There were eleven people at the dinner party, which broke up around twelve-thirty, possibly a little later in the early hours of Thursday morning. De Marigny graciously drove the two R.A.F. wives back to their cottages. It was drizzling as they passed through town. Just as they reached the cathedral she looked at her watch, which read twenty-five minutes past one; but when she looked at the car clock, it read only five past one; and this evoked conversation about the discrepancy between her watch and the car clock. When they reached the cottages, she and Jean Ainsley thanked de Marigny for a delightful dinner and evening. He courteously saw them to their respective doors, got in his car, and turned it around to head back toward Bay Street. They had no idea where he went, but his route, of necessity, took him past Westbourne.

There in all innocence and simplicity was the "opportunity" element of the Crown's case! The time sequences jibed closely enough with the doctors' estimates of time of death; two essential pieces of the Crown's jigsaw puzzle now meshed convincingly.

Godfrey Higgs rose with alacrity and distinct purpose, his first question on its way before he even completed the courtesy bow to the Chief Justice. Dorothy Clark's testimony, not a surprise at all, hurt the defense; he stood no chance whatsoever of having her back off from placing de Marigny at Westbourne at the critical time; so he set about to convert her into his own witness on at least two matters critical to the defense.

The dining tables were initially laid in the garden, Dorothy Clark responded easily to Higgs' question, but the party moved inside on account of the mosquitoes. This meant the tables were changed and set up in the studio or dancing room; the only lighting during dinner was supplied by candles.

Higgs walked to the registrar's table and lifted a stubby, nondescript candlestick, topped by a dirty glass shade approximately eight inches high with a diameter of some four inches. He handed it up to the witness, who examined it carefully, separating shade from candlestick, and revolving both thoughtfully in her hands.

Mr. Higgs: "I ask you if this is one of the candlesticks and shades used to light the tables at the dinner in the studio?"

"Yes, I am sure it is."

Mr. Higgs: "Did you notice whether there were three shades like it, or similar to it?"

"No, I did not. I only know that some of the candles were open and some were in glass chimneys, like this one. There were also some candelabra."

Mr. Higgs: "I put it to you. Did you see the accused light any of the candles?"

"Yes, I did."

This was Higgs' first point of converting Dorothy Clark into his own witness. He knew there would be testimony later on, police testimony, sinister and damaging, that burned hairs on de Marigny's arms were seen the morning Sir Harry's body was found. Higgs would claim, convincingly he hoped, that the burned and singed hairs came from lighting the candles at the party; and his claim was now dramatically buttressed by this report of one of the Crown's own witnesses.

Yes, Dorothy Clark continued, Georges, the Marquis de Visdelou Guimbeau, and Miss Betty Roberts were at the dinner, but they were not around when she left. She remembered seeing and talking about an ash-gray Maltese cat; she remembered petting the cat.

Higgs knew that the marquis and blond, buxom, sexy Betty Roberts were a vital part of de Marigny's tale; so he took this opportunity to introduce them peripherally to the jury through the Crown's witness.

When she and Jean Ainsley entered de Marigny's Lincoln in the falling rain, he was in the best of spirits. He was not intoxicated—no one at the party reached that condition; he was merely gay, happy, and relaxed.

Higgs again walked to the registrar's desk and lifted a tan linen sports jacket and a lighter-beige pair of slacks. These were complemented by tan-and-white sports shoes. The ensemble was in such perfect harmony that it could have come right out of a men's furnishings window. Dorothy Clark examined the wardrobe and declared it to be identical to that de Marigny wore at the party. He did not wear a raincoat or a hat, but there was a "very colorful tie" that she remembered, and a cream-colored shirt.

Higgs returned the clothing to the registrar and resumed his standing position behind the counsel table. Desperately, he wanted one more point from the Crown's witness.

He led her through her summons to Westbourne between nine-thirty and ten Friday morning, July 9. Mrs. Heneage and Mr. Hubbard were there, as were the Marquis de Visdelou and Betty Roberts. Lieutenant Douglas of the Bahamas police was there. They all sat in the west living room downstairs. She was questioned by the "American police," Captain Melchen and Captain Barker.

Mr. Higgs: "Did you see the accused, Alfred de Marigny, taken upstairs that morning?"

"Yes, I did."

Mr. Higgs: "I put it to you. Was it between eleven and twelve o'clock?"

"Yes, I am sure it was."

Godfrey Higgs could scarcely control his excitement. He knew that much of the Crown's case rested upon a latent fingerprint taken from the white Chinese screen that bordered the south side of Sir Harry's bed. The Crown claimed it was from Alfred de Marigny's right little finger. The "American detectives" swore that de Marigny at no time after the discovery of the body was permitted to go upstairs until *after* the screen was removed from Sir Harry's bedroom around three or four in the afternoon. Now, the Crown's own witness, Dorothy Clark, innocently and with no ax to grind for or against anyone, laid the plausible foundation for Higgs' assertion, if need be, that de Marigny's fingerprint could have been deposited on the screen during this trip upstairs *before* the screen was removed.

Higgs hesitated. He had what he needed in the form of a broad, general statement; could he fortify it with buttressing detail? Would he run any risks of mitigating the power of this generalized conclusion by further questions? He elected to take the plunge.

Mr. Higgs: "Where were you at the time you saw the accused taken upstairs by the American detective?"

"I was sitting in the western living room on a couch, on the south side of the room."

Mr. Higgs: "When did you next see the accused?"

"I was in the dining room, and the accused was talking to Miss Betty Roberts. I heard her ask him, 'Where have you been? You look as if you have been sleeping.' Mr. de Marigny replied, 'No, I have been upstairs with Captain Melchen.'"

This was better, far better, than Higgs dared to dream before putting this line of questioning!

Mr. Higgs: "How long would you say that the accused was out of your sight from the time you saw him taken upstairs by the American detective until you saw him next in the dining room?"

"I would say at least three-quarters of an hour."

❖   ❖   ❖

Then Dorothy Clark left the witness box, and Jean Ainsley, another person caught in an identical innocent interlude, became first a witness for the Crown in confirming de Marigny's opportune presence at Westbourne, and then for the defense on the matter of candles and de Marigny's trip upstairs before noon on Friday.

Constable Wendell Lamond Parker, badge No. 17 in the Bahamas police force, was another to report an innocent interlude, although his had a more relevant connection with the courtroom.

A policeman for six years, he knew the accused and spoke to him often. On Thursday morning, July 8, Constable Parker reported to his post with the traffic branch in the Central Police Station in downtown Nassau at seven o'clock. About half an hour later, de Marigny arrived at the station and spoke to him. Parker now remembered being "struck by his appearance": he was excited, his eyes appeared wide, and his lips were protruding. Never before had he been visited at such an early hour by anyone. De Marigny spoke about a truck, No. 651, formally passed and licensed on September 8 of that year; and de Marigny wanted to know if it was necessary to bring it up for inspection.

That was all: de Marigny's unusual appearance at the police station at an incredibly early hour of the morning! The Crown would argue that this portended guilt since fear of apprehension compelled him to use the truck ruse to find out if his dastardly deed at Westbourne was yet discovered.

Ernest Callender rose to cross-examine, adopting an attitude of derision. Constable Parker replied that the accused was not wearing dark glasses when he arrived at the station; he was positive because he remembered "being struck" by de Marigny's eyes which he looked at as he spoke to him. Yes, his lips remained protruding all the time he was talking; he did not think de Marigny was deliberately pushing out his lips. His eyes were open wider than he usually saw them, and they looked excited. He thought it was his professional duty as a constable to observe, and he made it a point to observe as much as possible. Callender turned nonchalantly to look down at his fellow counsel seated at the table.

Mr. Callender: "Do you remember ever having spoken to Mr. Higgs here?"

"No, I do not know that I ever spoke to him; but I have also seen him at Central Police Station."

Mr. Callender: "And I presume you looked also into his eyes, just as you looked into the eyes of Alfred de Marigny on the morning of Thursday, July 8, this year?"

"Yes, I am certain I did."

Mr. Callender: "And what, please tell us, is the color of Mr. Higgs' eyes?"

"They are blue."

Constable Parker fired the answer back so rapidly that it appeared an instinctive response, exaggerated by Higgs' bowed head so that the witness could not see his eyes.

"My lord," Higgs bowed respectfully as he slowly rose from his chair, "I am told they are hazel!"

Constable Parker's overeagerness to testify in a way to help the Crown was flagrantly exposed; but did it materially aid the defense?

Most trials collect a number of reports of innocent interludes; some are cluttered by them. Howard LeCato Lightbourn, a neighbor of de Marigny's on Victoria Avenue, returned to his home about twelve-thirty Thursday morning. He noticed a light burning in the southeast corner of de Marigny's house; and when he was awakened by his wife at one forty-five, the light still burned. He woke again about four in the morning and the same light was on in the same room. There was no activity of any kind either audibly or visibly perceptible.

Ernest Callender probed the witness with several irrelevant questions, without thrust or direction. Eric Hallinan would argue to the jury that the lights in de Marigny's house proved his "wakefulness on his return home," the result of a guilty conscience.

❖   ❖   ❖

The reports of these innocent interludes were necessary, or so the Attorney General thought, to set the stage for the description of the arrest of Alfred de Marigny. They also served as essential tiles in the mosaic of circumstantial evidence that was building toward the conclusion of de Marigny's guilt.

18

Why a Man Acts

The Common Law definition of murder does not require proof of *motive*, that illusory ingredient of what makes a man act. Centuries before Sigmund Freud paved the way for such terms as *id, libido, ego* and *superego, conscious* and *subconscious,* the early judges knew all too well that it was impossible to decide accurately any man's intuitive proddings, instinctive drives, and hidden goals that cause him to act. For these pragmatic reasons, the law's only technical requirement is proof that the killer *intended* the death of his victim. The *why* of the *intent* is too speculative for courtroom analysis.

No murder prosecutor, however, ever considers his task complete without presenting the jury some concept of motive, gossamer and conflicting though the evidence may be. And there are practical reasons: If the jury does not understand *why* the accused took the life of a fellow human being, it is reluctant to believe that he *did* snuff out that life. The jurors are supposed to reflect nothing more or less than the collective common sense and mores of the community, and the community always demands to know *why*. The usual motives for murder are hate, jealousy, and desire of financial gain, expressed through the modalities of extortion, robbery and blackmail; there are a dozen other precise categories carefully worked out over the past five hundred years that include vengeful violence and lying in wait.

In the fourteen points of his opening address to the jury, Alfred Adderley came down heavily on de Marigny's motive: hatred, humiliation, financial gain, all coupled with his own callousness. Having already established *opportunity* for the accused to commit the bludgeon murder at Westbourne, the Crown now proceeded to *motive*.

Lieutenant John Campbell Douglas, a trim Scotsman only two inches shorter than Alfred de Marigny, with hawklike features, a rolling burr in his voice that defied easy communication, and mischievous eyes that telegraphed his wry sense of humor before his punch lines arrived, stood easily in immaculate khaki uniform in the witness box and described himself as assistant superintendent of the Bahamas police.

Shortly after midnight—actually it was the early morning of Friday, July 9—more or less twenty-three hours after the Crown's time of death, Lieutenant Douglas arrived at de Marigny's house on Victoria Avenue. Police Commissioner Erskine-Lindop, the "two American detectives," and de Marigny's friend, J. H. Anderson, were there, although "the Americans" left within minutes after his arrival. One of them, Captain Melchen, took with him a brownish suit and a pair of brown-and-white shoes.

Colonel Erskine-Lindop instructed Douglas to spend the night and keep de Marigny under observation. Douglas remained awake for the entire time but the accused "slept fitfully."

Douglas testified easily, responding immediately to the Attorney General's questions, crisply and without any hesitancy. He was a professional witness in the most complimentary sense of the term, and what he said would obviously indelibly impress the jury.

It was bright daylight and a clear day when de Marigny awoke at six o'clock. He made a pot of coffee which Douglas shared before they entered de Marigny's Lincoln to drive to the chicken farm on East Bay Street. De Marigny showed him about with what Douglas interpreted as pride in his possessions and work. Among other activities, two or three blacks participated in a slaughtering and cleaning operation. Confidently, as though he knew what it was all about, de Marigny picked up a bucket of scalding water from one of the open fires, poured out the water, and replaced it.

They drove back to the Victoria Avenue house, puttered around aimlessly, drank more coffee, and left for Westbourne shortly after eight o'clock.

Mr. Hallinan: "Did the accused say anything to you about his relations with Sir Harry Oakes?"

"In the car, on the way to Westbourne, the accused talked about his chicken farm, and also of the strained relations between himself and Sir Harry Oakes which had resulted because of tales which his former wife, Ruth, had told Sir Harry."

Mr. Hallinan: "Can you tell us anything specifically that he said?"

"In the neighborhood of Westbourne, the accused said, 'That guy, Sir Harry, the old bastard, should have been killed anyway.'"

There was total silence in the courtroom, Lieutenant Douglas looking straight at the Attorney General, who did not lead with his next question for several seconds to permit the dramatic impact to seep in. The jurors, as jurors everywhere are wont to do when highly damaging evidence against the defendant comes in, studied Alfred de Marigny carefully. He sat tense in the prisoner's cage, his body flexed forward slightly, spine rigid, face immobile, his only motion being the stroke of his right hand moving slowly across his chin. The jurors next looked furtively at Godfrey Higgs and Ernest Callender; they were tense and rigid. Sir Oscar also cautiously shifted his gaze from witness to accused.

Mr. Hallinan: "Did you make any comment on the accused's remarks?"

"I made no comment whatsoever."

They drove past Westbourne but did not stop as it was too early, continuing on out along the beach where the waters above the coral reefs foamed into many shades of

green and blue. It was still too early when they came back
to Westbourne at eight-fifty; the police superintendent was
not yet there, and the special constables stood guard around
the house. They proceeded on to the golf-course clubhouse.

Everyone in the courtroom tensed with the realistic expectation that this recitation of minutiae led to something
sinister.

Mr. Hallinan: "Did the accused say anything to you at the
clubhouse?"

"He asked me if in a British court, a man could be convicted of murder if they could not find the weapon."

Mr. Hallinan: "And what, if any, reply did you make?"

"I said, 'Don't worry about it, Freddie.' "

De Marigny noisily shifted his position in the dock, a wry
smile playing across his face, his head moving in disbelief
from side to side.

Mr. Hallinan: "What happened next?"

"We walked from the clubhouse back to Westbourne and
on to its western porch. The superintendent had arrived by
that time."

Mr. Hallinan: "Did the accused say anything to you on the
porch?"

"He asked me if a man could be convicted on circumstantial
evidence alone."

Mr. Hallinan: "What did you say?"

"I told him, 'Yes, I think so. It's been done quite frequently in the past!' "

De Marigny once more altered his position and made a
grimace registering disgust.

Lieutenant Douglas' reiteration of the investigative events
the remainder of the day at Westbourne was an anticlimax.
He did describe delivering a parcel to the Miami, Florida,
Police Department on July 22. It contained three cuttings
from a pillow slip and towels. He was at Westbourne when
they were taken.

As Ernest Callender rose at the counsel table, he was well
aware of the old legal cliché, "Never cross-examine a Scots-

man!" But he dared not let Lieutenant Douglas' penetrating statements stand unchallenged. Although he knew he did not stand a chance in the world of getting Douglas to recant, his only alternative was an attempt to draw out some of their sting.

Mr. Callender: "On Friday morning before you went out, the accused prepared himself some breakfast?"

"He mixed up some milk concoction."

Mr. Callender: "I don't think you had anything, did you, you weren't feeling very well?"

"No."

Mr. Callender: "I think you said accused slept fitfully?"

"Yes."

Mr. Callender: "You were sitting on the couch, and only the light in the passageway was on?"

"Yes. There was an open colonnade and the light from the passage would shine right in the living room."

Mr. Callender: "You had a telephone call from the Central Station at each hour during the night?"

"I did."

Mr. Callender: "So there was nothing unusual in the accused sleeping fitfully?"

"It was slightly disturbing. It might have disturbed him."

If he went no further, that ploy helped immeasurably. The jurors now looked accusingly toward the Attorney General: Did he deliberately attempt to mislead them with the implication that de Marigny slept fitfully *without reason?*

Callender could see a new opportunity open for him. The burns which supposedly were observed on de Marigny's arms and beard when they were examined Thursday and Friday would assume alarming proportions. In Callender's quick mind, he now saw a chance to extract an admission from the Crown's own witness that might take considerable pressure off the defense on this score.

Mr. Callender: "When you got to the farm you say the accused went over to the fire. At that time, there were two little boys working around the fire?"

"Yes. I could not say that they were actually attending to the fire. They were in the vicinity."

Mr. Callender: "I suggest that accused went to the fire to assist these two little boys with the bucket?"

"I could not be sure."

Callender would use this simple extraction effectively later on, as would Higgs in his closing jury argument. Now, Callender felt compelled to go into the damaging admissions Lieutenant Douglas reported. He would not attempt to contradict them head-on, only to minimize them by showing their true and proper context.

Mr. Callender: "With regard to this conversation on the eighth at Westbourne, you say he asked you if a man could be convicted on circumstantial evidence. Hadn't you just been discussing the Glen Rogers case?"

"Not to my recollection; but I don't deny it either."

Mr. Callender: "And didn't you tell him that Glen Rogers had been convicted on circumstantial evidence?"

"I don't remember, but I don't deny that I said it."

Mr. Callender: "And wasn't it as a result of that, that he asked if a man could be convicted on circumstantial evidence?"

"I can't answer that in view of my last answer."

Mr. Callender: "You don't suggest that just out of the blue, he sprung that question on you?"

"I am making no suggestions."

Mr. Callender: "Then the question was put to you that in a British court, a man cannot be convicted if the weapon was not found. I put it to you that just before that you had been discussing Sir Harry Oakes' death. Had he not been asking you if they knew what kind of weapon had been used, a gun or a knife?"

"I cannot remember."

Mr. Callender: "You know the accused is a Frenchman, that they have different laws from the British?"

"I understand so."

The Lord Chief Justice was intrigued.

His Honour: "Well, I don't know. Did you know the accused came from Mauritius?"

"Yes, I did."

Mr. Callender: "And didn't he ask whether they had found any weapon?"

"I believe he did."

Mr. Callender: "Now, under the circumstances, wasn't it a perfectly normal question for him to ask if a man could be convicted without the weapon?"

"Nothing unusual."

Mr. Callender: "You paid no particular attention to those two remarks?"

"No."

Mr. Callender: "How long before giving your evidence in the magistrate's court on August 24 did you give a statement to the prosecution?"

"I told the police about the remarks when I came up from Westbourne shortly after the accused was arrested. I had paid no particular attention to them at the time of the conversation."

Sir Oscar Daly looked down approvingly at Ernest Callender. He would say later that this cross-examination was one of the most effective he ever heard during his thirty-plus years at the bar and on the bench. Callender was not through. His achievement to this point was gratifying—many cross-examiners would have stopped there—but Callender knew he could safely probe two other areas with a reasonable chance for gain.

Mr. Callender: "The night of July 9, you were off duty?"

"I was on call. I had just gone to bed."

Mr. Callender: "You were not very pleased to be called out of bed and have to stay up all night?"

"It didn't bother me, it was part of my duty."

Mr. Callender: "Did you not say to the accused on the ninth, 'Freddie, you have given me more trouble than you can imagine. Last night was my night off, and I had to spend the whole night watching you'?"

"I would not be surprised."

Mr. Callender: "Did you also say to the accused, 'They are making all this fuss about Sir Harry because he has dough. If it had been some poor fellow in Grant's Town [the ghetto for the native blacks], I would not have to make a lot of statements'?"

"I don't recollect saying anything to that effect."

Mr. Callender: "You also commonly use the word 'Bastard'?"

"I very seldom use that word."

Mr. Callender: "I put it to you, Lieutenant Douglas, that that is a favorite expression of yours?"

"I deny it."

Mr. Callender: "And I further put it to you that you were the one who said, 'That guy, Sir Harry, the old bastard should have been killed anyway?'"

"I deny it. It was the accused who made use of those words."

"That is all, my lord," Ernest Callender said quickly, before Douglas' last words faded from the room. There was no redirect examination by the Attorney General, and the jurors posed no questions. Granted, Ernest Callender's cross-examination was masterful; but no juror doubted the authenticity of de Marigny's words of hatred and animosity toward the slain baronet, his father-in-law. For the first time, the jurors noticed de Marigny's cast-down look and expression of defeat; he almost appeared to be embarrassed; certainly he was no longer cocky and defiant.

The Attorney General was not yet finished with *motive*. William Johannan Sayad stood in the witness box to describe himself as an eye, ear, nose, and throat specialist, who had been practicing medicine in Palm Beach, Florida, since 1926. In his mid-forties, Sayad could have been banker, lawyer, sales executive, any business or professional man. He was hesitant, almost timid, and his courtroom discomfort showed itself in an abnormal, backward arch of his spine, his hands clasped tensely behind him so that he swayed in the exaggerated position of parade rest.

De Marigny looked up at him uncomfortably, taking long, hard swipes at both sides of his face with his right hand in a strong rubbing motion.

In the early part of the year, perhaps in February—yes, it was February—Dr. Sayad responded in a tired monotone, he attended Mrs. de Marigny at the Good Samaritan Hospital in West Palm Beach. He operated on Nancy Oakes de Marigny's mouth on February 10, that year. He also did some work for the accused about that time, and it was proposed that he would remove de Marigny's tonsils.

On the thirteenth or fourteenth of February, some four days after Mrs. de Marigny's operation, Alfred de Marigny entered the hospital in the evening in preparation for the tonsillectomy to be performed the following morning. He occupied a room that adjoined his wife's suite. Dr. Sayad had a conversation over the telephone during the day with Sir Harry Oakes that did not mention de Marigny; but for some reason which he did not then understand, de Marigny moved out of the room in Nancy's suite and into a separate room, and he canceled the tonsillectomy.

The next morning, Sayad found de Marigny in the hallway of the hospital. They went into the serving kitchen for a talk, and de Marigny apologized for canceling the operation and explained it was because he was upset at what had occurred between himself and Sir Harry the preceding day.

Mr. Hallinan: "What did he say at that time about Sir Harry?"

"He said he would crack Sir Harry's head."

Mr. Hallinan: "What did you say?"

"I admonished him for making the statement, owing to the age of Sir Harry, and that he was his father-in-law."

Mr. Hallinan: "Did you consider that remark to be made in jest or in anger?"

"I considered it in anger."

The jurors hardly heard Eric Hallinan hand over his witness. They watched Alfred de Marigny continue to stroke his face with great swipes of his right hand while glaring through his barred cage up at the witness. Several of the jurors thought they could read anger and hostility into de Marigny's glower, a reaction that clearly did the defense no good whatsoever.

Godfrey Higgs rose quickly in an effort to emulate Ernest Callender's masterly performance with the preceding witness.

Mr. Higgs: "Did you make any inquiry of the accused as to what was said between him and Sir Harry in the telephone conversation the preceding day?"

"Yes. The accused told me that Sir Harry had called him in the hospital room and told him to get out."

Mr. Higgs: "Is that all? Wasn't there something stronger said?"

"Yes. The accused said that Sir Harry told him that if he did not get out of the room, Sir Harry would kick him out."

Mr. Higgs: "What did the accused tell you about his wife that morning?"

"He told me that Mrs. de Marigny was considerably upset."

Mr. Higgs: "Did he tell you that she had requested that she did not want to see her father or mother in her room?"

"Yes. He also said that he had given instructions to the nurse to tell *everyone* that Nancy did not wish to see *any* visitors."

Mr. Higgs: "And what did you say to that?"

"I told him that I certainly would not stop Sir Harry or Lady Oakes from visiting their daughter."

Mr. Higgs: "And at this point, did you not have some harsh words with the accused?"

"I suppose you can say that."

Godfrey Higgs was making every effort to show bias and prejudice on the part of the witness against the accused, emotional feelings that might color and taint the objectivity of his testimony.

Mr. Higgs: "Did not the accused tell you that if you allowed Sir Harry to come into the room and upset Nancy, the accused would lose his patience and knock Sir Harry out of the room?"

"I do not remember that."

Mr. Higgs: "Did not the accused use the words 'knock him out of the room' instead of 'crack Sir Harry's head'?"

"I am absolutely positive that the accused said he would crack Sir Harry's head."

Godfrey Higgs now walked dramatically to the registrar's table and found two stapled sheets of foolscap. Carefully he examined the writing; and now with a flourish he waved the papers up in front of the witness box, but did not actually hand them to Dr. Sayad.

Mr. Higgs: "Did you not give a written statement to the prosecution some months ago?"

"Yes, I believe I did."

Mr. Higgs: "In that statement you said the accused used words *to the effect* that he would crack Sir Harry's head. In your statement, you were not as positive then as you are now about the accused's words?"

"I was just as positive when I made the statement as I am now that the accused made the statement that he would crack Sir Harry's head."

Godfrey Higgs let the witness go. There was really nothing else to do with him; the slight insinuation of bias and prejudice might be enough to leach out some of the sting of de Marigny's intemperate threat to "crack Sir Harry's head."

Three of the jurors were uncomfortably indisposed with colds, so the Lord Chief Justice ordered a doctor sworn who could administer to their medical needs; and he recessed court just before noon.

As the jurors made their way into the dining room of the Rozelda Hotel, their rather comfortable place of confinement, they noticed a redheaded girl, tastefully dressed, at a table in the far corner of the room. She lunched there every day with the heavy-set, gray-haired, beak-nosed man they saw in court behind defense counsel. They knew who the girl was, although they were not yet acquainted with the man. It was Raymond Schindler taking his daily report to Nancy Oakes de Marigny, who was barred from the courtroom as a witness for the defense.

No one else knew it but other progress reports were going forth daily: Christie and Barker kept the Duke informed of major developments; and in Baltimore, the Associated Press quoted the Duchess as being fascinated with Erle Stanley Gardner's acounts of the trial.

19

The American Police

It early became apparent that Captain Melchen, the original Mr. Five-by-Five with florid face and jowls in lieu of neck, was merely the administrative forerunner for Captain James Otto Barker, who would develop into the most important witness in the case. Although technically subordinate in rank and table of organization to Melchen, Barker was the stronger and more sinister of the two "American police." Now approaching fifty, Barker was tall and slender, with a high forehead, deep-set eyes, and full head of wavy gray hair. A dapper dresser, he appeared almost an identical twin of the actor Robert Ryan. Although he had never stood in a British witness box to give evidence, he was perfectly at ease in his new environment. He spoke clearly, confidently, and convincingly. His entire demeanor conveyed sincerity and elicited belief.

Alfred de Marigny sat transfixed in his dock, realizing fully that his life literally depended upon what Barker said and what Godfrey Higgs could extract from him on cross-examination. Higgs leaned forward tensely, both elbows resting on the counsel table so that the backs of his hands could support his chin, but this studied posture did not quite conceal a nervous, spastic motion of his fingers which he tried to stop by interlocking his hands. He was impatient with his task, as though trying to rush the Attorney General along with Barker's direct examination so that he could have at him on cross.

Barker stood fearlessly, his hands resting gently and confidently in the pockets of his gray, wide-lapelled, double-breasted suit that matched the color of his hair, his thumbs thrust forward and downward in a relaxed 45-degree angle.

The Attorney General's questions were crisp and automatic, so precise that they sounded as though they were scripted in advance, each word a forceful tribute to Eric Hallinan's skill with the English language.

Captain Barker explained that he had been Superintendent Detective of the Bureau of Criminal Investigation of the Miami Police Department since 1930. His responsibilities included fingerprint records and criminal and technical investigations.

At 11:10, the morning of July 8, Captain Melchen told him to be ready to leave for Nassau by noon. Their mission was "to investigate the death of a prominent citizen of Nassau. It was not designated as a crime. The possibility of suicide was mentioned."

During the next fifty minutes at his disposal, he assembled the tools of his trade: Speedgraphic camera, flash bulbs, a pair of calipers, a firearms-examination outfit, and a "small fingerprinting-processing outfit and also some film."

Upon reaching Westbourne at 2:05 P.M., Barker first endeavored to establish the manner of death; and for the first time he formed the definite opinion that the case was not a suicide. This discovery threw an entirely new and different light on his investigative procedures and attitude.

Fundamentally a fingerprint technician with some degree of expertise acquired over the years, Barker reacted instinctively by attempting to obtain fingerprints from Sir Harry's body. Prints of the left fingers only were available because of the burning of the right hand. He fingerprinted Major Pemberton, Harold Christie, and Dr. Quackenbush; and he then turned to other objects in the room, processing first a drinking glass on the night table between the two beds. The

glass yielded two legible prints which he immediately identified as belonging to Dr. Quackenbush and Major Pemberton.

He processed some books, magazines, and the Chinese
screen near the south side of Sir Harry's bed; he dusted the
dresser top in Sir Harry's room and attacked the mosquito
spray gun, as well as the door in the east bedroom where
Harold Christie stayed the night and a window sill of the
south window in that same room.

Everyone in the courtroom tensed at the mention of the
Chinese screen. From the evidence presented at the preliminary hearing, it was common knowledge that the entire
case might rise and fall on one of de Marigny's fingerprints
that the Crown would claim was raised from this screen.

Alfred de Marigny sat frozen like a marble statue, his eyes
fixed through the barred window of the dock on the witness
whose poise conveyed truthfulness and sincerity. Godfrey
Higgs and Ernest Callender were also totally immovable:
Both realized that unless this clear-voiced, professional man
standing in the witness box could be destroyed in the eyes
of the jury, their client would likely hang.

He made some attempt to process the screen at that time,
Barker continued easily, but the extreme dampness of the
surfaces presented a hazard: He was afraid his dusting
powder would smear or obliterate any latent prints deposited
on the screen. He thought it advisable, therefore, to defer his
technical processing until the following day when, hopefully,
the humidity conditions would be improved.

Godfrey Higgs made a brief note at Barker's next statement: When he came into the room, the clean side of the
screen faced the south, away from the bed. Obviously, this
meant that the screen had been moved before Barker arrived
since there was ample testimony that the smudged, burned
side of the screen faced south, away from the bed, when the
first witnesses arrived.

Shortly before the screen was moved, Barker marked the
second panel from the left on the clean side, "Outside.
Handle with care." His initial examination of the screen in-

dicated the possibility of latent fingerprints on the second panel, the one on which he wrote, and the end panel on the smoked side. He wrote "Outside" on the panel to establish its location at the time he found it. Shortly after this, someone folded the screen before the removal of Sir Harry's body. Two O's were placed on the end panels by Captain Melchen, and the screen was moved to the hallway near the cabinet on the west side.

Eric Hallinan elected to drop the screen at that point, to leave the matter dangling in midair so that the jury would eagerly anticipate later elaboration. He was proceeding with Barker's chronological description of his activities at Westbourne instead of attempting to departmentalize them by subject matter.

He formed the opinion, Barker continued, that the condition of the room as a result of the fire would assist in the identification of a person present at the time the fire started. He expected to find burned hairs on this person, so he examined the arms of Harold Christie with a small lens, particularly looking at the back of his fingers, hands, and forearms, then proceeding to his forehead, eyebrows, head, hair, and portions of his chest.

Mr. Hallinan: "What did you discover, if anything?"

"I did not find any traces of burned hair."

At around ten o'clock on Thursday night, Alfred de Marigny arrived at Westbourne and voluntarily submitted to an examination, removing his coat and shirt and placing his arms under the microscope. First Barker studied the left arm, the back of the fingers, the hand, and the outside of the forearm; and then he proceeded with his search of the right arm. He next examined de Marigny's moustache, his Vandyke beard, his eyebrows, and the hair on his head. De Marigny jokingly told him he was growing the moustache and beard as a surprise for his wife who was in the States; she had always known him to be clean-shaven.

The Attorney General now carefully laid his foundation to enhance the force of Barker's observations.

Mr. Hallinan: "Is it part of your work at the Bureau of Criminal Investigation in Miami to examine suspects for burned hair?"

"Yes, I have examined many times and observed the results of burning on hair. The degrees of burning are extreme brilliance or shiny impressions on the outside of the hair, which is called the cuticle. There is also a type of burning which is called curling. Next, there is singed hair; and finally, the hair may be completely burned or carbonized. The carbonization appears at the top of the stump of the hair."

Only the real professionals in the courtroom realized exactly what was happening to Captain Barker: He was succumbing to the intoxicating vapors and endemic infections of the witness box; soon he would have a full-blown case of "witness box-itis" which magically transforms witnesses into experts on all phases of any subject. Throwing caution to the winds, they get caught up in playing the game of Win with This Witness or This Witness Must Win. The disease grows out of a frailty of human nature, and the only antidote is the Common Law medicinal of cross-examination.

The Attorney General was now ready for his stinging thrust.

Mr. Hallinan: "What did you find upon your examination of the hair of the accused?"

"I found traces on the accused embracing all the degrees of burning I have just mentioned. There were traces on the back of the fingers on both hands, and on the outside of both arms; also in his beard and moustache on the left side, his left eyebrow and the forepart of his head. The hairs on the forepart of the head only showed burns. I could not detect brilliance or the lesser degrees of burning. A few hairs were burned which left stumps of varying lengths."

The flow of words lulled the jurors hypnotically. The rhythm of the Attorney General's questions meshed perfectly with the responses of the witness to set up a cadence obtained only by skillful actors with the ability to spark each other to masterful performances.

Barker told de Marigny matter-of-factly of his discovery, and de Marigny asked to see the burned hairs on his arms through the microscope. He denied being able to do this.

Mr. Hallinan: "What did you say to the accused and what did he say to you?"

"I asked him if he could offer any reasons as to how the burnt hairs got on his body. His first reply was that he did not know how he got them. Three or four minutes later, he' said he thought he knew how he got them. He thought he might have burned his moustache lighting a cigarette and said that he had his hair singed at the barber's three or four haircuts back. Some time later, he stated that he might have got his arms burned at his chicken farm where he assisted occasionally in scalding chickens in a kettle over an open fire. I asked him about the size of this flame, and he indicated a two-foot blaze. When I asked him the time that he had done this, he replied, 'Not recently, but occasionally I give them a hand at the farm.' "

One of the Attorney General's most effective courtroom techniques employed the stratagem: "Never Overkill!" Skillfully he extracted each new subject matter from his witness almost hurriedly so that the jury never became tired or bored by it. He moved immediately to cinch up the peculiarity of the missing shirt.

Barker asked the accused what clothes he wore at the dinner party the night before, and he described a two-piece ensemble. He also wore sport shoes, a shirt, and a tie; but there was an important gap in Barker's memory: He could not recall exactly how the accused described the missing shirt and tie.

It was now between twelve-thirty and one in the morning of July 9; and the officers decided to go to de Marigny's house on Victoria Avenue to examine the clothes he wore the preceding evening. Godfrey Higgs would later argue to the jury that the officers next performed an incredible investigative blunder: They permitted de Marigny to leave Westbourne alone in his own car, ahead of them. Some time later

when the officers arrived at the accused's house, he admitted
them through the front door. The implication was clear: Now
that he realized he was under full suspicion, de Marigny took
advantage of this opportunity to destroy the shirt and tie,
soiled from his murderous actions and available to incriminate him.

Barker went on to relate how the accused produced a coat
and pair of trousers like those in the courtroom; they were
neat at the time and not any more soiled than they were
now. He next produced a pair of tan-and-white shoes, also
like those exhibited in the courtroom. The shoes were dry
and there was no mud on them.

At this point Godfrey Higgs made another note, remembering the heavy rainstorm that fell *before* de Marigny drove
Dorothy Clark and Jean Ainsley back to the Hubbard Cottages west of Westbourne.

Barker went on to describe de Marigny's exaggerated efforts
to locate the missing shirt and tie. He found a hamper of
dirty clothes in the laundry room just off the kitchen but said,
"It's funny, I can't find the shirt I wore last night."

Attorney General Hallinan shifted to still another separate
matter.

Shortly after the officers were admitted by the accused,
Barker recalled, de Marigny said to him, "I have something
here which will amuse you very much. I just love candles."
The accused then showed him two hurricane-lamp shades,
the candle in one about five inches shorter than the top of
the shade. The other candle was nearer to the top. He did
not see a candle that was burned as far down as the one now
in the courtroom. De Marigny lit a match and put it between
two fingers of his right hand before proceeding to light the
candle in one of the shades, explaining that he must have
burned himself this way. He withdrew his hand from the
shade, but Barker told de Marigny he was not convinced;
it was not possible for him to burn his hand in that manner.

Up to this point, Barker's only damage to the defense was
the enumeration of actions by de Marigny from which the

jury could infer motives prompted by guilt: the destruction
of incriminating evidence and deliberate lies to explain away
the burned hairs on his body.

It was now time, both in chronological sequence and
dramatic impact, for the Attorney General to return to the
Chinese screen and the fatal fingerprint.

The next day, Friday the ninth, at about eleven o'clock,
Barker continued, easily bracing himself like an actor approaching his dramatic climax, he resumed his search for
latent prints at Westbourne. The screen was in the same place
in the hallway all the time he examined it. He lifted between
fifty and seventy latent prints from the screen; but "just a
few were legible." All were taken off with Scotch tape except
the last three prints, which were raised with a strip of
gummed rubber which was then covered with a transparent
plastic sheet, similar to the piece in the courtroom.

Mr. Hallinan: "Why did you use rubber strips instead of
Scotch tape on these last three prints?"

"I had run out of Scotch tape by that time, and the rubber
is quite as effective as the Scotch tape."

The three prints raised by the rubber came from the right
end panel on the smudged side of the screen, on the top
part of the panel. He wrote the word "screen," the date, and
his name on the back of the rubber lift.

Mr. Hallinan: "Did you make any note as to where these
prints had come from?"

"Yes, I did."

Mr. Hallinan: "On the night of the ninth, when you examined these latent prints, did you find any one which you
considered worth processing?"

"I did."

Mr. Hallinan: "Did you find on the screen an impression
which bore any similarity to the fingerprint of the accused?"

"I did. I discovered this similarity after I had finished working on the screen in the hallway, which was around one-
thirty P.M."

Barker then detailed only in highlights his visit to the
R.A.F. laboratory to make some photographic enlargements

of a latent impression that bore certain similarities to the fingerprint of the accused. The accused was arrested about six o'clock on July 9.

The next day, the tenth, Barker returned to Miami. During the following week, on Tuesday, he paid a visit to Bar Harbor, Maine, at the request of Lady Oakes, who had telephoned him. He returned to Miami from Bar Harbor on Friday, July 16, and left Miami on Saturday, July 17, at noon for Nassau to confer with the prosecution in this case.

When he returned to Miami on July 10, he took the raised (lifted) latent-fingerprint impressions with him and placed them under lock and key; and he did not examine them again until Monday, the nineteenth. On this re-examination, he found a rubber lift bearing a raised latent print of the accused's No. 5, the little finger of the right hand.

Mr. Hallinan: "You told us that on the ninth, you had found a raised latent print that bore certain similarities to a fingerprint of the accused. What fingerprint in your opinion was that?"

"Finger number ten of the accused, that is, the little finger of the left hand."

Mr. Hallinan: "Of these two prints, which do you think was the clearer for presentation in court?"

"Number five."

Mr. Hallinan: "With regard to this number-five print, had you examined it on the ninth?"

"Yes."

Mr. Hallinan: "And how was it that you did not identify it as the number-five digit of the accused on the ninth?"

"I discovered on the nineteenth that this print which was removed on the rubber was reversed in pattern."

Mr. Hallinan: "Did you take a photograph of the rolled impression of accused's number-five finger on July 9?"

"Yes."

Mr. Hallinan: "Did you take a photograph of the latent number five which you discovered on July 19?"

"Yes."

Godfrey Higgs rose slowly, made his Tudor bow to the

bench, and said: "My lord, I reluctantly ask leave to interrupt my learned friend; but I must in all candor point out that this is the first time the defense has heard anything about *lifted* prints. When the evidence was submitted in the Magistrate's Court, I assumed that the fingerprints referred to were photographs of prints on the screen. I only learn today officially of something on rubber."

The Lord Chief Justice shared Barrister Higgs's concern.

The Chief Justice: "When was the photograph of latent number-five print taken?"

"The photograph was taken July 9."

"My lord," Higgs continued, warming to his task, a smile of hope spreading across his face, "that is exactly what I object to. This piece of rubber is not the best evidence; and I know of no case in which it has been produced in court before. The proper evidence would be to produce the print *on* the article on which it is found, and I submit that there is no print now on that screen."

Higgs' robed arm swept toward the screen at the corner of the bench in a motion of defiant challenge.

"We have only this witness's word to suggest that the print in question came from that screen," Higgs pushed on. "We for the defense are in a position to prove that a photograph of a lifted print cannot be produced as the original latent raised print of number-five digit of the accused, and that the best evidence is the screen itself on which the print should be produced, and on which there is now no sign of a fingerprint."

Higgs next argued *authority* to the Chief Justice, prior decided cases recorded in the form of opinions by appellate-court justices. None was directly in point; Higgs was forced to argue from analogy.

The Chief Justice: "You would not object to a photograph of a raised print on that screen?"

"I would not, my lord, and that is precisely my point. By a 'raised' print, I mean a print that has been dusted with powder and is visible. It can then be photographed *in situ*. The original fingerprint can be preserved by covering it with

Scotch tape. The original fingerprint in this way is not destroyed. It is there for all to see; and in addition, if need be and helpful, the photograph of the print *in situ* may be received."

The Chief Justice: "Your point is that they should have powdered the print, left it there, and taken a photograph?"

"That's it precisely, my lord."

The Chief Justice: "What you say is that since they did not powder the print and leave it on the screen, it might be a forgery?"

"That is exactly my fear and my contention. Whether this print came from that point on the screen which the witness describes now depends upon the uncorroborated evidence of the witness himself."

The Chief Justice: "It seems strange to me that no case on this exact point has come before the courts, either in England or America?"

"I have searched the authorities, my lord, and assure the court that I can find no case in point."

Chief Justice Sir Oscar Bedford Daly was having difficulty controlling his Irish impatience.

The Chief Justice: "Why was the print not powdered, photographed, and left on the screen?"

The Witness: "I did not have my fingerprint camera with me so I had to lift the print from the screen."

The Chief Justice: "And why did you not have your fingerprint camera with you?"

"As I was proceeding originally on the theory that the case was a suicide and did not involve any criminal act, I saw no need to bring the latent-fingerprint camera with me from Miami."

The Chief Justice: "Would it not have been easy to powder the print and leave it there?"

"There is always a chance that it will be accidentally smudged or destroyed."

The Chief Justice: "Could you not have had a latent fingerprint camera flown over from Miami in a relatively short period of time?"

"Yes, I suppose that I could have."

The Chief Justice: "So by your process of lifting this print on the rubber matting, you deliberately destroyed the best evidence which was the print itself?"

"This manner of lifting the print does destroy it, yes."

The Chief Justice: "And a photograph of this print *in situ* taken with a latent-fingerprint camera would also have shown the background so that there would be no doubt where the print came from now?"

"Well, the background doesn't always positively tell you exactly where the print came from."

The Chief Justice: "I have no hesitancy in admitting that I am taken by surprise. It seems highly unlikely that no court has ever been called to pass upon this exact question in the past, but if counsel assure me that they find no cases for precedent, I accept their representations. It occurs to me that I may well admit this print, Exhibit J, into evidence and let the jury decide whether it is legitimate and what weight to give it. If they have reason to doubt its genuineness, they can discard the print, and for that matter, the testimony of this witness altogether. We approach the hour of adjournment. The court needs time to reflect upon this critical matter. You will have my decision when we sit again on the morrow."

Raymond Schindler tried hard not to show his apprehension as he reported the developments of the day to Nancy Oakes de Marigny in her house on Victoria Avenue. A snide remark that she was attempting to influence the jury made Godfrey Higgs instruct her to go no longer to the Rozelda Hotel for lunch. She now passed her ordeal alone with her black maid, fearful that any social activity might be construed as levity and lack of concern for her husband's plight.

Her eyes that day were red and swollen from crying. She went to the airport to meet her mother, who flew in to hold herself in readiness to appear as the Crown's witness. Lady Oakes received special customs clearance and departed the airport by a side door to be driven to Maxwellton House, another of the Oakes mansions only a mile away from Victoria Avenue. Nancy suspected that her mother had deliberately evaded her at the airport; and her gall was made even more bitter as she tossed sleeplessly with the realization that the Chief Justice's ruling on Exhibit J the next morning might well be her husband's death sentence.

Every daily newspaper in the States detailed the judge's dilemma with the fingerprint. The Duke did not need a special call from Christie or Barker to know that the crucial point of the trial was at hand.

Erle Stanley Gardner classed Barker as one of the most effective witnesses ever to perform in a courtroom. If Exhibit J was admitted into evidence, de Marigny was finished, unless Higgs could demolish it; and this in turn would demand Barker's destruction.

20

Exhibit J

Sir Oscar Bedford Daly savored his dramatic role. Within minutes, the wire services would flash around the world his decision to admit or exclude Exhibit J as evidence. Raymond Schindler stood poised next to the main door, ready to rush to a telephone to tell Nancy Oakes de Marigny whether the jury would be permitted to consider the raised fingerprint of her husband's right little finger as almost conclusive evidence of his guilt in murdering her father. By his own voluntary statement at the time of his arrest, de Marigny positively barred himself from Westbourne for the preceding two years. If Exhibit J was legitimate, de Marigny was not only impeached, he was positively placed in the murder room with both opportunity and motive, by his own irrevocable signature.

The Lord Chief Justice reluctantly broke the pall of silence by clearing his throat nervously.

The Chief Justice: "During our recess, I have carefully considered the cases and textbooks on fingerprinting provided me by Mr. Higgs and the Attorney General. Surprisingly enough, I find that none of the cases are directly in point; as I believe I stated yesterday, I am amazed that this question has not been settled either in England or in the American courts. I deem it not my duty to pass upon the technical propriety of what this police officer did or did not do. It may well be that his techniques and processes leave much to be desired; and other fingerprint technicians may well have done it differently. I am faced only with this one fingerprint, Exhibit J, and the whole question is whether it can safely be received into evidence. It is my ruling that Exhibit J is admissible; and it is formally received. I must point out to the jury, of course, as I will instruct them in greater detail at the close of the evidence, that the mere fact that the fingerprint is admitted does not mean that it must be accepted as legitimate and genuine by the jury. The weight to be given this particular item as evidence is a matter for them and them alone to decide."

Raymond Schindler slipped quietly out of the courtroom to seek a telephone, as did James Kilgallen, the distinguished crime reporter for International News Service (Hearst papers), representatives of the Associated and United Press, and reporters from dozens of newspapers and magazines in the United States, the British Isles, Canada, and Australia, and Reuters French News Service.

Alfred de Marigny visibly sagged in the prisoner's cage, his head held between the palms of both hands; he said later that it was all he could do to keep from becoming violently ill. Godfrey Higgs anticipated the ruling and was ready for it; as a matter of actual fact, his barrister instincts welcomed it. The Attorney General next asked three or four perfunctory questions about the latent print photographed July 9 but not identified as de Marigny's until July 19, and the rolled prints of de Marigny's ten fingers made July 8 by the police at Westbourne.

Mr. Hallinan: "And what did you do with the pictures you made of the fingerprints?"

"I made duplicates of both the latent print and the known rolled print of the accused's number-five finger and forwarded them on July 23 to Detective Frank Conway, who is head of identification for the New York City Police Department."

Mr. Hallinan: "And why did you do that?"

"To get his additional opinion as to whether the raised
latent print found on the screen was made by the accused's
right little finger."

Corroboration by another distinguished expert rang omi-
nously in Higgs's ears.

"My lord, that is all," Eric Hallinan said as he bowed to
the bench and nonchalantly resumed his seat at counsel table.

As a British barrister trained at the ancient Inns of Court
in London, Godfrey Higgs did not minimize his task, nor was
he overwhelmed by it. Day in and day out, he lived for and
by the courtroom, for his clients, the solicitors, the "office
lawyers" who were not permitted to practice in the superior
courts. Only 10 percent of the British lawyers are barristers,
the men who present cases in court, and Higgs had elected
the trial side of the law profession, first for its glamor, second
for its dramatic opportunities, and finally for its professional
and financial rewards.

The Common Law method of deciding the facts is an *adversary proceeding*, the trial a *contest* between two parties.
In a criminal case, the Crown is the party-plaintiff, the accused the party-defendant.

The contentions of each party are advanced by an advocate in the person of a barrister who has one fundamental
purpose for existing: To present his client's side of the controversy as convincingly as possible. He is partisan and
makes no pretense of neutrality.

The British barrister's first duty and loyalty is to the court,
secondarily to his client, the solicitor who hired him. Under
no circumstances may he mislead the court by an act of either
commission or omission. If he knows of a decided case ad-
verse to his client's position, for example, he must bring it
to the court's attention if his opponent fails to cite it; he dare
not, under pain of disbarment, conceal a witness or item of
physical evidence material to the case, regardless of whether
that evidence will help the opposing side more than his own.

He need not believe in either the guilt or innocence of the
accused in a criminal trial, or the justice of his client's cause
in a civil matter. The barrister has one duty only: To present

the evidence of the side that employs him in the most lucid, persuasive manner possible. This designation of duty means that he could just as well be representing the opposing side to the controversy if hired first by them. Insofar as the actual performance is concerned, Godfrey Higgs could assume the role of Attorney General and Eric Hallinan could become the chief counsel for the defense of Alfred de Marigny. Regardless of the counsel table at which he sits, the barrister's prescribed responsibility is to "lead," as the British phrase it, the evidence of his side.

Any other role practiced by the barrister in the Common Law system vitiates it. The adversary concept rests on the proved fact that if both parties to the dispute marshal their evidence and present their arguments aggressively, the independent fact-finder, the jury, will reach the correct verdict nine times out of ten. To permit the barrister to refuse to accept the accused's case because he thinks him guilty, or for the Attorney General to fail to call a witness because he thinks him erratic and unstable, perverts the adversary system into trial by barrister or trial by attorney.

The jury must decide the facts, not the barrister!

We know from eight hundred years of experience that in the crucible of the contest, the truth will emerge far more often than not when the aggressive contentions of both sides of the dispute are laid bare for marketplace analysis.

It follows, therefore, that any party forced into the courtroom needs the most convincing barrister he can find; and regardless of the potentials of his witnesses and other evidence, the case will not be persuasive if presented by a lackluster barrister. Being another man's articulate spokesman is a noble and moral calling!

Although Alfred de Marigny first wanted Alfred Adderley as his chief defense counsel, he could not know then that the evidence would develop in such a way that Godfrey Higgs' cross-examination of Captain James Otto Barker would go down as one of the most brilliant in Common Law history.

Eric Hallinan had barely settled in his chair before Higgs' first words flew from his mouth.

Mr. Higgs: "You are not prepared to say that the finger-print came off the area marked 5 in the second panel?"

"I am not."

Mr. Higgs: "Do you know what portion of that top panel you took the print from?"

"I can only say with certainty that it came from the top portion."

Such an opening was an engraved, bonded invitation to an eager cross-examiner like Higgs. It presented him the stance of the tired boxer who drops both hands for one split second, enough to permit his opponent to move in for the kill.

Mr. Higgs: "Captain Barker, will you please walk over to the screen and point out area number five marked in blue pencil at the top of the panel?"

All eyes followed the witness as he descended the witness box and made his way across the well of the court, in front of the bench, in front of the registrar's desk, to begin his studied inspection of the screen. Alfred de Marigny strained his face between two bars of his cage so that he could follow the immediate sequence of events which he knew could prove fatal. Barker shifted his position three times, his confident demeanor visibly melting away, and looked up quizzically at the Chief Justice.

Captain Barker: "I wish to inform the court that this blue line which I now see on the screen was not made by me."

Mr. Higgs: "I beg your pardon!"

Captain Barker: "There has been an effort to trace over a black line with blue pencil. That is not my work. I made the black line in the presence of the Attorney General in the police station on August 1."

All the light and power in the room focused on Barker as he stood by the screen, drawn there like rays of the sun through a glass in potent enough convergence to cause burning. Barker again concentrated on the panel of the screen while running his right hand across the sides of his head and face. Godfrey Higgs elected not to disturb his discomfiture by offering the solace of a question. The Chief Justice ap-

peared sympathetic, cleared his throat, and was on the verge
of speaking when Barker himself broke the silence.

Captain Barker: "I now withdraw what I said about the
alteration of the blue line. I find my initials where the blue
line is."

The Chief Justice: "My sympathies to you, sir. I have often
been confused in such a way myself."

The Chief Justice's understanding words were some help to
Barker, but he flushed in professional embarrassment. He
knew enough of the psychology of the courtroom to realize
that his gratuitous *faux pas* was great.

Mr. Higgs: "You have that area marked in two colors, in
black pencil and blue?"

"Yes, the area was marked by me on two occasions, the
first time in black and the second time in blue."

Mr. Higgs: "And in what color did you mark the spot
where your initials are now visible?"

"That was in black."

Mr. Higgs: "You have the date 7/9/43 marked in black
pencil?"

"Yes, the American way of writing July 9. That is the date
on which I found the print. I made the inscription on August
1, at Nassau police headquarters. At the same time, I marked
the figure 5 with a black pencil within the area marked on
the black line."

Mr. Higgs: "So until August 1, there was nothing to indicate where that exhibit came from?"

"Nothing except my memory."

Mr. Higgs: "On August 3, in the Magistrate's Court, you
swore on your oath that 'I marked the spot on the screen
where latent impressions of the print above referred to was
found with pencil and it is now within the area marked with
blue pencil and signified by the number 5 and initialed and
dated 8/3/43'?"

"Yes."

Captain Barker remained standing at the edge of the screen,
nervously shifting his weight from one leg to the other, hope-

ful that the command for his return to the witness box would come quickly.

Mr. Higgs: "Will you look again to your marking on the panel under the date of 8/3/43. What color does that now appear to be in?"

"I marked this area in blue in the magistrate's court; and that is where the print in question came from."

Mr. Higgs: "You were certain then that that print came from this area?"

"I certainly was."

Mr. Higgs: "And why are you not certain now?"

"Detective Conway of the U.S.A. and I last Saturday examined the area marked 5, but we could not find evidence of ridges which enabled us to say with certainty that that print came from within the marked area. Therefore, I had to confine myself to saying that it came from the top of the panel."

Higgs glanced at the jurors out of the corner of his eye, the experienced barrister's technique to measure his hold on this captive audience. As one man, they glared at Barker with periodic looks to Eric Hallinan and Alfred Adderley at the Crown's table to study their reactions. Higgs was pleased since this was the classic response of the suspicious jury.

Higgs now led Barker carefully over the screen, pointing out a number of marks beside area No. 5. Barker explained that some of these markings were not of a powdered latent-fingerprint impression; it appeared as if someone had placed a fingerprint over a dusted area. He would say with absolute certainty only after a microscopic examination, which he had not made.

Mr. Higgs: "You say you cannot say that this print, Exhibit J, came from that area number five on the screen?"

"I cannot say with certainty."

Mr. Higgs: "Are you not saying positively that it did because you *know* it did not come from that area?"

"I doubt very seriously if it would be possible for the fingerprint to have come from area number 5."

Mr. Higgs: "Don't you think the defense should have been

told that you were going to move the location of the print?"

The Chief Justice: "I believe, sir, that that matter is for the prosecution to say rather than the witness."

Mr. Higgs: "Very well, my lord. Thank you."

While the Chief Justice's question succeeded in protecting the witness momentarily from serious embarrassment, Higgs' thrust was understood by the jurors who nodded their heads in appreciation.

Mr. Higgs: "Did you know that the defense had also photographed area number five for experimental purposes?"

"I did not know that."

Mr. Higgs: "You made a trip to Nassau in September?"

"Yes, about this case. I came on a Saturday."

Mr. Higgs: "I put it to you that this was two days after the defense conducted these experiments?"

"That is a coincidence."

The jurors readily caught the implication.

Mr. Higgs: "I would say it was highly coincidental."

Barker offered no response, but his flushed face now dripped perspiration, and he dabbed at his forehead with his handkerchief. Alfred de Marigny still peered immobile through the two bars of his cage, his right hand and arm dangling completely outside.

Mr. Higgs: "Was it on that trip to Nassau that you realized that you could not get the print out of this area?"

"No."

Mr. Higgs: "When did you first discover that Exhibit J could not have come from the area marked?"

"A week ago last Saturday."

The cross-examination was going far better than even Higgs dared hope. Barker was exposed and vulnerable because of his own defections in investigative performance; Higgs exaggerated his pursuit.

Mr. Higgs: "What made you re-examine the screen that day?"

"I knew that I would be called upon to produce the exact spot, therefore, I examined the screen."

Mr. Higgs: "Did Mr. Conway, who is chief of the identifi-

cation bureau of the New York Police Department, tell you
that it could not come from there?"

"He agreed with me."

This, of course, was the real reason for Barker's change of
position: He knew that Conway, who stated vehemently that
he intended to testify truthfully, would contradict him if he
held to his original claim that Exhibit J came from the No. 5
area of the screen.

Mr. Higgs: "Realizing that you would be called upon to
say where the exact spot was the print came from, you did
not find out until two days before the trial began that you
could not find the exact spot?"

"That is correct."

Mr. Higgs: "When did you decide to change your
evidence?"

"Immediately."

The witness who changes his evidence is always suspect
in the eyes of the jury, and this suspicion is magnified geo-
metrically when that witness is a police officer. Jurors, whether
rightly or not, demand a professional performance from the
police far in excess of that required of the lay witness; and
it may well be that, in reality, policemen seldom can live up
to the rigorous requirements of the lay jury.

Mr. Higgs: "Where do you say *today* that Exhibit J came
from?"

There was just the right ring of sarcasm in Higgs' inflection, not enough to be supercilious, but sufficient to cast an
aura of doubt.

Captain Barker: "From the top portion of the end panel
with the mark 5, but I cannot locate it any closer."

Barker was now responding uncertainly and with hesitance,
a man backed against the wall, who could not say how many
lifts altogether came from the top of No. 5 panel.

"My lord, I think the witness may now resume his position
in the box," Higgs said graciously with a deferential bow.

The Chief Justice: "Quite! Quite! Please resume the box,
Captain Barker."

The order could not have come too soon for Barker. The

jury now knew that he not only had changed his testimony since the preliminary hearing, he could not say with certainty exactly from where Exhibit J came; the Crown's most salient item of evidence was in considerable jeopardy.

Higgs changed the subject, moving cautiously into a potentially dangerous area, the personal and professional background of the witness. His attack could not be unkind and in poor taste, or else the jury would embrace the witness with its sympathy and react hostilely toward the cross-examiner.

Mr. Higgs: "I believe you told us you have been with the Miami Police Department since 1925?"

"That is correct."

Mr. Higgs: "What was your first assignment?"

"I was a motorcycle patrolman."

Mr. Higgs: "And then what?"

"I became an emergency-call dispatcher."

Mr. Higgs: "Are the duties of the Superintendent of the Bureau of Criminal Investigation in Miami the same as Captain of Detectives, except that the rank of captain gives the officer control over subordinate officers in examining crime scenes?"

"Yes, I think that is a correct explanation."

Mr. Higgs: "You were assigned to the Bureau of Criminal Identification as a clerk in 1929?"

"Yes."

Mr. Higgs: "How long did you remain in that post?"

"For five months."

Mr. Higgs: "And what was your next assignment?"

"I was ordered back to uniform duty, and about a year later I was named to the position of Superintendent of the Identification Bureau."

Mr. Higgs: "Is it customary in Miami to appoint superintendents with such meager qualifications as you have described to us?"

"No, I do not think that it is."

Godfrey Higgs did not pursue this subject further since he was not sure what the explanation would be. His point with the jury was clearly established without taking any chances: Barker must have been elevated to this position of high-echelon administration through internal political shenanigans; it could not have been on professional merit alone.

Mr. Higgs: "Why were you ordered back to uniform duty?"

"Because the work in the department had been brought up to date. There were only two of us, the boss and myself."

Mr. Higgs: "And how long did you continue as Superintendent?"

"Until March, 1933."

Mr. Higgs: "And what was your next assignment?"

"I was sent back to uniform patrol duty."

Mr. Higgs: "And why was that?"

"It was claimed that I had been insubordinate to a superior officer."

Mr. Higgs: "How long did you remain out of the Bureau of Identification at the time of this assignment?"

"For eleven months."

Skillfully, with tact and without insult, Godfrey Higgs continued to undress the professional soul of Policeman Barker.

Mr. Higgs: "Do you term yourself a fingerprint expert?"

"As the term applies, I think I am."

It was obviously a hedging answer, practically the only one the witness dared to give in view of his lack of technical training and background as established by Higgs's earlier questions.

Mr. Higgs: "Have you ever, in testifying, produced the object in court with the print on it?"

"Yes, when the objects were movable."

Mr. Higgs: "Would it not be highly advantageous to have the print in this courtroom today still on the screen?"

"Yes, I suppose it would."

Mr. Higgs: "Why did you not introduce the screen in this court? Is it not movable?"

"It can be moved."

Barker could hardly answer otherwise since the screen now stood no more than a dozen feet from Sir Oscar's right hand.

Ably and with finesse and cunning, Higgs was already at

a persuasive posture in his cross-examination: He had managed to turn the burden of proof around, shifting it so that it was now the practical obligation of Captain Barker and the Crown to prove the authenticity of Exhibit J if they were to salvage its damning advantage for them.

Higgs next decided to play the same theme but from a different point of departure and at a change of pace. He wanted his attack to be cumulative so that Barker's integrity would be completely demolished, but in a gracious way.

Mr. Higgs: "What equipment did you bring with you to Nassau on July 8 from Miami?"

"I had a small dusting kit, and tape, and a Speedgraphic camera."

Mr. Higgs: "Did you not come prepared to look for fingerprint evidence?"

"Yes."

Mr. Higgs: "But you left your fingerprint camera behind?"

"Yes. I thought the kit I brought sufficient to take care of a murder case. The fingerprint camera would have been desirable, but I did not know the conditions."

There were raised eyebrows in the jury box. They remembered Melchen's and Barker's testimonies on direct that they thought they were coming to Nassau to investigate a *suicide*, not a criminal matter.

Mr. Higgs: "When you examined the screen on Thursday afternoon, did you not know that you were investigating a case of homicide at that time?"

"Yes."

Mr. Higgs: "Could you not easily have got a camera flown over from Miami by Friday morning?"

"I believe I could."

Mr. Higgs: "And you never made that effort?"

"No."

Godfrey Higgs walked to the registrar's desk, picked up a photograph marked "Exhibit 4." It was a picture of area five on the panel screen. He passed it up to Captain Barker and asked him to study it carefully.

Mr. Higgs: "I put it to you, sir, could not the camera that took that picture have been used to photograph the finger-print *in situ* on the screen?"

"Yes, of course, it could have."

Mr. Higgs: "I tell you that the camera which took this photograph belongs to Mr. Stanley Toogood, a commercial photographer here in Nassau. Could you not have borrowed a camera from him to photograph the fingerprint on the screen before you lifted it?"

"Yes, I suppose I could."

Barker continued to shift uneasily and to dab at his face with his saturated handkerchief, no longer the cool, firm professional witness called by the Attorney General the day before.

Barker could not be sure if he dusted the head of Sir Harry's bed or the thermos on the nightstand. He agreed that the thermos would have been a good surface for fingerprints, but he could not explain why he did not dust it. Nor did he dust the stair rail.

Higgs' attack now was to take the jury along and have it figuratively look over Barker's shoulder as he toyed with the crime scene Thursday, July 9. He wanted them to sense and feel Barker's incompetent investigative lapses so that they could wonder how any trustworthy police officer could be so slovenly. Almost parenthetically, Higgs got the witness to admit that he did not recall performing any processing after one-thirty; he was sure that by this time he had finished all surfaces that might yield latent prints valuable to the investigation.

Higgs darted in and out like a champion boxer toying with an amateur sparring partner. Over and over again, he came back to the screen, supposedly the source of Exhibit J, in his effort to show Barker's continued incompetence. By this time the jury was asking, "Why? Why? Why?" This now became the pressing mystery for which they wanted clarification.

Mr. Higgs: "I suggest that there were numerous objects in that room that you did not process?"

"I suppose that is correct."

Mr. Higgs: "If accused left a fingerprint on the screen, don't you think it likely that he might have left other prints in the room?"

"Yes, under ordinary conditions, but the very nature of the crime in my opinion would most likely prevent the assailant, in his press of emotion and hurry, from handling a lot of objects in the room. In this case, there was no necessity for the assailant to handle many objects, in my opinion."

Higgs had accomplished another goal: to force the witness into illogical explanations for conduct which should be easily explainable.

Mr. Higgs: "Well, why did you process in the downstairs powder room?"

"We could not exclude anything in an investigation of this type."

Mr. Higgs: "But you did exclude a number of articles in Sir Harry's room?"

"In my opinion, yes."

Mr. Higgs: "Had you excluded the possibility that accused might have an accomplice?"

"I have not excluded the possibility of accomplices, nor have I advanced the theory that he had accomplices."

Higgs was now ready to move deftly into a related, almost peripheral issue, the thrust again to illustrate incredibly inept performance on Barker's part.

Mr. Higgs: "In identifying a criminal, you require the rolled impressions of as many persons as possible who were at the crime scene?"

"Yes, for elimination purposes."

Mr. Higgs: "And on Thursday, you only got the rolled impressions of Major Pemberton, Dr. Quackenbush, and Harold Christie?"

"That is correct, and the right hand of Sir Harry Oakes."

Mr. Higgs: "Why did you not obtain the rolled fingerprint impressions of Dr. Fitzmaurice?"

"Because I was informed that he had not touched anything and had arrived only a short time before."

Mr. Higgs: "Did you roll the fingerprints of Mrs. Heneage?"
"No, I did not."

Mr. Higgs: "Why?"
"I was not told that she had been in the room."

Mr. Higgs: "Did you roll the prints of Mrs. Kelly?"
"No."

Mr. Higgs: "Why?"
"I was not told that she had been in the room."

Mr. Higgs: "But you now know that she had been in the room several times?"
"I know it now, but I did not know it then."

Using the same technique, Higgs established that Barker did not roll fingerprints of the Attorney General, Police Commissioner Colonel Erskine-Lindop, Corporal Muir, the coroner, Constable Knowles, Constable Nottage, Constable Kemp, Constable Tynes, Mrs. Gale, Frank Christie, Captain Melchen, Mabel Ellis, the maid, or His Royal Highness the Duke of Windsor, all of whom were in the upstairs hall and Sir Harry's bedroom after the body was discovered.

Mr. Higgs: "How many latent fingerprints that you raised did you identify?"
"The accused, Dr. Quackenbush, Major Pemberton, and myself."

Mr. Higgs: "You did not find a single fingerprint of Harold Christie in that room?"
"No, I did not."

Mr. Higgs: "You knew that Mr. Christie handled the glass and the thermos?"
"I knew at the time."

Mr. Higgs: "Is not a glass considered to be an excellent surface on which latent fingerprints can be found?"
"Yes, but I found no identifiable prints on the glass."

Mr. Higgs: "Although Mr. Harold Christie and Sir Harry had been living there together for several days, you found no fingerprints of Mr. Christie?"
"No."

Barker asked for a glass of water which the crier handed up to him. He accepted it gratefully, drained its contents in a single gulp, and asked for another. Higgs stood motionless until the water pantomime was completed. It gave him an opportune time to shift to an entirely different matter.

Through it all, the jurors sat in stunned expectation, completely baffled by the hopelessly inept performance of the witness. They continued to ask themselves, "Why? Why? Why?"

21

The Other Physical Evidence

James Otto Barker, taut, drawn, face and shoulders sagging, had aged a lifetime in the preceding forty-eight hours. The night before, he huddled with Major Pemberton while Professor Leonarde Keeler, head of the first Police Crime Laboratory in the United States at Northwestern University, pioneering polygraph operator, fingerprint expert and Raymond Schindler's assistant, experimented under Godfrey Higgs' shrewd direction, with area five of the screen as the Lord Chief Justice had directed the previous morning. Barker seemed to sense that instead of his ordeal nearing its end, it was only beginning.

Godfrey Higgs' voice dominated the courtroom from the split second Sir Oscar gave him leave to begin.

Mr. Higgs: "With regard to the hand prints on the northern wall, did you measure these prints?"

"No."

Mr. Higgs: "Why not?"

"It would not have furnished us with evidence."

Mr. Higgs: "Why not?"

"There were no visible ridge marks or fingerprints for identification."

Mr. Higgs: "Did you not at least determine the size of the hand that might have made the prints?"

"It would have been difficult to determine the size of the

hand. You could not necessarily get the length. It would all depend on how the hand was placed on the wall."

Mr. Higgs: "Might not it be the palm print of a man in the room on the night of the murder?"

"It appeared to be an average hand, neither large nor small."

Mr. Higgs: "Wasn't it a small hand?"

"I would say an average adult's hand, medium height in size as I recall. If I had made a complete examination then, I could form an opinion as to whether the marks on the northern wall were those of a large hand or a small hand."

With this opening, Higgs now took advantage of an opportunity to stage a dramatic courtroom demonstration, simple though it was.

Mr. Higgs: "My lord, I ask permission to have the accused hold up his hand."

The Chief Justice: "Very well."

Higgs signaled the uniformed guards who stood at parade rest on each side of the prisoner's dock, and they lifted the hinged lid. Mechanically, like a jack-in-the-box uncoiling in slow motion, de Marigny rose to his full 6 feet 5 inches. Not since his plea of "not guilty" within minutes after his trial opened days earlier had he stood before the jury face to face, in a sense challenging them to read guilt or innocence in his face. For the first time in several hours, the jurors were brought back from Barker's performance at Westbourne to the direct realization that the man for whom they would vote guilt or innocence stood less than thirty feet away.

Mr. Higgs: "Would you please hold up your hand, both of them? [Accused holds up both hands to exhibit to jury.] Would you say that those were long hands?"

The Witness: "Yes, I would say that those are long hands."

Higgs motioned to de Marigny who slowly sat down, and the guards lowered the lid of his cage to lock him in, creating an eerie illusion, like closing the lid of a coffin.

Higgs was not finished with his discussion of bloody prints, but dramatically, and by way of effective suggestions, he shifted the site of his interest.

Mr. Higgs: "Did you see the bloody prints on the southern door of Mr. Christie's room?"

"Yes."

Mr. Higgs: "Did you dust those prints?"

"Part of them."

Mr. Higgs: "Was the blood moist or dry?"

"I am not sure. It appeared to be dry."

Mr. Higgs: "And doesn't dusting bloody prints obliterate them?"

"A portion of the marks on the south door of Mr. Christie's room were clearly bloody to the naked eye. Another portion appeared to be a delta formation, which is favorable for identifying fingerprints."

Mr. Higgs: "And did you try to identify fingerprints on the door before you processed them?"

"Yes, I could not identify them."

Mr. Higgs: "And so you then processed and obliterated them?"

"A portion of it."

Mr. Higgs: "And did you dust all the marks on those doors?"

"I dusted the outside of the glass door, but I cannot recall dusting the screen door."

Mr. Higgs: "I suggest that you examined both sides of the door and obliterated the marks?"

"I may have done it."

Godfrey Higgs did not have to look at the jury out of the corner of his eye to sense their reaction of hostility toward Barker's incompetence. He was building it purposefully, letting it rise slowly to a steady simmer before agitating it to a rolling boil. Higgs elected to jump in and out on several matters, treating them in cursory fashion, but directing them all to form the total mosaic of Barker's incredibly slothful investigation.

Mr. Higgs: "Did you notice the heel marks of a shoe in Sir Harry's room?"

"No."

Mr. Higgs: "Do you recall seeing a bloody towel in Sir Harry's bed?"

"Yes. Exhibit E appeared to be the one I saw."

Mr. Higgs: "Did this towel appear to be burned along the edge?"

"I would not say it was burned, but it appeared to have been subjected to heat. It should be examined under a microscope to give a definite answer."

Mr. Higgs: "Have you made such an examination of the towel under the microscope?"

"No."

Mr. Higgs: "This would not appear to you to be an important part of your investigation?"

"No, not at that time."

At no time did Barker become agitated or hostile. He performed now like a man in a trance, always ready to admit the things asked him by Higgs. He did not examine the stairway all the way down, nor was he sure whether he examined the screen outside the powder room downstairs. He did not recall seeing smoke smudges on it or any fingerprints.

It came as a welcome relief for all in the courtroom when Godfrey Higgs suggested that this might be an opportune time for Captain Barker to demonstrate to the jury the techniques of lifting a fingerprint. For the next thirty minutes, Barker shifted back into his role of pedagogue with his kit of visual aids: dusting powder, camel's hair brush, Scotch tape, and rubber lifting pads. It was a creditable performance, as he had individual jurors lay down their own prints on table tops, the top of the bars surrounding the jury box, the rail in front of the witness box, and the edge of the defense counsel table. Barker was caught up in the enthusiasm of his own performance, his spirits sweeping upward in contrast to his cowed, defeatist attitude moments before. He failed to anticipate just what Higgs was doing with him and to him by this maneuver: He would point out adroitly in his closing argument to the jury that something was drastically amiss when a man who could perform so skillfully in the courtroom (as Barker had demonstrated he could do) could act ineptly when the chips were down during a real-life investigation at Westbourne. Over and over again, Higgs would ask, "Why? Why? Why?"

After the lunch recess, Higgs spent another hour on Barker's examination of de Marigny's burns. It was an uncomfortable interval that Barker would never forget during which he contradicted himself three separate times as to the position and severity of de Marigny's burned hairs. This set the stage for Higgs' parting thrust.

Mr. Higgs: "Then you could not say that the reddening on accused's skin was due to burns or not?"

"No."

Mr. Higgs: "I suggest that you never examined accused's arms?"

"That is incorrect."

Mr. Higgs: "Why didn't you show these hair burns to Major Pemberton, head of the local C.I.D.?"

"Our highest authority in the United States is the chief of police, and I therefore showed the hairs to Colonel Lindop."

Mr. Higgs: "Colonel Erskine-Lindlop is now conveniently out of the Colony?"

The Chief Justice interrupted to suggest that the fact that the former Commissioner of Police was "conveniently out of the Colony" was not within the purview of knowledge of this witness. Higgs knew that Erskine-Lindop had been transferred to another colonial post two weeks before the beginning of the trial, and Island rumor mills had it that the transfer was to prevent him from appearing in the witness box: He was so provoked with the interference of "the American police" at the behest of the Royal Governor that he would do the Crown's case no good whatsoever.

Mr. Higgs: "So the only person who can corroborate the fact that you even examined the accused's arms for burns is no longer available in the colony?"

"I don't know about that."

The sinister suggestion of Higgs' question nettled the

jury, who glowered at the Attorney General and then back at Captain Barker in the witness box.

Mr. Higgs: "Did you not take specimens of hairs from the accused's arms, from his beard, from his moustache, and from his hair?"

"Yes, I did."

Mr. Higgs: "Was this so that these hairs could be examined under the microscope?"

"Yes, and to preserve them as evidence."

Mr. Higgs: "And where are those hairs now? Do you propose to let us all see them here in open court?"

It was a dramatic foray and something of a gamble on Higgs' part, although he knew that the hairs were not produced at the preliminary hearing; he would have a reasonable ground for objection if they now entered the picture by way of surprise. He need not have worried.

The Witness: "The hairs were in Captain Melchen's custody."

Mr. Higgs: "He has already testified, and there was no mention of the hairs. Do you know what happened to them?"

"If Captain Melchen does not have them, I don't know where they are. It could be that they have been misplaced."

Mr. Higgs: "Would these hairs from the accused's body not be important evidence to you in this case?"

"No, not really. I saw them myself so I know that he had varying degrees of burned hairs on his arms, face, and head."

Mr. Higgs: "But we now have no other witness to corroborate what you tell us you saw?"

"I know what I saw, and I know that I saw burned hairs from his body, and I know that I clipped off a substantial number of these hairs."

Higgs again shifted to another area of investigative discrepancy: the shirt and the tie de Marigny was supposed to have worn the night of his own party and Sir Harry's murder. Barker could not remember how de Marigny described them.

Sir Oscar's patience was reaching the breaking point. In an obvious effort to illustrate disgust and displeasure, he swiveled his chair so that he faced the far corner of the room, his back to the witness and jury, giving counsel and the accused only an oblique profile view. He quickly swiveled back 180 degrees to his left and broke in abruptly.

The Chief Justice: "Who was in charge of the investigation?"

"Captain Melchen and I were working together, but neither of us was under the other."

The Chief Justice: "That's so! That's so!"

The Chief Justice swiveled again to his right to turn his back on the witness, his last remarks in the form of a censoring exclamation, a tortured groan aloud over the report of this incredible investigation.

Mr. Higgs: "I put it to you that the accused told you he could not identify the shirt he was wearing that night?"

"That is untrue. I can remember his exact words: 'It is very funny that I cannot find the shirt I wore.'"

Mr. Higgs: "And isn't it very funny that you can remember those identical words but cannot remember his description of the shirt?"

"It isn't very funny."

Mr. Higgs: "The accused could very easily have picked up any one of those shirts and said, 'This is the shirt I wore last night'?"

"Yes, as far as I was concerned."

Higgs now shifted to the matter of the tie, which bore basically the same status as the shirt. His thrust and Barker's response were identical for the tie.

The minute Higgs asked the next several questions, the jurors grasped their grotesque insinuations.

Mr. Higgs: "Would you have expected to find burned hairs on the legs of anyone who was in that room the night of the fire?"

"Not necessarily. It would be unlikely. The legs would be covered by his trousers which would protect them."

Mr. Higgs: "I take it, then, that is the reason you did not examine the accused's legs to see whether the hairs on his legs were burned?"

"That is correct."

Mr. Higgs: "Is it safe to assume that you examined and found burned hairs on his arms because you considered his arms bare at the time the fire was started?"

"I did not consider it at that time. I just asked to see his arms."

Mr. Higgs: "I put it to you that if you found singed or burned hairs on the arms of the accused, this would mean that he would have had to remove his jacket and shirt?"

"Unless the jacket and shirt were burned."

Godfrey Higgs now walked slowly to the registrar's table and deliberately picked up the jacket and trousers already identified as those worn by Alfred de Marigny during his own party on Victoria Avenue the night of July 7. Draping the trousers over his robed arm, he first spread out the jacket in front of the jury box, then reversed it like a torero flaunting his cape before an onrushing bull. He passed it up to Captain Barker in the witness box.

Mr. Higgs: "I put it to you, show us some burns on the sleeves of this jacket or any place else on the jacket."

Barker sent back his answer without the slightest effort to inspect the jacket, obviously knowing in advance what the examination would produce.

The Witness: "There are no burns on it."

Mr. Higgs: "And would you be kind enough to point out the burned marks on these trousers?"

The sarcastic rebuke penetrated softly, just enough to elevate the simmer of the jury's hostility toward Barker into a medium boil.

The Witness: "I don't see any."

Mr. Higgs: "But, sir, you did not take time to carefully examine either the trousers or the jacket. Are we to assume that you knew beforehand that there were no burns or soil marks on either one?"

"Yes, I had examined them before. There are no burn marks."

Mr. Higgs: "Did you not tell us that the fourth-degree burning of the hairs, easily recognizable by the fact that residue was adhering to the shaft, was found on the accused's forearms?"

"I may have said it."

Mr. Higgs: "When you examined the accused, did you see ash residue appear on the shaft of the hairs on his forearms?"

"I did."

Sir Oscar Daly swiveled his chair back to the left, looked critically up at Captain Barker, cleared his throat in an effort to bring his voice under control, and spoke.

The Chief Justice: "Where? Where? In all the affected areas?"

"Yes, in all the affected areas but not on all the burned hairs."

Mr. Higgs: "And would you have expected to find ash residue on the burned hairs of the person's body after he took a bath?"

"Yes, I've seen it."

Sir Oscar half rose from his chair, apparently motivated to declare a recess, obviously desiring escape from the confinement of his bench. Higgs sensed the Chief Justice's intention and leaped into another matter. He still had much ground to cover and did not wish to give any respite whatsoever to the witness, which might happen if Sir Oscar declared a recess at this time.

Hour by hour, question by question, Higgs pushed methodically on, the cross-examination lasting another day and a half. Barker admitted that Exhibit J contained absolutely nothing in the way of background impressions and consisted entirely of fingerprint friction ridges, as clear and pristine as any ever seen.

But then Higgs showed Barker two photographs of prints lifted experimentally by Schindler's expert, Leonarde Keeler, from area five on the panel of the screen from which Barker swore Exhibit J came. Clearly, circles from the painted scrollwork of the screen showed in the background of the prints. Barker could not explain how Exhibit J could be neat and clean and without background markings, whereas the other lifted prints clearly showed the pattern of the scrollwork on the screen.

Higgs' questions were decimating.

Mr. Higgs: "You told us yesterday, I believe, that you dusted some magazines and books. Did you think that the assailant was reading books and magazines in Sir Harry's room?"

"I thought he might have touched one."

No one could be quite sure whether Higgs' question was a veiled jibe at Harold Christie, who testified that he read *Time* before crawling under his mosquito netting on Wednesday night.

Mr. Higgs: "But you didn't think he might have touched the headboard of Sir Harry's bed since you didn't dust there?"

"He might have touched it. I did not dust the headboard of Sir Harry's bed; tue heat from the fire would have destroyed the latent friction ridges."

Mr. Higgs: "Why would a latent fingerprint be preserved on the screen which is blistered due to heat, and not on the headboard of Sir Harry's bed?"

"I could tell by looking for certain that there would be no fingerprints left on the bed."

Mr. Higgs: "And you did not dust the foot of the bed either?"

"There is no foot of the bed there."

Higgs now enjoyed one of the pleasurable interludes in a cross-examiner's lifetime. He went to the registrar's desk, picked up one of the Crown's own pictures of the bedroom with Sir Harry's body still on the bed. He thrust the photograph up to Barker and tried hard to control the rasped tone of his voice.

Mr. Higgs: "What, pray tell, is that?"

"I see that the bed does have a footboard. I did not dust it."

Mr. Higgs: "Wouldn't you say that would be a likely spot for the assailant to have touched?"

"Unlikely, in my opinion."

The Chief Justice: "Why did you think the assailant might have touched the screen?"

"The screen was an obstacle that the assailant might meet as he came into the room, and so might touch it on going toward Sir Harry's bed."

Godfrey Higgs now faced the real problem of all cross-examiners: How far is enough and when should he stop? He did not want to turn Barker loose until he was completely discredited, at least from every angle and on every subject, peripheral or substantive, that gave hope for success; but on the other hand, he did not dare "overkill" the jury. The jury is a captive audience, and because of this peculiar relationship with judge and barrister, its attention span collectively is somewhat limited. It cannot depart the courtroom in physical body, but it can mentally begin to woolgather if the attorneys are not sensitive to jury interest. There were additional technical matters about the procedures of fingerprinting that some of the jurors would appreciate; others would become bored, and Higgs dared not lose one single member of his audience.

With a sweeping glance left to right and right to left that instantaneously caught every eye in the jury box, he decided on a few preliminaries to set up his kill; and then he would let Barker go.

22

The Accusation

Everyone in the courtroom, spectator and participant alike, sensed that Barker's time was at hand. As a cat tarries in his game with the mouse, Higgs could make his kill any time he wished. He could drag out the torture for several more hours, or he could administer the *coup de grâce* at once. Barker had been around enough courtrooms to realize that the time for the blow was rapidly approaching; he could not anticipate its exact form since this was his first appearance in a British court.

Mr. Higgs: "Did you identify on Friday, July 9, all the lifted prints that you took?"

"I did identify all the legible prints, except the one, Exhibit J, on the screen. I did identify another print of the accused, but it was too dim and it might have been contestable. I thought it might have been a fingerprint of the accused, but I could not be positive."

Mr. Higgs: "Please tell us again when you discovered the impression that is now Exhibit J."

"On July 9; but I did not mark the area."

Mr. Higgs: "And this is the only print that you did not identify on that date?"

"On Thursday afternoon, I could see traces of fingerprints on panel five and I processed them. This is the reason that I had the screen folded the way it was."

Mr. Higgs: "And you did not mark the area from which Exhibit J came until August 1?"

"That is correct."

Mr. Higgs: "And you left that panel to the last to work on?"

"I did."

Mr. Higgs: "You said Captain Melchen folded the screen to protect area number five?"

"It was folded to protect all areas, not number five particularly."

Mr. Higgs: "Can you indicate where any other legible prints came off that screen?"

"I don't think I could now."

Mr. Higgs: "Would it not have been wise to mark on the screen where the lifted prints came from?"

"It would have been."

Mr. Higgs: "I suggest there are only two spots on the screen where lifts came from?"

"It would have been possible for Exhibit J to have been lifted from the area marked on the screen. It could not have come from the space above the molding. From a closer examination which we made in court the night before last, I still say that Exhibit J could have come from the area from the left of the red line which I made at that time."

The jury was now properly confused by Barker's references to red lines, blue lines and black lines made with both pens and pencils.

Mr. Higgs: "Is it a coincidence again that you can find no lifted area corresponding to Exhibit J?"

"I cannot find any such area."

Mr. Higgs: "Since you knew that you could not photograph the fingerprint *in situ* on the screen, wouldn't it have been simple to have lifted part of the background along with the print?"

"I did not attach the importance or significance to it at the time. If I had identified the print then, that day, yes."

Higgs now moved cleverly to set up an anticipatory impeachment of one witness and an anticipatory rehabilitation

and strengthening of another: Lady Oakes and Nancy Oakes
de Marigny.

Mr. Higgs: "You said that you took three rubber lifts off
the panel on July 9. Have you got the other two?"

"No."

Mr. Higgs: "You said that you did not identify the print
described as Exhibit J before you left Nassau?"

"No."

Mr. Higgs: "Will you please explain what you did with it?"

"I realized that it was a legible print. I took it with me to
Miami, but I did not re-examine it until July 19."

Mr. Higgs: "Why did you wait until July 19 to re-examine
it?"

"I left Nassau on July 10 and immediately resumed un-
finished work which I had left in Miami to come over here
the first time. I left for Bar Harbor at the request of Lady
Oakes on the thirteenth and did not get back to Miami until
the sixteenth. I returned to Nassau the next morning and
remained here until Monday, July 19. I found out at that
time from the prosecution that there would be an early preliminary hearing. Consequently, I started to work on all the
prints on July 19 and examined all the lifts. There were some
latent prints which needed further examination. I was not
entirely satisfied with my original examination made on the
ninth. I came to Nassau again toward the end of September."

Mr. Higgs: "Did you and Captain Melchen visit Lady
Oakes in Bar Harbor the day of the funeral?"

"Yes, we did, at her request."

Mr. Higgs: "This was after the funeral?"

"Yes."

Every eye in the courtroom now focused on Barker. Up
to this point, Lady Oakes had been left entirely in the background, almost totally ignored, as was Nancy insofar as formal
courtroom evidence unfolded. Now they would be thrust to
the forefront; that this initiative was being taken by Higgs
implied tacitly that the defense hoped to gain something
by it.

Mr. Higgs: "Mrs. de Marigny was there with her mother as well as other members of the family?"

"Yes."

Mr. Higgs: "And did you tell Lady Oakes and Mrs. de Marigny that the assailant had entered the garage and picked up a stick from a pile of railings, crept upstairs, and struck Sir Harry on the head with it, and sprayed the bed with insecticide and set it afire?"

"I did not, nor did I hear Captain Melchen say that. I am positive of this. He might have said that some liquid had been used."

Mr. Higgs: "And did you tell them that Sir Harry was revived by the flames and tried to fight off his attacker; that Sir Harry had been in great agony, and his assailant finally killed him?"

"No, I did not say that."

Mr. Higgs: "That his assailant had knocked over the screen, and replaced it, and that you had examined the screen and found several prints of the accused on the screen?"

"I did not say that."

Mr. Higgs: "I put it to you that you and Captain Melchen did say these things in order to arouse Lady Oakes's hatred of the accused?"

"I did not say this. We did not go up there on our own initiative. Mr. Paul Ellis, brother-in-law of Sir Harry, Lady Oakes, and Mrs. de Marigny were there. I spoke to all three at once, and they were asking for details."

Mr. Higgs: "Did you tell them about finding the finger-print of the assailant on the screen?"

"I believe I did mention this to Lady Oakes and the accused's wife."

A timid cross-examiner might have stopped at that point, but Godfrey Higgs was anything but timid.

Mr. Higgs: "Did you not tell Lady Oakes and Mrs. de Marigny, and whoever else was present, about finding a fingerprint of the accused on the screen?"

"I believe I may have mentioned that we found such a fingerprint."

Mr. Higgs: "And the funeral and your conversation were on July 15?"

"Yes, that is correct."

Mr. Higgs: "But you have told us not once, but several times, that you did not positively identify the accused's print, Exhibit J, until July 19. How do you account for your statement to Lady Oakes and Mrs. de Marigny on the fifteenth that you had found a fingerprint of the accused on the screen?"

"I knew of this legible print on the screen, and I thought it was the accused's."

Mr. Higgs: "Yet you told Lady Oakes and Mrs. de Marigny positively that you had found the accused's fingerprint on the screen?"

"I believe I did."

Mr. Higgs: "When did you first tell Captain Melchen that you had positively identified Exhibit J as the fingerprint of the accused's right little finger?"

"I believe he heard it for the first time when I told Lady Oakes and Mrs. de Marigny."

An audible gasp en masse arose from the courtroom. Sir Oscar's jaw fell open; he looked as though he wanted to intervene but was not sure what his proper posture should be.

Mr. Higgs: "I put it to you, if you were in a position to tell Lady Oakes positively that a fingerprint of the accused had been found on the screen, you must have made your identification before you left for Bar Harbor on July 13?"

"Well, I wasn't entirely one hundred percent positive at the time. I thought it was the accused's print, but I did not make sure until July 19."

Mr. Higgs: "Yet you told Lady Oakes and Mrs. de Marigny that you had positively found the accused's print on the screen. I put it to you that the only possible reason that you could have made this allegation to them on July 15 was to prejudice them against the accused in order to arouse their hatred of him?"

"I would not say that."

Mr. Higgs: "I suggest that you chose the psychological

moment to prejudice Lady Oakes' mind against the accused?"

"I would not do that."

Mr. Higgs: "After you returned to Miami from Nassau on your first trip, did you see and consult with Captain Melchen?"

"Yes."

Mr. Higgs: "And you rode together on the plane to Bar Harbor from Miami?"

"Yes."

Mr. Higgs: "And you were with Captain Melchen in Bar Harbor some thirty-six hours from the time of your departure in Miami until you told him in the presence of Lady Oakes and Nancy de Marigny that you had positively identified the accused's fingerprint on the screen?"

"Yes, if you say it was thirty-six hours, I will not object to that."

Mr. Higgs: "Did you not think the discovery of the accused's fingerprint on the screen was an important item of evidence in this case?"

"Yes, I did."

Mr. Higgs: "Do you think it was quite the proper thing for you not to mention this fingerprint to your coworker, Captain Melchen, after you found it until this conference with Lady Oakes and Mrs. de Marigny?"

Barker, now shifting his weight nervously in the box and mopping his sweating brow, did not respond. This gave Sir Oscar an opportunity for intervention.

The Chief Justice: "Isn't it strange that you did not tell Captain Melchen about the fingerprint of the accused that you found on the screen?"

The witness still made no response, and a pall fell over the courtroom as the personal battle between the witness and the Chief Justice developed.

The Chief Justice: "You did not answer that question, Captain Barker."

"Yes, it is strange."

Higgs turned as though ready to release his witness, then shot a parenthetical question.

Mr. Higgs: "Did not His Royal Highness visit you at West-bourne and come to Sir Harry's room at the time you were processing for fingerprints?"

"Yes, he came up to see the crime scene."

Mr. Higgs: "I do not think it would be proper for me to inquire as to why he came or what was said."

Higgs operated under the unwritten law that pervaded the entire British Empire: The Royal Family is immune from criticism, direct or implied.

He was ready to administer his *coup de grâce*.

Mr. Higgs: "While you were working on that screen on Friday morning, did not Captain Melchen bring the accused upstairs?"

"I understand he did."

Mr. Higgs: "And did Captain Melchen take the accused into the northwestern bedroom?"

"I understand he did."

Mr. Higgs: "Did not you go to the door of that room and open it while they were there together?"

"I did not."

Mr. Higgs: "I put it to you that you did, and that you asked Captain Melchen if everything was O.K.?"

"I did not."

Mr. Higgs: "I put it to you that Captain Melchen said yes."

"I did not even know he was in that room until the next day, I believe."

Mr. Higgs: "Wasn't accused's latent print, Exhibit J, obtained from some object in that northwestern bedroom?"

"Definitely not."

Mr. Higgs: "But it was after he left that room that you claimed to have discovered his print, was it not?"

"Yes."

Mr. Higgs: "I suggest that you and Captain Melchen deliberately planned to get the accused alone in order to get his fingerprints?"

"We did not."

Mr. Higgs: "I suggest that Exhibit J did not come **from that** screen."

"It did come from that screen, from the number five panel."

The voices were rising through a loud crescendo, and for the first time Barker was shouting back at Higgs hysterically, without any attempt to maintain composure.

Mr. Higgs: "You can show none of that scrollwork from the screen on Exhibit J, can you?"

"I cannot."

Mr. Higgs: "Do you usually withhold a lift? You never told Captain Melchen about it, did you, until the day at Bar Harbor?"

"No, I did not."

Mr. Higgs: "This is the most outstanding case in which your expert assistance has ever been requested, is it not?"

"It has developed into that."

Mr. Higgs: "May I suggest that your desire for personal gain and notoriety has caused you to sweep aside truth. I put it to you, sir, you have fabricated evidence?"

"I emphatically deny that."

Godfrey Higgs turned on his heel with such a flourish that his robe flared out in a rolling spin. The Attorney General's attempt at rehabilitation of his witness was masterful; but Captain James Otto Barker left the witness box a demoralized man, debased not by Godfrey Higgs but by his own indiscretions.

Foreman Sands polled his fellow jurors, who offered no questions to put to the witness. This alone was an unbridled tribute to Higgs' masterful cross-examination, which placed an entirely new complexion on the Crown's case. Higgs did not know how or by whom Sir Harry was killed, but he was reasonably sure of his client's innocence, which meant that something was morbidly wrong with the Crown's evidence.

23

The Fight To Save
Exhibit J

As the Crown's case rushed toward its grand finale, everyone even remotely familiar with it realized that unless Attorney General Hallinan could salvage Exhibit J, he would have absolutely no chance for a conviction. Motive and opportunity simply were not enough; de Marigny's presence in the murder room, in contradiction to his own sworn statement that two years had elapsed since his last visit to Westbourne, would have to be proved by his fingerprint on the Chinese screen next to Sir Harry's bed.

The savior of Exhibit J stood in the witness box in the person of Frank Conway, Chief of the Bureau of Criminal Identification, New York City Police Department. Conway rose almost as tall as de Marigny, but more spindly, almost as Irish in brogue and senile as the Lord Chief Justice sitting immediately to his right, with black wavy hair, long face, and longer nose, steady blue eyes and an imperturbable voice.

His qualifications as a fingerprint expert went back to 1927, and they were impressive. He knew the technical jargon of his trade and handled it easily. At Hallinan's prompting, he lectured to his fascinated audience on the science of fingerprints.

There are three methods of identifying latent fingerprints. First, the print may be brought up by dusting with contrasting powder so that it can be photographed *in situ;* the photograph of the latent print is then compared with a known, rolled impression of the suspect. Secondly, the latent print may be dusted with contrasting powder and the comparison made in its location with the known prints of the suspect. Thirdly, Scotch tape may be carefully placed over the powdered latent print and pulled off in such a way that the entire impression adheres to the bottom surface of the Scotch tape. Rubber lifting tape may also be used, but this technique produces a reversed image which must be turned around through an intermediate photographic process before comparison is attempted.

Detective Conway, adapting easily to the British environment, said that there could be absolutely no doubt that the fingerprint represented by Exhibit J was identical to the known fingerprint of the accused's right little finger. There were thirteen major points of identity and similarity between the two prints, and good practice demanded only a minimum of twelve points of identity.

As if anticipating what would happen on cross-examination, Hallinan let Conway explain that the lifting method was good practice in dealing with latent fingerprints; and if a fingerprint camera was not available, he would recommend lifting the print as Barker did rather than attempting to work with it on the screen in making his identification with the known fingerprint impression of the accused.

It was as far as Hallinan or the witness dared go at that moment.

Ernest Callender now rose in an effort to cast further doubt upon the legitimacy of Exhibit J.

Mr. Callender: "If the surface on which this fingerprint was deposited, the Chinese screen, was soiled, would the lifter bring up part of the background?"

"Yes, I would expect it to."

Mr. Callender: "Would you not agree that the upper portion of number five panel of the screen appears to be particularly soiled?"

"Yes, it does appear so."

Mr. Callender: "If a lift had been made from that portion of the panel of the screen on July 9, would you expect the pattern to show?"

"If there was a pattern under the background, yes. If the tape was sufficiently large, it would bring up the pattern beyond the area of the latent print."

Mr. Callender: "If there was a slight bit of dust on the area, it would still show on the lifting paper?"

"It should."

Ernest Callender asked Jury Foreman Sands to leave his seat in the jury box and walk to the screen and deposit his thumb print in the area marked No. 5. Callender then asked Conway to dust and lift the print.

Mr. Callender: "Is that as heavy as you would ordinarily dust a print for lifting purposes?"

"No."

Mr. Callender: "Then please dust it as heavily as you ordinarily would."

Once more, Conway took the fingerprint brush, dipped it into the jar of powder, and redusted the print.

Mr. Callender: "Now, would you please lift that print for us."

Conway applied the Scotch tape, lifted the print, and examined it carefully.

The Witness: "That is not a very clear print because it was not a clear impression to bring up."

Mr. Callender: "You yourself pressured the foreman's finger?"

"I pressed his hand, yes."

Mr. Callender: "And there is still some background showing on that lift?"

"Yes."

Mr. Callender: "And even though you were careful to dust only the print, the pattern came up as well, the background pattern?"

"The dirt from the panel has appeared, and shown the pattern of the scroll."

Mr. Callender: "If in taking a lift, you pick up a certain amount of background, you would then be able to photograph that lift with the background around it?"

"Yes."

Mr. Callender: "But Exhibit J has absolutely no background pattern of any nature in it whatsoever?"

"No, it does not."

Callender would not let the jury forget the precise, clear, pristine nature of Exhibit J, especially since he had Foreman Sands' own raised latent print, lifted before the eyes of the jury just moments earlier, by way of contrast; Foreman Sands' raised print clearly showed the background pattern of the scrollwork of the screen.

Callender now moved into another matter, his thrust to have Police Expert Conway indirectly attack the efficiency of the work of Police Expert Barker.

Mr. Callender: "But before lifting a print, do not you mark the object with the date where the print is lifted?"

"The best practice calls for running a line around the lift before it is lifted, and if there is more than one lift to be made, a number is given to the lift and also to the spot where it came from."

Mr. Callender: "So if you made fifty lifts from the screen, you would have fifty identifying marks on the screen?"

"If I lifted fifty prints on the screen, I would mark the area of each print with a pencil before lifting."

Mr. Callender: "And at any future time, you could go back and say with certainty where each print came from?"

"Yes."

Mr. Callender: "And that is your method, and the practice of experts generally?"

"Yes."

Just as medical doctors are reluctant to criticize the professional practice of a colleague, policemen tend to stick together, giving each other immunity from critical comment. The fact that Conway was willing to criticize Captain Barker was most unusual. Callender wanted Conway to comment on one additional facet of Barker's technique.

Mr. Callender: "Isn't it the general rule in New York and elsewhere to produce the objects in court on which the fingerprint is deposited if this is at all possible?"

"Yes, if it is movable."

Mr. Callender: "And it is also the general rule to photograph the print on that object?"

"Yes, if it is possible. When it is not photographed, it is because it is in some inaccessible place like the inside corner of a cash box."

Mr. Callender: "How many cases can you name where a lifted print not showing background pattern has been successfully introduced in court?"

"I believe St. Louis had one around 1930. It was a murder case. I was not engaged in that case, so I have just heard of it. I have never been engaged in a case where a lifted print without background material was used, and I have testified in hundreds of cases."

Mr. Callender: "And this is the first case in which you have taken part where a print of this sort was produced without either being photographed *in situ* or having a photograph that showed some background material for purposes of identifying the site from which the print came?"

"Yes."

Ernest Callender held back from asking the fatal question; Alfred Adderley put it for him on redirect examination.

Mr. Adderley: "In your experience, do you know of any cases where the photographs of a print were produced in court and not the original object with the print?"

"Yes, because it is not always possible to bring the object to court. If it were an automobile or a safe, for instance, photographs only would then be produced."

Mr. Adderley: "You have been asked to examine that number five panel on several occasions. Would you expect to find the upper part of panel five in the same condition as it was on July 9?"

"Oh, no, I would not. Even two weeks ago there were a number of fingerprint ridges there that I don't see now."

Mr. Adderley: "Can you say with reasonable certainty that

this fingerprint, Exhibit J, could *not* have come from panel five of the screen?"

"No, I cannot say that it could *not* have come from the screen."

Mr. Adderley: "Then can you tell us whether it *could* have come from panel five of the screen?"

"Yes, in my opinion it *could* have come from that location on the screen."

Mr. Adderley: "Even though it contains no background pattern of the screen and its scrollwork?"

"Yes. It is *possible* that the lifting process did not bring up any background patterns even though the fingerprint came from that location in that panel on the screen."

Mr. Adderley: "The mere fact that there is no background pattern in Exhibit J, then, does not automatically exclude it from having been lifted from panel number five on the screen?"

"No, it does not. It *could* have come from the screen."

"Could have" or "in all probability did" were the conflicting lines of argument between Crown and defense at this posture of the evidence. The mere fact that James Otto Barker performed with amateurish techniques did not, in and of itself, prove that Exhibit J did *not* come from the screen; his incompetence merely opened the door to the defense to allege fabrication of the fingerprint evidence. Exhibit J, although considerably dishonored, was still alive, and continued to figure prominently in the jurors' minds.

Erle Stanley Gardner concluded that even though Higgs and Callender had performed masterfully, the odds still favored the jury's acceptance of Exhibit J, for the simple reason that it is hard for most people to believe that a policeman would deliberately frame an innocent person of a crime that might cost him his life.

24

The Housekeeping Witnesses

Eric Hallinan presented half-a-dozen housekeeping witnesses to tidy up his loose ends.

The manager of the bank where de Marigny maintained his checking account detailed the accused's precarious financial condition. From time to time, overdrafts in the amount of $20,000 were recorded; but on July 7, 1943, the manager admitted under cross-examination, de Marigny's account showed a credit balance of around $5,000.

He also knew of the threatened lawsuit by de Marigny's second wife, Ruth Fahnestock, to recover some $125,000 she claimed de Marigny appropriated from her during the course of their marriage. The banker was asked by de Marigny to attempt to work out a compromise of some kind with Ruth.

Walter Foskett, Sir Harry's legal adviser for the preceding thirteen years, with offices in Palm Beach, a medium-sized, spare-shouldered man in his fifties, was also family confidant as well as professional adviser.

When Sir Harry and Lady Oakes were out of the United States, they received mail at Foskett's office, which Foskett opened and selectively forwarded to them.

While Sir Harry and Lady Oakes were in Mexico attending Nancy's serious illness in the fall of 1942, Foskett received a letter addressed to Lady Oakes from Ruth Fahnestock de

Marigny. He elected not to forward it as he was somewhat shocked by its contents.

The Oakes returned to Palm Beach in November of 1942, and Mr. and Mrs. de Marigny arrived there in January, 1943. He saw the accused one time at his office. De Marigny reported an estrangement between himself and Sir Harry and Lady Oakes; they were not receiving him properly; he was ignored, treated with indifference in a manner quite annoying to him. As Nancy's husband and a member of the Oakes family, he was entitled to acceptance and treatment as such; he would appreciate it if Foskett would use his influence to create a more friendly relationship between himself and Sir Harry and Lady Oakes.

Foskett told de Marigny that since this was a highly personal matter, he thought de Marigny should attend to it himself. De Marigny stated that he considered himself a gentleman, he wanted to be treated like a gentleman, and he was not being so treated by the Oakes.

Foskett apparently could not control his desire to castigate de Marigny, so he lectured him on his personal disapproval of the manner in which de Marigny married Nancy: De Marigny was a man of mature years, much older than Nancy; he had been twice divorced; he had pursued Nancy while she was a schoolgirl of seventeen in New York; he invaded the Oakes home by taking Nancy in marriage two days after her eighteenth birthday, without the knowledge and consent of her parents. Foskett's terse summary reflected the feelings of most Bahamians, including the jurors, about de Marigny.

He next told de Marigny about the letter which Ruth Fahnestock de Marigny had written to Lady Oakes in which she made serious charges against him. De Marigny demanded a copy of the letter, but Foskett would not give it to him. He told de Marigny that up to that time, neither Lady Oakes nor anyone else had seen Ruth's letter.

The accused told him that he was satisfied that everything in the letter must be false and untrue, and that he could prove it and would like to have an opportunity to do so, but he could not unless he knew the contents of the letter. He

then asked Foskett to tell him what was in the letter, and
Foskett gave him a summary of its contents.

De Marigny immediately stated that everything Ruth alleged was a lie; she was tremendously jealous of Nancy and
would do anything to injure him. He could and would prove
that Ruth's lies were untrue, but he needed to go to New
York to obtain documentary proof.

Foskett explained that he never sent a copy of Ruth de
Marigny's letter to Sir Harry; but he mailed a photographic
copy to Lady Oakes in late June, 1943.

On February 15, 1943, he drew up new last wills and
testaments of Sir Harry and Lady Oakes in West Palm Beach,
Florida.

Higgs and Callender elected not to cross-examine Foskett.

Lady Oakes was permitted to sit in the witness box, and
a chair was solicitously supplied by the crier at the suggestion of the Chief Justice.

Her black silk dress, black hat, and black gloves suggested
mourning; and her pale sallow face sagged as though she
had lost many pounds quickly over the past few weeks; even
her expensive dress hung loosely.

She spoke softly, at times almost inaudibly. Eric Hallinan
treated her with regal respect. Before long, it was evident that
her contribution would be more psychological and emotional
than substantive.

The only sound in the entire room other than her confident
voice as she began her recital was the swish of fans with
which the audience attempted to beat out the oppressive
humidity.

Mr. Hallinan: "You are the widow of the late Sir Harry
Oakes?"

"Yes, I am."

Nothing more was needed to establish her hold on everyone within earshot.

She was the mother of five children; and Sydney, the second oldest, was now sixteen. She seemed to be deliberately
ignoring Nancy in her calculations.

Lady Oakes was reliving an unpleasant nightmare as she continued. She received a telephone call from Nancy in May, 1942, telling her that Nancy and the accused had been married earlier that day; Nancy was but two days past her eighteenth birthday, still a child and schoolgirl. Before the call, neither she nor Sir Harry had any inkling whatsoever that the marriage would take place. They were frightfully upset; but at her instinctive invitation, Nancy and the accused came to stay with them at Bar Harbor. As she and Sir Harry thought over the dilemma, they elected not to break with their daughter but to make the best of what they considered a bad situation.

During the Bar Harbor visit, the accused was "very nice" to the children, playing and sailing with them; they liked him a great deal. After a two-week visit, the accused and his wife returned to New York and then proceeded to Mexico. They learned shortly thereafter that Nancy was gravely ill with typhoid fever. She and Sir Harry arrived in Mexico City by the middle of August and remained there until October. The accused was extremely attentive to Nancy during her illness and gave her two transfusions before the Oakes arrived.

She gave the accused around four thousand pounds to pay for all the medical expenses. She refused to accept it when he tried to return it, thinking it was Nancy's money instead of his.

In January, 1943, she was anxious for Nancy to have an operation on her mouth and sent her to Palm Beach so that she could receive proper medical attention. The accused arrived and took Nancy to the hospital where she had two operations. Sir Harry came to Palm Beach shortly thereafter. She told Sir Harry how much Nancy had suffered, and he was terribly resentful. "I told the accused before Nancy left Mexico to take the utmost care of her, and there was no question as to what my meaning was." There was a telephone conversation between the accused and Sir Harry; and the relations became more strained and the accused left their house. He never stayed with them again, asking for permission to come and get his clothes.

After leaving the hospital, Nancy came to Nassau. Lady Oakes knew from her secretary that a letter from Ruth de Marigny was awaiting her, although she did not learn its contents until some time in June.

Lady Oakes received a letter from Nancy on June 9, the first written her since Nancy left Palm Beach in March; it was dated May 26. She cabled the accused for Nancy's address, but he never sent it to her. After reading Nancy's letter, she definitely got the impression that Nancy did not want to have anything more to do with the family, or to receive help, financial or otherwise, unless the accused was accepted into the family. She had already sent Nancy a birthday gift and understood that it was to be returned.

At the time she received Nancy's letter, the accused was not accepted by the family. This was because of his irresponsible actions in his care of Nancy—"after all, he got her pregnant"—and because of certain statements contained in Nancy's letter, they considered that the accused had been "so unfair." Lady Oakes also felt that the accused was alienating Sydney from the family, from herself and Sir Harry. When going through Sydney's clothes after he returned from school, she found a letter from the accused to Sydney; it was a "horrible" letter for anyone to have written to a sixteen-year-old boy about his father. It was "the most diabolical thing that could be written to a boy who was sixteen about a parent."

Now Eric Hallinan led Lady Oakes into one final subject. At sixty-eight years of age, Sir Harry was in perfect health. She had not seen him for two months prior to his death; but both went to Hot Springs, Arkansas, earlier in the year where they took "a cure" and both felt in top shape. Responding to a specific question, she explained that everyone who knew Sir Harry agreed upon his moderate habits with respect to drinking.

Godfrey Higgs realized he would be treading on eggshells

in any cross-examination of Lady Oakes, so he asked not more than half-a-dozen questions. He concluded:

Mr. Higgs: "Did you at any time ever hear the accused make any threats to do grave bodily injury to Sir Harry?"

"No, of course not."

Mr. Higgs: "To your knowledge, was the accused's only complaint that he was not accepted by you and Sir Harry into the family?"

"I assume that was all."

"My lord, I have no further questions."

And the Crown decided it had no further witnesses.

That night, Nancy Oakes de Marigny sent her black servant to the jail on Rawson Square with a steak-and-kidney pie. Even worse than in other areas in the Caribbean world, the prisoner's cell was alive with vermin: mice and centipedes, cockroaches and spiders, gnats and flies, all combined with the stench of decaying conch shells on the quay a block away to make the air virtually unbearable.

Long before the sun fell into the ocean, Nancy cried herself to sleep. Raymond Schindler reported each day's events to her factually with his own shrewd analysis: Lady Oakes' low-key, convincing recital of interfamily relationships could not help but strengthen the Crown's allegations of motive; and the psychological persuasions of her appearance alone could not be discounted. They might well be enough to tip the scales for the Crown, to create a general aura of credibility to embrace Exhibit J and bless it with authenticity.

25

The Accused's Own Story

At the nod of the Chief Justice, the uniformed constables raised the hinged cover of the prisoner's dock; and Alfred de Marigny, without prompting, slowly stretched out his lanky frame. Every eye in the courtroom burned him in its glare. Beyond any doubt, the critical point of the trial was at hand.

Sir Oscar Daly cleared his throat nervously, as was his habit before making an important announcement.

The Chief Justice: "Marie Alfred Fouquereaux de Marigny, hear me carefully as I must now advise you of your rights under British law. You may elect to do one of three things. You may choose to make no statement whatsoever, which means that you will remain silently in the prisoner's dock where you now are until your counsel announces that your case has been completed. Secondly, you may stand where and as you are now and make an unsworn statement to the jury. If this is your choice, the Attorney General is not permitted to cross-examine you. Thirdly, you may decide to testify under oath from the witness box. If this is what you choose, I must warn you that after you give your evidence, you will be subject to cross-examination by the Attorney General. Mr. Higgs, have you advised the accused of his options?"

Mr. Higgs: "I have, Your Honor, and he is ready to make his election."

The Chief Justice: "And what say you, Marie Alfred Fouquereaux de Marigny, what do you elect to do?"

The Accused: "I will testify under oath."

The Chief Justice: "Very well, you may advance to the witness box to be sworn."

As he walked swiftly to the witness box, the time-honored ritual mesmerized the courtroom, everyone watching de Marigny, in tan linen suit, brown-and-white shoes, a multicolored print for a tie. He exuded a haughty confidence bordering on defiance, which was exaggerated by his broad, toothy, now forced smile. Somehow, his confidence appeared out of order.

Godfrey Higgs' problems with his witness were substantial. He was an admitted "foreigner," a man whose life style, manner of speaking, moral and social philosophy differed drastically from those of the twelve jurors occupying positions as members of a cross-section of the community about to judge a fellow resident of that same community. They would be gauging with jaundiced eye and critical appraisal not only the substance of de Marigny's words but his method of saying them, watching for any sign that could be interpreted as evidence of guilt; each nuance of voice, turn of head, roll of eye, or movement of body would be scrutinized for possible betrayal of falsehood. Perhaps Higgs' greatest hurdle was to show these twelve men in the jury box, through the witness's words and demeanor, that while he might be "foreign" and "different" from them in attitude and action, he was not a murderer. Even though he could have hated and detested his father-in-law, and would gladly have made use of his money, still this did not prove that he bludgeoned him to death at Westbourne, and then attempted to cover his crime by fire.

Higgs began by having de Marigny recite essential items of biographical data: His birth, education, move to the Bahamas, his first meeting with Lady Oakes, the introduction to Nancy at the Oakes' party at the British Colonial Hotel, his courtship of Nancy in New York and California, their marriage, the Bar Harbor visit to Sir Harry and Lady Oakes, the ill-fated Mexico City honeymoon, the unpleasant episode in Palm Beach, his ostracism by Sir Harry and Lady Oakes from the family, his visit to Attorney Foskett's office asking him to intercede for him, his conversation at the hospital with Dr. Sayad, the return to Nassau, his decision to go into the poultry business, and then the visit of Sir Harry and Sydney to the de Marigny house on Victoria Avenue in March.

De Marigny talked easily, almost jauntily, without any show of nervousness whatsoever. He did not remove his eyes from Godfrey Higgs' face so that the jury received the impression that it was eavesdropping on an intimate conversation between the accused and his barrister. The heavy French accent almost seemed to lend a halo of truth to the English words.

Higgs knew that he must answer each and every charge of the Crown convincingly from the mouth of the accused. There was no other way. As good a place as any to begin was the evening of the dinner at the de Marigny home.

De Marigny described the dinner by explaining that "Sir Harry was rather rude to everybody." When Sir Harry left at ten o'clock, de Marigny walked to the car with him. On the way out he told de Marigny that de Marigny and Nancy were "a couple of asses" not to have gone to a cocktail party at Government House given by the Duke and Duchess of Windsor. He emphatically told de Marigny that the Duke expected them to go, and it was the height of offense when they elected to ignore the invitation. Their conduct made it difficult for him and Sydney; and if they did not go out and meet people socially, they would never get anywhere.

He then said that insofar as he was concerned, Nancy would never get anything from him at any time—nothing; "and he spelled the word N-O-T-H-I-N-G in a very loud voice."

When they reached the car Sir Harry said: "You have written a filthy letter to Lady Oakes and your lawyer has done the same thing too; and if ever any of you two dare

repeat such a thing, I will have you both whipped. That girl
in your house [referring to Nancy], she has caused enough
trouble to her mother." Sir Harry then said "something to
the effect that he did not want her to have anything to do
with the family." De Marigny thought that Sir Harry was
going to hit him. De Marigny told Sir Harry, "Sir Harry, you
must be either drunk or insane to speak that way." This was
the end of the conversation because Sir Harry shouted for
Sydney and they raced off in the car.

Higgs next led de Marigny to the episode involving Sydney.

It was March 29, de Marigny's birthday, and some twenty
of his friends stopped by the Victoria Avenue house for a
drink. Sydney also came; and de Marigny received a present
that morning from Lady Oakes, some beautiful glassware. The
cocktail party did not break up until midnight, and Nancy
asked Sydney if he would like to stay the night. At this time,
there were two beds in the "spare" room (later it was converted into a dancing room for parties). Sydney went to bed.

At about four in the morning, there was a terrible pounding at the front door and someone was shouting, "Open the
door or I'm going to break it down." De Marigny opened the
door and Sir Harry walked in, demanding to know where
Sydney was. As they reached the guest room, Sir Harry pulled
Sydney by the foot, dumping him on the floor, and said, "Put
your clothes on and get out of this house." They left.

From that morning of March 30 on, he had never spoken
to Sir Harry.

In May, Nancy left for the United States for medical treatment; and he made arrangements to begin his poultry-raising
operation. Nancy would return to Nassau as soon as her medical condition permitted; so she unknowingly set the stage
for his dinner party Wednesday, July 7.

De Marigny rose early, around six-thirty, since he expected
three to four hundred chickens to be hatching in his incubator that morning. While at the chicken farm, he telephoned
Harold Christie, discussing with him a permit for the farm,
and he also invited him to his dinner party that evening. Mr.

Christie declined, explaining that he had a prior engagement with Sir Harry, and that he was spending the night with him at Westbourne.

In view of the prearranged meeting that same evening between Christie, Sir Harry, and Meyer Lansky's lieutenant, de Marigny probably spoke the truth; but no one in the courtroom that morning believed him. Harold Christie already had testified otherwise, and the word of the Island's number-two citizen easily outweighed the unpalatable "foreigner" whose case was now fraught with even greater hazard: In the eyes of the jury, a witness who lies about one matter can be reasonably expected to pervert the truth on all other topics.

After his day at the farm, de Marigny continued, he returned to the Victoria Avenue house, shaved, bathed, and dressed. His servants were capable of preparing for the party that evening. He "wore those clothes there," pointing to the coat and trousers in the courtroom, "and I wore a shirt of the same texture and color as the one I have on today. I always wear these shirts in the evening. They are a creamish shantung. I wore those shoes," and he pointed to Exhibit ZZ.

He owned so many ties that it was impossible for him to remember which one he wore the night of his party, and this intrigued the Chief Justice.

The Chief Justice: "Five or six ties?"

"I have dozens of them."

The ones in his bedroom were only part of his supply; Mr. Higgs had part of them with him.

At this point, Raymond Schindler spread out across defense table two or three dozen ties, all bright, multi-colored. Higgs waited until Schindler completed his performance and was about to speak when de Marigny interrupted.

The Witness: "Would you please wrap all of those ties in paper, Mr. Schindler, so that they do not get soiled!"

The implication of his concern slowly dawned on all in the courtroom, and understanding, sympathetic smiles immediately gave way to loud guffaws. The guards rapped for order.

De Marigny continued his description of the evening's events in his easy conversational manner, his recitation flowing out spontaneously and unrehearsed in the manner of a man confidently relating the facts.

He drove to the Yacht Club to inquire about a disqualification in that day's races, and then he went to the Hubbard Cottages to pick up Mrs. Ainsley and Mrs. Clark by prearrangement. By the time they arrived back at the house on Victoria Avenue, his other dinner guests were there: Mr. Freddie Ceretta, Mr. King, Mr. Oswald Moseley, Georges de Visdelou, Betty Roberts, Alva Brook and his wife, and Mr. Donald McKinney.

It was his plan to eat outside in the garden, but because of the mosquitoes, the three tables were moved inside, where all ate in the dancing room.

During the dinner they used candles as lights; "there are three of the hurricane shades." There were also several candelabra.

De Marigny lit the candles himself. One of the shades stood in front of Mrs. Clark, one in front of Mr. McKinney, and one in front of Mr. Moseley. The tables were arranged in a U shape; he placed the candelabra among them. He lit the candelabra on the left with his left hand and those on the right with his right hand. He was ambidextrous; perhaps this would explain why he acted as he did. When he lit the candles in the hurricane shades, he burned his hands.

Godfrey Higgs paused, like a scriptwriter signaling the end of one act and the beginning of another. They were approaching the time sequence which, according to the Crown's theory of the case, was fatal.

The party broke up around twelve-thirty, de Marigny continued his recital, speaking easily and showing no signs of nervousness whatsoever as he approached the crucial period. Mr. Moseley was the first to leave, then Georges de Visdelou and Miss Roberts. He offered to take Mrs. Ainsley and Mrs. Clark home, and he invited Freddie Ceretta to accompany them.

The implications of this new material permeated the court-room immediately: If de Marigny had formulated a premeditated intent to kill his father-in-law, it would have been rather stupid for him to invite a witness to ride along.

He and the two women left his house about one o'clock, and he drove to their houses at the Hubbard Cottages in his Lincoln, which had been parked in front of the house on Victoria Avenue on the left of the driveway. He did not get out of the car at the Hubbard Cottages because it was raining. He could fix the time by a conversation with Mrs. Clark. As they passed Lightbourn's Pharmacy on George Street, Mrs. Clark said it was 1:20 or 1:25; and he looked at the luminous dial on his watch and corrected her, saying it was only 1:05. The time on his watch also corresponded to the clock in the car, and Mrs. Clark mentioned something about her watch running fast.

After dropping the women at the Hubbard Cottages, he drove straight home, got undressed shortly after he arrived, and went to bed.

Sir Oscar Daly hung on every word of the accused and could not restrain himself.

The Chief Justice: "Which way did you go home?"

"The same way, by Bay Street."

When he arrived home, he found de Visdelou's car, the Chevrolet, parked in the driveway in the same place it had occupied all evening, opposite the steps leading to the porch, facing toward the garage. He got out of the Lincoln, drove the Chevrolet onto the lawn at the back, and parked the Lincoln in the garage.

He next went upstairs to see if de Visdelou wanted him to take Miss Roberts home, since de Visdelou had a cold and might not want to go out in the rain. De Visdelou declined his offer.

All the servants were still there. He went to his room and went to bed. It was now no later than 1:40 or 1:45.

He did not sleep through the night. At three o'clock, Georges de Visdelou's cat and his own puppy were having a fight. They came into his bedroom and the gray Maltese cat, named Grisou, jumped at the Venetian blinds, making a horrible noise that frightened him.

At about the same time, he heard the Chevrolet backing out of the drive and assumed it was Georges taking Betty home. He knew that Georges would return shortly; and as Georges always liked the cat in his room, he knew he would take it with him, so de Marigny did not get up to throw the cat out.

In approximately fifteen minutes, de Visdelou returned. He entered through the dining room, and de Marigny called to him to please remove the cat. He went back to sleep and may have wakened again, but he did not remember. He suffered burning pains in his stomach, almost a nightly affair, so every morning he awakened to take alkalizers and other medicine; and the early morning of July 8 was no exception.

He was up by six-thirty to go to the incubator in the garage to see whether a batch of chicks had hatched. He made his own breakfast, which he usually did since the servants did not come until nine o'clock. It included two poached eggs, Ovaltine, and toast, the identical breakfast he had 365 days of the year.

Everyone knew that de Marigny had passed successfully over the critical period; and the jury strained in a sincere effort to believe him, although they knew him still as the unpleasant "foreigner" with the haughty, overbearing superiority who elected to hold himself above the structured customs of the Islands.

Godfrey Higgs now approached a series of direct confrontations between the accused and the Crown's witnesses. Wherever possible, defense counsel prefer to avoid these head-butting contests, but often it is not possible. A single unqualified conflict between the accused and the Crown's witnesses over a salient fact is not morbid; even two do not doom the accused; but when the accused must lay his veracity on the line three, four, and five times in an offer to the jury to choose between his truthfulness and that of several other

witnesses, the jury is hard put to believe that *all* the other
witnesses lie or are mistaken, and the accused is the sole
accurate, truthful reporter in the courtroom.

Higgs did not back away from the first confrontation, almost approaching it confidently.

De Marigny described putting a number of chicks from
his garage on Victoria Avenue into the Chevrolet and driving them to the chicken farm, where he remained until 8:45.
Then he drove down to the Central Police Station, parking
his car by Moseley's book shop. He ran into Basil McKinney
and another friend; they talked racing for a while before he
went to the Central Police Station.

Mr. Higgs: "Constable Parker said you went to the police
station at seven-thirty. Is that correct?"

"No. It was much later, about 9:05 A.M."

He spoke to the constable at the station, but did not know
his name. There might have been others there since he paid
no particular attention.

The jurors shifted in their chairs, visibly uncomfortable for
the first time since de Marigny's evidence began, realizing
the magnitude of their task: Should they believe de Marigny
or Constable Parker and his associates at the Central Police
Station, or was this comparatively immaterial information on
which reasonable men might honestly differ on the facts?

They also remembered de Marigny's direct challenge to
Harold Christie over whether Christie declined de Marigny's
party invitation by describing his prior commitment to spend
the night with Sir Harry at Westbourne; and didn't Dorothy
Clark say that de Marigny escorted her to the door of her
cottage, but de Marigny just said that he did not get out of
his car because of the rain? Who was to be believed?

De Marigny returned to the chicken farm, then headed
uptown where, he continued, he met his friend Anderson at
the Pan American Airways office, who told him of Sir Harry's
death.

Mr. Higgs: "What did you say?"

"Anderson did not look serious to me, so I said, 'You're

kidding me, Andy!' But he said, 'No, I have confirmed it with Dr. Fitzmaurice.' "

Mr. Higgs: "And what was your response?"

"I asked if he knew what he had died of, whether a stroke, or something like that, and he said he did not know."

He and Anderson drove to de Marigny's house on Victoria Avenue where they told Georges de Visdelou of Sir Harry's death; and then de Marigny asked Anderson if he knew where Sir Harry had been staying so that they might go to him. Anderson suggested that it might be either The Caves or Westbourne, and they proceeded to Westbourne not really knowing whether they would find Sir Harry there.

The jurors studied de Marigny carefully. Clearly, his confident poise was masterful. Erle Stanley Gardner, James Kilgallen, and other members of the press had already hung the labels "cool," "a cool cucumber," "a cool Frenchman," and "the cool count" on de Marigny's performance. His casual, parenthetical asides colored the main themes of his story with probity: If de Marigny really did not know whether the scene of death was at The Caves or at Westbourne, obviously he could not be the murderer.

When they reached Westbourne, there were many cars in the yard, so Anderson suggested that "it might be here." They drove in, stopped the car by the tennis court opposite Mrs. Kelly's house, and he walked toward Mrs. Kelly's porch some twenty-five feet away. When he reached Mrs. Kelly, he told her he had received the bad news and asked her if she could give him some details, whether Sir Harry had been sick "or something like that."

Mrs. Kelly assured him that Sir Harry had been in perfect health the evening before, playing tennis up until six o'clock. He asked Mrs. Kelly if Lady Oakes had been advised, and Mrs. Kelly assured him that since Mr. Foskett had been notified by telephone, he would make all necessary arrangements for communication with Lady Oakes. De Marigny told Mrs. Kelly that he would cable Nancy to go immediately to her mother; but Mrs. Kelly replied that the censors had been given orders that no telegrams about the case were to leave Nassau.

Once more the jury pondered this parenthetical interlude: How could Mrs. Kelly know, assuming that de Marigny spoke the truth, that the censors would not pass cables discussing Sir Harry's death at what must have been around eleven o'clock, Thursday, July 8?

Erle Stanley Gardner wondered at this juncture if de Marigny might have gone too far, if he had employed an embellishment that would tax the jury's acceptance of his credibility.

Higgs rushed on, and de Marigny conveyed the impression of actually enjoying his ordeal, at least appearing to experience no discomfort.

De Marigny then walked to Westbourne, where the first person he met was Harold Christie. Christie was seated at the telephone in the hall, "telephoning all the time and he did not tell me anything at that time." De Marigny moved into the east room where he saw Frank Christie, Mr. Dew, and a number of other people. Major Pemberton may have spoken to him that morning, but he had no recollection of it. From someone and somehow, he did not remember from whom, he learned that Sir Harry had been found dead with a wound in his head and burned. He may have remained at Westbourne for ten minutes, but then returned to Mrs. Kelly's cottage. He asked her for some water as he was not feeling well; he had just heard of the unexpected death; Sir Harry had been burned; it was morbid; and he was upset by the news.

The jurors thought back to Mrs. Kelly's testimony, about the second day of the trial, in which she described de Marigny's statement that he was about to be sick as "over-dramatic."

Once again, the jury was forced to a choice between two conflicting interpretations of the same event.

De Marigny and Anderson left to drive to his home on Victoria Avenue, but on the way there, he stopped and sent a telegram to Nancy in Florida, urging her to fly to her mother.

De Marigny spent the rest of the day in zombi fashion with de Visdelou and Freddie Ceretta—lunch at the Prince George, a trip out to the chicken farm, and aimless wandering around Nassau in a state of shock.

De Marigny and Anderson returned to Westbourne, between three and three-fifteen, a few minutes before Sir Harry's body was removed. Harold Christie was still there, and for the first time, de Marigny asked Christie about the details. Christie told him quickly that he had entered Sir Harry's room that morning, seen it in a terrible mess, and Sir Harry was "burned with wounds in his head." Christie told him that Mr. Foskett was expected on the five o'clock plane, and de Marigny suggested to Christie that he would be happy to fetch Foskett. This offer was refused.

Lady Oakes telephoned to speak to Christie; de Marigny asked to speak to her and did; and then he and Anderson left Westbourne immediately after the conversation with Lady Oakes.

At around ten in the evening, while he was at the Prince George, he received a telephone call from Colonel Erskine-Lindop; and he and Anderson returned at the Colonel's request to Westbourne. Major Pemberton was there, as was the Attorney General, and for the first time he met Captains Melchen and Barker.

"The American police" asked him to subject himself to both questioning and physical examination, and he readily agreed in an effort to shed any light on the case he could. Both men proceeded to examine his body, first Captain Melchen and then Captain Barker, looking at his hands with a lens, then his head, especially the front of his hair, his moustache, and beard. They thoroughly examined the front part of both forearms about six to eight inches from the wrist. He was instructed to place his hands under a microscope.

After this detailed inspection, Captain Barker asked if he

could cut some hair from de Marigny's head, beard, moustache and hands; and de Marigny told them they could take anything they wished. Captain Barker asked him to leave the room for about ten minutes, and when he returned at Captain Melchen's request, Melchen told him they had discovered signs of burned hair on his hands, and face, and head. They asked him how the burning came about. At no time was he shown any of these burned hairs, nor was any suggestion made to him that he look at them.

Here was another head-butting confrontation between the accused and the Crown's principal witness: Barker was certain, and so informed the jury, that de Marigny asked to see the burned hairs on his hands and forearms, which the police pointed out to him.

By way of explanation, de Marigny said he told Melchen that he smoked heavily, perhaps half-a-dozen cigars a day; this would account for the burns on his beard and moustache, possibly his hair. He told them he often did some of the cooking around his house, which he enjoyed, and he used a gas stove. This might account for some of the burned hair on his hands and forearms. Then he thought about the open fires at the chicken farm that heated the boiling water for scalding the chickens; he thought maybe this might account for some of the burning.

Melchen asked to examine his feet and the lower part of his legs. He remembered, and told Melchen, that he had attended a fire at the farm that day since they had filled a large order for chickens, and it was on the books of record of the farm.

Here was another confrontation: Barker had testified that *no* examination was made of de Marigny's feet and legs. Could de Marigny be correct on *all* the areas of conflict with *all* the Crown's witnesses? The jury could be expected to wonder.

The subject changed as Barker and Melchen asked de Marigny about his clothes. He described to them a two-piece brown matching suit.

The Chief Justice: "Of the same color?"

"No, I meant 'matching'—two shades of brown that matched and did not clash. I have never possessed a brown suit of the same shade."

Clearly, de Marigny came through as a clotheshorse. The jurors remembered how he earlier had asked that his two dozen multi-colored ties be carefully wrapped in paper; here in the midst of his stress in the witness box, he emphasized, even with the Chief Justice, his concern over the exact match of his two-piece ensemble.

De Marigny explained to Melchen and Barker that he wore a light cream shirt, tan-and-white shoes, and a tie to match the suit. They asked if they could go with him to the Victoria Avenue house to find the clothing. He rode with Major Pemberton; Anderson and the others followed in different cars. Just as they left Westbourne, he was fingerprinted by Barker.

Here was another serious conflict: Barker claimed de Marigny went on home in his own car without police supervision; de Marigny claimed that Major Pemberton was with him, which would rule out Barker's insinuation that de Marigny could have destroyed the shirt and the tie after he reached home ahead of the officers.

As he drove through town, he suddenly remembered lighting the hurricane lamps the preceding night at the party, and he mentioned this to Captain Barker when he next saw him. Now, they were all in his house—Melchen, Barker, Colonel Erskine-Lindop, and Major Pemberton. They were in the bedroom, opening doors, looking in drawers, and moving all about. When they reached the dining room, Major Pemberton asked him to light the candles and the hurricane lamps he had described to him in the car; so de Marigny lit three of them, two on a side table and one in the hall. He asked Captain Barker if he would like to try the experiment so he could see how his hand could be easily burned, but Barker declined.

Afterwards, Captain Melchen asked about his clothes, so they went back to his bedroom to see if they were in the clothes closet; they were not. He led them to the pressing room where the butler pressed the clothes; this was a room just behind the kitchen. As they went through the kitchen, Melchen asked him about the gas stove. He opened it and showed it to them. Then they reached the pressing room, where the clothes were hung either before or after being serviced. There were clothes there, and as he gave them what they wanted, he did not remember making any remark of any kind.

Melchen asked for the shoes he wore the preceding evening, and he pointed them out on a stand where his shoes were kept. They asked him for his shirt, and he found dirty linen in the basket on the floor in the pressing room. There were a few shirts in it, perhaps five or six, and two of them were cream-colored shirts, the same kind he wore the preceding night. While he stood talking with Captain Melchen, he discovered more dirty shirts in the bottom of a rack with sheets and other linen, and there were two or three more shirts of the same kind, only made of silk.

He told Melchen that the shirt he had worn must be one of these, but he truthfully could not remember; the shirts were all alike, more or less. He owned two or three dozen of these shirts.

Raymond Schindler once more began to open packages at defense counsel table. Within minutes, he spread out a dozen cream-colored shirts, some clean, some wrinkled and dirty. There were two shades, one slightly darker than the other.

Mr. Higgs: "Are these all your shirts?"

"Yes, they are."

Mr. Higgs: "Did you own each and every one of these shirts prior to the night of July 7, this year?"

"Yes, I most certainly did."

Mr. Higgs: "And are these the shirts that you pointed out to Colonel Lindop, Major Pemberton, Captain Melchen, and Captain Barker when they searched your house on Victoria Avenue on the night of July 8?"

"Yes, they are."

Mr. Higgs: "And is it from this batch of shirts that you told Captain Melchen and Captain Barker that you were unable to select the exact shirt you had worn the preceding evening during your party?"

"Yes, that's it exactly. I said it must be in there, but I could not tell which one it was for sure, they are so much alike."

The jury's suspicions were somewhat neutralized: Higgs' simple courtroom demonstration took much of the sting out of the Crown's insinuation that de Marigny deliberately destroyed the shirt to get rid of incriminating scorch marks or blood spatters; but this possibility still remained, particularly since de Marigny's account conflicted directly with the reports of half-a-dozen witnesses.

Captain Melchen was not satisfied with either the search or de Marigny's explanation, so they went downstairs to a room that was built originally for a garage but was not used by the servants. Captain Melchen rummaged it thoroughly and asked if any laundry had been done there recently.

When Captain Barker also questioned him about the shirt and tie, de Marigny got the impression that Barker's questions were made deliberately to irritate him. Then, just as all the officers were ready to leave, Colonel Erskine-Lindop asked if he would mind having Douglas "as my guest for the night."

The jurors smiled at Erskine-Lindop's delicate handling of his surveillance of de Marigny.

As de Marigny began to explain his actions the following morning, a light of recognition dawned as the jurors anticipated another frontal assault by de Marigny on testimony of a Crown witness.

Lieutenant Douglas accompanied him to the chicken farm where he helped two little boys fix a five-gallon boiler of water on the fire. On the way back to Victoria Avenue, Douglas led a conversation by complaining about having to watch de Marigny the whole night since it was his night off. Douglas continued: "What boils me is that they are having all this fuss about Sir Harry because he is a rich man and has lots of money. If he was a poor colored fellow in Grant's Town, I would just be asked to go and take his statement, and that would be all there would be to it."

They talked of other things, the trouble de Marigny had with Sir Harry, which he explained was owing to his former wife, Ruth. He knew Douglas extremely well and readily admitted to him his difficulties with Sir Harry.

Mr. Higgs: "Did you say to Douglas: 'That guy, Sir Harry, the old bastard should have been killed anyway'?"

"No, sir, I did not use the word 'guy' or 'bastard' at all in speaking to Douglas or anybody else. Those words are not in my usual vocabulary."

Somehow the jurors obtained the impression that he spoke truthfully, they reported later: This suave, debonair, haughty Frenchman would not sound quite right spewing out such terms as "guy" and "bastard."

Mr. Higgs: "Do you remember whether anyone used the expressions 'guy' or 'bastard' that morning?"

"Yes, Lieutenant Douglas used both words when he was describing his general dissatisfaction."

There was the challenge! Would the jury believe de Marigny's version, or would they accept Lieutenant Douglas' allegations as gospel? De Marigny was forcing them into an uncomfortable corner.

They reached Westbourne about nine-forty after intermediate stops along the beach and at the Country Club House, de Marigny continued.

Mr. Higgs: "Did you say anything to Lieutenant Douglas about the case?"

"Yes, I asked Lieutenant Douglas if he knew what had been used to kill Sir Harry, whether he had been shot, or stabbed, or what. The public did not know at this time how Sir Harry had been killed. Douglas said he did not know himself. I asked him if they had found a weapon or anything in the room, and he said he did not know. So I asked him, 'If they don't find a weapon, can they proceed with the case?'"

Mr. Higgs: "What did Lieutenant Douglas say?"

"He said that he thought so."

Here was another morsel for the jurors to dissect. De Marigny's version of the conversation corresponded identically with Douglas'; but was the question asked from idle curiosity, as de Marigny and Higgs contended, or did it grow from frightened guilt, as the Crown alleged?

When they arrived at the porch of Westbourne, they were discussing the Glen Rogers case; and he asked Douglas to describe it to him since he was not in Nassau at the time. Specifically, he asked the grounds "on which they got Rogers." Douglas explained that the Rogers case rested entirely on circumstantial evidence, and de Marigny thought he replied something about circumstantial evidence not being sufficient to convict a man of murder under French law.

Mr. Higgs: "Did you ask Lieutenant Douglas whether it was possible for a man to be convicted under English law on circumstantial evidence alone?"

"I do not remember. I could well have since we were discussing the Glen Rogers case, and it brought circumstantial evidence to my mind. That was all."

When they reached the living room at Westbourne, several witnesses were being interrogated. He was questioned by Captain Melchen, who took him upstairs to the northwest living room, and he remembered seeing Constable Knowles standing in front of the steps downstairs.

Mr. Higgs: "And what time was this?"

"This must have been eleven or eleven-fifteen."

He and Captain Melchen walked upstairs and he did not see anyone in the upstairs hallway, not a soul!

When they reached the northwest room upstairs, Captain Melchen told him that since he did not know anyone in Nassau, de Marigny might be able to furnish information that might be helpful. De Marigny agreed. Captain Melchen then asked him if he knew Harold Christie and whether Christie was indebted to Sir Harry Oakes, or whether he had any grievance against him whatsoever. De Marigny responded that so far as he knew, Christie was one of Sir Harry's best friends, and "I am certain that Mr. Christie would confirm this himself."

The Chief Justice: "One of your best friends?"

"Yes, Mr. Christie is one of my best friends."

There seemed to be a conversational block between the Chief Justice and the witness as they debated several more questions as to whether Christie was one of Sir Harry's best friends or one of the witness's best friends. The witness finally suggested that Christie was "both our best friends." This conclusion caused raised eyebrows in the jury box as well as throughout the courtroom: De Marigny was apparently the only man in the colony who would claim that Harold Christie was one of *de Marigny's* best friends.

Higgs next led de Marigny through a description of his interrogation by Captain Melchen.

Mr. Higgs: "What did he next ask you?"

"He asked me suddenly, out of a clear blue sky, after talking about my boyhood on Mauritius, 'Did you see any lights at Westbourne when you drove by?' I told him that I did. I saw the outside porch light on. Then he said, 'Did you see how many cars were there?' I told him I did not see any cars that I could remember. These were the regular sort of police traps."

De Marigny became quite dramatic, gesturing and imitating what he described as Melchen's next question to him: "He pointed his finger at me and said: 'Are you sure you did not come to Westbourne last night? Didn't you want to have things straightened out with Sir Harry, and then you had an argument with him, and then you hit him?' "

Mr. Higgs: "How did you respond to that accusation?"

"I told him that if I had wanted to see Sir Harry, I would certainly have come in the daytime and not in the middle of the night. I knew I would not get anywhere with him by interrupting his sleep at night."

Mr. Higgs: "What did he say next?"

"He told me, 'You were out that evening around three o'clock, and your friend was up too. How do you account for that?' I told him the suggestion was absurd. He said to me, 'What would you say if I told you that you were seen coming in here last night?' I replied, 'I defy you or anyone to suspect me.' "

De Marigny's voice assumed a Shakespearean quality as he arched his back while turning his body obliquely toward the jury, obviously re-enacting his interrogation by Melchen at Westbourne.

Melchen sat opposite him in the room, de Marigny continued, near a table to the left which contained a tray with two glasses and a pitcher of water. Over the preceding period of time, Melchen had offered him many cigarettes from a packet of Lucky Strikes; and Melchen finally asked de Marigny to pour Melchen a glass of water. He poured a glass for each one of them. He distinctly remembered the glasses being on the table, turned upside down, when he entered.

The jury understood Higgs' thrust: The real source of Exhibit J was some object in this room that Melchen was able to get de Marigny to touch during his interrogation.

Melchen next shifted the conversation to generalities; and Captain Barker pressed his head through the door, coming halfway in, and asked, "Is everything okay?"

Melchen replied, "Yes."

De Marigny interpreted Barker's appearance as a prearranged signal because, almost immediately, Melchen took him out of the room, back downstairs, where they talked for a few minutes in the living room. Mrs. Clark, Mrs. Ainsley, de Visdelou, Miss Roberts, and Lieutenant Douglas were there. Miss Roberts sauntered over to ask where he had been, and he told her he had been upstairs with Captain Melchen.

Colonel Erskine-Lindop implied that he was to be released from his "sort of tentative custody," and he said to Erskine-Lindop, "Colonel, I left this morning before my servants arrived. If you are interested in what shirt I wore, I could ask them if they knew in what basket they had put the shirt —so that I could bring the bundle there and they could have it."

Mr. Higgs: "What did Colonel Lindop say?"

"He said not to worry about it, that they had the coat and trousers, and that was all they wanted."

De Marigny idled away the day until his arrest at six-fifteen that evening, when he was officially notified of the murder charge against him. Captain Melchen invited him into the west living room at Westbourne to ask if he had anything more to say. De Marigny replied that he did not know what else Melchen wanted him to say; and "Captain Melchen shut me up very rudely and said, 'I want to warn you about one thing. In this case, nobody is too small or too big to be arrested, and even after we have gone away, we will come back and keep on investigating the case.' I said that was all right with me."

Higgs next asked him about the money that went into the chicken farm, half of it supplied by Nancy Oakes de Marigny. He wasn't impoverished, as was implied by the Crown; he had money in the bank and his future prospects were excellent. He was not afraid to work hard, in fact he rather enjoyed it, and he and Nancy looked forward to earning their way together.

Not a sound emanated from the crowded room when Higgs slowly turned his back to the witness to look out absently over the audience, through the glass windows in the rear, out onto the crowded courtyard. His demeanor telegraphed the arrival of his dramatic climax. Almost as a soldier doing an about-face, he whirled, and before his robe came to rest, his words flew almost visibly at de Marigny.

Mr. Higgs: "Did you on the night of July 7, or the morning of July 8, go to Westbourne?"

"I did not."

Mr. Higgs: "Did you kill Sir Harry Oakes?"

"No, sir."

"My lord, that is all!"

It came and went with stunning rapidity, this necessary denial of guilt or even remote complicity. De Marigny stood immobile, his head elevated and chin thrust forward in an unconscious Wagnerian pose. All jurors joined the Chief Justice in quizzical appraisal. Higgs was seated at counsel table before the spell broke. De Marigny sagged slowly as he looked toward the advancing Attorney General, whose task it was to discredit him.

26

Fake, Cad, and Gigolo

It was clear from the Attorney General's first questions that he planned to impeach de Marigny's character generally rather than attack his alibi and explanations of his actions frontally and specifically. After all, this cross-section of the community seated in the jury box was not likely to vote a verdict of guilty unless shown that the black heart or depraved conscience of the accused would permit him to do the heinous murder. Eric Hallinan also needed to feel out his witness, to see whether he was possessed of a soft underbelly vulnerable to cross-examination.

The Attorney General: "Your father's surname?"

"Fouquereaux."

The Attorney General: "And where did you get the name de Marigny?"

"From my mother. Her name was Desbeaux de Marigny."

The Attorney General: "And I suppose your mother's name is more distinguished than Fouquereaux?"

"No."

The Attorney General: "Why did you not keep your father's name? Did you think the name Fouquereaux bourgeois?"

"Not in the least. I took it for a simple reason. My mother and father were divorced when I was a little boy, and I had been given in custody to my father. I first met my mother when I was eighteen years old. When I saw my mother for the first time, she asked me to do so to please her, to use her name as part of my name."

The Attorney General: "When you came to this colony first, you were styled Count?"

"I never used it."

The Attorney General: "Why were you **then** called Count?"

"In the family of my mother, the de Marigny family, there are lots of titles."

The Attorney General: "Does it come from Fouquereaux?"

"It came from both sides. They had it too."

The Attorney General: "I put it to you that Fouquereaux is a bourgeois name?"

"I do not agree."

The Attorney General: "How is it that you became publicly known as Count de Marigny?"

"My former wife, Ruth, who was in New York at the time, called herself Countess de Marigny against my desires. I discussed the matter with the *Guardian* and the *Tribune* here, and I asked them not to use it, and the *Guardian* never did afterwards. I have never used this title in Nassau, or anyplace else."

Eric Hallinan knew immediately that his adversary was formidable. Clearly, de Marigny won the opening sally; the jurors were impressed.

Hallinan then spent the better part of an hour on de Marigny's financial condition, and the round ended as something of a Mexican standoff. Certainly his cash position was mercurial, plunging from credit balances of $5,000 to overdrafts as high as $20,000. His funds, Nancy's funds, and questions about £25,000 from his former wife, Ruth, left everyone properly confused. He admitted soliciting the aid of his friend, John Anderson, to prepare an account for his former wife, Ruth, touching upon monies due Ruth. It was a faked and fabricated account.

The Chief Justice: "A fabricated one?"

"Some of the items are not correct. I used the word 'fabricated' by mistake. It was under the advice of Mr. Anderson that I sent this account to him to send a copy of it to Ruth, though I knew then that some of the items were not correct."

The Attorney General: "So I take it that you did not lose any money on this expenditure?"

"No."

The Attorney General: "And therefore, any money you received from Ruth has been spent on nonbusiness matters?"

"Yes."

Now the jurors appeared vexed. Willful defalcations, whether labeled "fabricated" or not, do not augur well for the believability of a witness. He was spared further embarrassment by the Chief Justice.

The Chief Justice to the Attorney General: "What do you say the object of your cross-examination is?"

The Attorney General: "My lord, my object is to show the way of living of accused."

The Chief Justice: "I do not think that's important. Pray be on to something else."

The Attorney General shifted into new ground.

The Attorney General: "You told us that in March, 1942, you were having medical treatment in New York, and that Nancy saw you often in the hospital?"

"Yes."

The Attorney General: "And then you went to California?"

"No, before we went at the invitation of Miss De Rapp."

The Attorney General: "Nancy at that time was about seventeen?"

"Seventeen and ten or eleven months."

The Attorney General: "And how old was Miss De Rapp?"

"Eighteen or nineteen."

The Attorney General: "You would not regard her as a chaperone?"

"No."

The Attorney General kept up the attack in his effort to show de Marigny's moral degeneracy.

The Attorney General: "After you got your divorce, you continued to live with your former wife?"

"What do you mean?"

Mr. Higgs: "My lord, I must interrupt my learned friend and object to the questions as being prejudicial."

The Attorney General: "I submit they are material, my lord, in view of the fact that the Oakes family knew of these conditions; and they were part of the bone of contention between the accused and Sir Harry and Lady Oakes."

The Chief Justice: "Very well, you may put your question again."

The Attorney General: "I put it to you, after you got your divorce from your former wife, Ruth, you continued to live with her?"

"For a short period of time, yes."

The Attorney General: "I put it to you that you were living with her up to December, 1941, and everybody knew it?"

"No, certainly not."

The jurors recalled de Marigny's earlier statement that he met Nancy for the first time at a party given by Lady Oakes at the British Colonial Hotel in December, 1941.

The Attorney General: "When did you cease to live with your wife, on your oath?"

"We were divorced in Miami in March, 1940; and I ceased to live with her in December, 1940."

The Attorney General was ready, after his basic questions involving de Marigny's life with Ruth, to shift to his relations with Nancy and the Oakes family.

The Attorney General: "Did you inform either Sir Harry or Lady Oakes of your intention to marry their daughter?"

"No, I did not."

The Attorney General: "Did you and Nancy talk over the need to inform her parents of your intention to marry?"

"Yes, we did. We discussed it while I was still in the hospital in New York, and she went to Canada to talk it over with her mother."

The Attorney General: "And did Nancy mention to her mother that she was going to be married?"

"She did not discuss it with her mother."

The Attorney General: "On Nancy's return from Canada, did you ask her if she had discussed it with her mother?"

"She had not discussed it."

The Chief Justice: "I do not believe that communications between husband and wife should be introduced here or referred to."

The Attorney General: "Thank you, my lord. I will leave them be. *[To the witness]* Before you married Nancy, did you know that you had the consent of her parents?"

"No."

The Attorney General: "I put it to you that you waited until after she became of legal age because you knew you could not get that parental consent?"

"No. She was of legal age and could marry when she wanted to, then or six months afterwards, it made no difference. I had never thought of it."

This line of questioning scored well with the jury. They thought de Marigny's answers flippant and irresponsible and now, most of all, they could not accept his easy explanation for his failure to obtain the consent of Sir Harry and Lady Oakes for the marriage. His conduct did not conform to either British or Bahamian standards of manners and good taste.

The Attorney General next wanted to emphasize motive, and there were a number of items on which de Marigny appeared vulnerable.

The Attorney General: "When Sir Harry turned you out of that room in the hospital in Palm Beach, and when he spoke in that rough way to you before the neighbors in the Victoria Avenue house, and when Sir Harry removed Sydney from your house, I take it you were humiliated?"

"No, not in the least. I knew Sir Harry was a man who was very moody and had a violent temper, and everyone knew it. He used to lose his temper for nothing."

The Attorney General: "He was speaking loudly outside the house in Victoria Avenue so that people in the neighboring houses could hear?"

"Nobody was around. I don't think the neighbors could hear."

The Attorney General: "Did he call you a sex maniac?"

"Quite possibly."

Sir Oscar could not resist entering the fray.

The Chief Justice: "Did this make you angry?"

"I realized that he was very angry, he was losing his temper more and more, and there was no sense in getting angry. I thought he might not have meant what he said. If he had spoken coldly or in an insulting way, I might have been angry."

There were more vulnerabilities on motive.

The Attorney General: "Did you refuse the offer of the Jones property and other properties for purely business reasons?"

"Yes."

The Attorney General: "I thought you said that your main reason was that Nancy and yourself might be cut off from your friends?"

"It was so far away, it was difficult for servants, for food and everything."

The Attorney General: "I put it to you that Sir Harry was disgusted after you refused his offer of making good on the Jones property?"

"I did not think so at all."

Then there was the question of de Marigny's social conduct, as viewed from the eyes of Sir Harry and Lady Oakes.

The Attorney General: "You said Sir Harry said he did not approve of your not accepting the invitation to Government House?"

"He did."

The Attorney General: "He said you should go out if you were to get anywhere?"

"I did not go out with the society set in Nassau. I kept to my own friends and stayed there. I am very happy with them."

In a sense, de Marigny was challenging, figuratively thumbing his nose at the jurors and their wives. Even those who were not active in the so-called social set respected it and would defend it, certainly against "foreign" attack. Still, they could not help but admire de Marigny's courage and, at least, his pretext of integrity.

The Attorney General: "Do you think Sir Harry relished the idea of his daughter living in the house with Betty Roberts and the marquis, who were not man and wife?"

"They were not living in our house. They were living in a separate apartment upstairs."

This was an effective, deadly character assault by implication. These two Frenchmen obviously did not respect Nassau and British social convention, at least as applied to the matrimonial bed.

The Attorney General: "Did not you share meals with them?"

"On rare occasions, they would eat with us and would then go up to the apartment again."

The Chief Justice: "Did Sir Harry ever speak to you about it?"

"No, as a matter of fact, he came to lunch when they were there and took them driving afterwards."

The Attorney General: "Were Betty Roberts and de Visdelou present at the dinner at which Sir Harry was present on March 27?"

"Yes."

Eric Hallinan moved next to de Marigny's direct relationship with Sir Harry, emphasizing the last months of his life.

The Attorney General: "You said Sir Harry was a man of violent tempers and they passed. But after March, he seemed to have ignored you?"

"I did not see him."

The Attorney General: "He did not seek your company?"

"Not that I know of."

The Attorney General: "He never made any attempt to communicate with you?"

"Not the slightest."

There were now several vulnerable matters in the family relationship: Nancy's birthday present from her mother, the two thousand pounds in government bonds, Nancy's letter to her mother in May, and the letter de Marigny wrote to Sydney.

The Attorney General: "Do you think the letter to Sydney was a proper letter to write a boy of sixteen?"

"I was answering his letter."

The Attorney General: "I am asking you a very simple question. You don't think it was disloyal or encouraging disloyalty to his parents?"

"I don't think so."

Hallinan now moved to a discussion of de Marigny's relationship with Christie. De Marigny said that Christie had dined at his house on "several occasions but I did not keep track of them all."

The Attorney General: "If he said once, he is telling a lie?"

"I wouldn't say that."

The Attorney General: "You have known him since you came to the colony in 1938?"

"Yes."

The Attorney General: "Are these the sort of people you would have invited Mr. Christie to be with?"

"Why not?"

The Attorney General: "His age, his taste?"

"Certainly, I see nothing wrong."

The Attorney General: "And you issued an invitation to him that morning?"

"Yes, I knew him well. I used to go to his house at six or seven o'clock in the morning when he was in bed, dozens of times."

The Attorney General: "You had this group, and then suddenly thought you would ask Mr. Christie?"

"I was speaking to him on the phone, and just thought of it then."

Eric Hallinan realized there was little more he could do with the witness, so he rushed his cross-examination to a rapid conclusion.

The Attorney General: "Captain Melchen says you brought

the coat and trousers that are here in the courtroom out of the bedroom and handed them to him?"

"Melchen lies when he says that."

Once more, de Marigny elected to contradict head-on the testimony of one of the Crown's chief witnesses; and it was the extreme form of confrontation, calling that witness a liar. Godfrey Higgs sat worried at counsel table: How many direct contradictions of how many witnesses could the accused get by with and still be believed by the jury?

Eric Hallinan's questions virtually screamed, "Cad, gigolo, and fake!" He knew he would get nowhere by asking de Marigny directly about a visit to Westbourne after dropping off Mrs. Ainsley and Mrs. Clark in the early morning of July 8. Obviously, the frontal attack would avail nothing; and the jury sat in wonderment about de Marigny as a man charged with killing his fellowman: As one, they all agreed that he was a cad, gigolo, and fake; but did this also make him murderer?

Jury Foreman Sands proposed the most dramatic courtroom demonstration of the century. The three hurricane lamps which supplied the light for the party de Marigny gave July 7 sat in a row on the bench in front of Sir Oscar Daly, their yellow candles of varying lengths, the one nearest the witness box only an inch tall. At Sir Oscar's request, de Marigny stepped down from the witness box, walked around to the front of the bench, and stood facing Sir Oscar, his back to counsel table and his right side to the jury box. He took a wooden match from a box in his pocket, placed the match in his right hand between his thumb and index and middle fingers, and struck it. The low height of the candle forced him to push his hand deep down into the shade. As Sir Oscar watched transfixed, the jurors standing in their box to see better, and robed barristers and court attendants hovering around the front of the bench, the flame suddenly caught on the wick and curled upward over de Marigny's hand. Instinctively and reflexively, he jerked his hand upward and outward, almost knocking over the lamp in the process. Something similar to "ouch" burst from his lips, although the Reuters reporter called it "a French oath."

Earlier testimony alleged him ambidextrous; so de Marigny next took another wooden match and placed it between his left thumb and the appropriate fingers. Striking it, he pushed his left hand down into the second lamp shade. The candle was taller and nothing untoward developed, although it was obvious that de Marigny could not hold his hand inside the shade after the wick caught fire without running the risk of being burned.

If Melchen and Barker had, indeed, found burned hairs on de Marigny's hands and forearms when they examined him Thursday afternoon at Westbourne, here was an easy explanation of their source. This "cad, gigolo, and fake" offered the jury an alternative to the Crown's theory that his burned hairs came from the fire at Westbourne, and the simple demonstration spoke louder than any words Godfrey Higgs or Ernest Callender might have used in explanation.

Erle Stanley Gardner concluded that de Marigny evoked no sympathy whatsoever from the jury; still he helped his own cause immeasurably by his bold, unequivocal responses. There was an intangible quality to his courage that implied truthfulness. The unanswerable question at that point was whether he had given the lie to too many individual witnesses by head-on confrontations to leave himself any measure of credibility. More and more, Exhibit J loomed as the controlling item of evidence.

27

The Alibi Witnesses

As with a great many things in life, the great problem of an alibi is its *timing*. In the spurious alibis, the defendants know better than to cut them from whole cloth; rather, they take an event which actually happened and juggle it in time sequence to exculpate themselves: If the crime took place at *h* hour on *d* day, the accused obviously is not guilty if he was with Witness 1 in a restaurant in another city at *h* hour, *d* day. In the false alibi, the alibi event (the visit to *x* restaurant) actually takes place, but it happened a day before or a day after the crime.

The legitimate alibi frequently fails to convince because it is run-of-the-mill, undramatic routine, provable only by relatives, neighbors, or friends, so that each of the alibi witnesses is biased beyond belief in the defendant's favor.

Both these problems faced Godfrey Higgs as he attempted to buttress de Marigny's alibi that would prove him physically incapable of the murder.

Charles Rolle, de Marigny's black butler, was entirely credible, except for his obvious bias in de Marigny's favor.

The Victoria Avenue house party broke up at twelve-thirty in the morning, Rolle explained naturally, and he saw de Marigny leave to take the two girls home. He busied himself cleaning up and washing the dishes and heard de Marigny return about an hour later. Time was not a significant reck-

oning with Rolle that morning; there was absolutely nothing
positive to which he could hang a time identification of de
Marigny's return. He confirmed that de Marigny parked his
Lincoln in the garage after moving de Visdelou's Chevrolet
out of the driveway. De Marigny came through the house,
as if on a quick inspection tour, and told him good-night
before going to his bedroom. There was no cross-examination.

Betty Roberts was next. Blond, fair-skinned, blue-eyed,
buxom, cocky, and sexy, she insisted that her real home was
with her mother, although she lived part of the time with
Georges de Visdelou in the apartment over the de Marignys'
house on Victoria Avenue.

Betty Roberts' flippant, nonchalant, cavalier attitude toward
sex and marriage, long before the hippie attitudes of the
Sixties and the sexual permissiveness of the Seventies, intrigued the jurors, but it did not particularly lend credence
to the alibi. She, of course, was at the party de Marigny gave
July 7. Georges de Visdelou was not feeling well because of
a cold; he retired to his bedroom early, maybe around eleven.
At about the same time, she went upstairs to an adjoining
room and fell asleep on the couch. She did not awaken until
almost three the next morning, when she asked de Visdelou
to drive her to her mother's home, which he did in the
Chevrolet.

When Alfred Adderley asked Betty on cross-examination
why she elected to sleep on the couch in the room adjoining
de Visdelou's, she replied matter-of-factly, "I told you he had
a cold that night!"

Godfrey Higgs knew that he must call Georges de Visdelou,
but he well realized the attendant risks. De Visdelou was born
with darting eyes, and there was no way in the world for
him to alter their impression of shiftiness and untrustworthi-
ness. It was he rather than de Marigny who looked the role
of cad, gigolo, and fake. His brow was wide, his face narrow,
and his chin pointed; his black wavy hair rolled in perfect
marcels; there was a cast of femininity in his demeanor, hand

motions, and voice; and the French accent, captivating and intriguing on de Marigny, shouted out arrogance and deception when emitted by de Visdelou.

Godfrey Higgs questioned him only seven minutes on direct, and his appearance was neutral. Nothing about it permitted it to be described as good; it just wasn't bad.

But then Alfred Adderley pulled no punches on cross-examination.

He went into de Visdelou's transatlantic trip with de Marigny and his wife; de Visdelou's "threesome" arrangement with de Marigny and his second wife, Ruth; and finally de Visdelou's arrival to participate in the marital arrangements, at least to live under the same roof, with Nancy. Adderley did not once need to insinuate either by direct word or nuance of voice: The admitted facts of the tacit relationships screamed their own incrimination. De Marigny was virtually made guilty by his strange association with de Visdelou, since it implied both his and Nancy's approval of de Visdelou's keeping a sixteen-year-old girl in the apartment above the de Marignys. This did not exactly call out jury sympathy.

Courtroom observers were totally at sea when Adderley led de Visdelou once more through his confirmation of the alibi events: De Visdelou's retiring from the party, his talk to de Marigny about the cat, his taking the cat from de Marigny's room after he drove Betty Roberts home in the Chevrolet—but then Adderley ran in his sword.

Mr. Adderley: "I will ask you, sir, if you did not give a statement to the police on July 11, this year?"

"I gave a statement at some time; but I do not remember exactly when."

Mr. Adderley: "I hand you now this paper and ask you to examine it closely and tell us whether it bears your signature?"

"Yes, it is my signature."

Mr. Adderley: "Does it not bear the date July 11, 1943?"

"Yes, that's on it."

Mr. Adderley: "Will you look at the paper carefully and

tell us whether this is the statement you gave to Colonel
Lindop of the Bahamian police?"

"Yes, it is."

Mr. Adderley: "My lord, by your leave, I will read from
the statement: 'As I had a slight cold and was not feeling
well, I retired to my room from the party a little after eleven
o'clock. At this time, I said good-night to Mr. de Marigny
and all of his guests. I did not see Alfred de Marigny from
that time on until about ten o'clock the following morning.
. . .' I put it to you, did you make that statement to the
police?"

"Yes . . . yes . . . yes. I did then, but my mind was vague.
I was terribly upset; my best friend, there, had been arrested.
I didn't know exactly what I would say. It is not right, what
I said then in this statement. What I say now is right. I did
talk to him about the cat, I got the cat out of his room after
I took Miss Roberts home. I did! I did! I did! I'm French. I
get emotional. I forgot about the cat until Mr. de Marigny
reminded me of it."

De Visdelou shouted his answers hysterically, rubbing his
hands dramatically; it looked as though tears would burst
from his eyes at any minute. He was not a believable witness, his courtroom story now smacking of complete fraud
when weighed against the prior statement to the police, in
writing and signed by him, July 11.

The jurors could not help but wonder whether de Marigny
might have tampered with this witness in a desperate effort
to support his alibi, and de Marigny's rather favorable appearance in the witness box was now considerably undone
by de Visdelou's emotional failure as an alibi witness. Clearly,
the defense would have been much better off if de Visdelou
could somehow have made himself unavailable for the trial.
Erle Stanley Gardner thought the odds against de Marigny's
acquittal now were almost insurmountable.

28

The Frontal Assault
on Exhibit J

More and more as the case rushed madly to its finish, Exhibit
J loomed as the controlling item of evidence. Maurice B.
O'Neil, Superintendent of the Bureau of Identification of the
New Orleans Police Department and a past president of the
International Association of Identification, was Raymond
Schindler's choice as expert to give the defense's theory on
Exhibit J.

Of medium height, gray-haired, and pedantic in appearance, stocky in build but sharp-featured, O'Neil was equally
as believable as Conway.

Mr. Higgs: "Do you, based upon reasonable certainty, have
an opinion as to whether Exhibit J could possibly have come
from the screen?"

"I do."

Mr. Higgs: "Please tell us what that opinion is?"

"In my opinion, Exhibit J could *not* have come from the
screen."

O'Neil's statement evoked no audible response around the
courtroom; it was as though everyone knew in advance exactly what to expect and adjusted for it. Higgs plunged on
professionally and in a matter-of-fact tone.

Mr. Higgs: "On what do you base that opinion?"

"I have spent several hours closely examining panel five of the screen. I can find evidence of two lifted prints about six inches from the top of the screen in this panel; but I am unable to find any area on the screen other than these two that I have described that does not have discernible circles in the background of this particular scrollwork on the screen. Exhibit J has no discernible circles in its background pattern at all, nor is there anything else in its background pattern. I don't see how it is possible for Exhibit J to have been lifted from the screen."

Everyone in the courtroom tensed for the next line of questioning which all knew Higgs dared not omit.

Mr. Higgs: "Do you have an opinion where Exhibit J might have come from?"

"It could have been lifted from almost any surface that the accused touched."

Mr. Higgs: "Would this include a packet of Lucky Strikes which he handled in the northwestern room upstairs at Westbourne?"

"Yes, most certainly."

Mr. Higgs: "Could Exhibit J have come from a glass tumbler in that same northwestern bedroom upstairs at Westbourne which the accused handled?"

"Yes."

Mr. Higgs: "Could Exhibit J have come from the thermos bottle in the northwestern bedroom upstairs at Westbourne which the accused handled?"

"Yes, it could have."

Mr. Higgs: "Could Exhibit J have come from the wooden arm of a chair in which the accused sat while he was interviewed by Captain Melchen in the northwestern bedroom upstairs at Westbourne?"

"Yes, it could."

Mr. Higgs: "Could Exhibit J have come from a magazine that the accused touched when he was in the northwestern bedroom upstairs at Westbourne being interviewed by Captain Melchen?"

"Yes."

Godfrey Higgs decided this was enough and stopped.

Eric Hallinan asked virtually the only question possible of an expert witness under the circumstances.

The Attorney General: "Your statement that Exhibit J could not have come from number-five panel on the screen is nothing more than your own opinion?"

"Yes, that is correct."

The Attorney General: "By that, you mean your opinion as a fingerprint expert?"

"Yes."

The Attorney General: "Not all expert witnesses have the same expert opinion?"

"That is correct."

The Attorney General: "I put it to you that expert witnesses of the same qualifications may have exactly the opposite opinions on the same item of evidence?"

"Yes."

The Attorney General: "Then it is up to the jury to decide which of the opinions of the two experts is to be believed?"

"Yes, that's always the case."

The Attorney General: "There is nothing unusual particularly in having a conflict of expert opinion over a technical matter of evidence?"

"No, there is not."

The jury's task with Exhibit J could not have been spelled out more clearly: Would they believe Police Expert Barker, or would they accept the opinion of Police Expert O'Neil? As with all things human, whether they elected to go with Barker or O'Neil depended on factors extrinsic to the mere words of the two American policemen. Fact-gathering and fact-finding are not mathematically precise, prognostic events that occur with computerlike prediction in the sterility of a vacuum tube. Fact-finding is perhaps the most human and vulnerable of all occupations; and the great strength of the Common Law system is the award of the fact-finding task to twelve laymen representing a cross-section of the community, instead of entrusting it to a single professional judge whose biases and prejudices control. Better it is to have twelve sets of bias to counterbalance one another democratically than to be limited to the totalitarian decision of a single judge, or of a small number of jurors.

29

Harold Christie's
Midnight Ride

Godfrey Higgs was master dramatist. He built the case for
the defense with a gradual increase in suspense worthy of a
gifted playwright.

Freddie Ceretta, until July 7 an almost nameless, faceless
nonentity who had attached himself hopefully to de Marigny,
was in the witness box less than five minutes; yet his contribution to the defense was monumental.

After describing the party, the dinner, and the departure
of the guests, he was ready for Higgs' single potent but
seemingly innocuous question.

Mr. Higgs: "When accused got ready to take Mrs. Clark
and Mrs. Ainsley home at around twelve-thirty, did he say
anything to you?"

"Yes. He asked if I would like to ride along."

Did this sound like the actions of a man whose mind already premeditated the murder of his father-in-law—Higgs
would argue to the jury in his final summation—this invitation to a witness who could surely give damning evidence
against him later on? Did de Marigny pause at Westbourne
to say: "Pardon me one moment, I'll be right back. I must
run in and murder my father-in-law, that guy, the old
bastard!"

Captain Edward Sears next stood in the witness box,

his named called loudly by Godfrey Higgs. He was a contemporary of Harold Christie's, of the same age, a general
similarity in build and appearance, and an almost identical
family background. Sears and Christie grew up together,
played together, went to school together. Their paths separated at the choice of careers: Christie followed the Bay
Street route to Island fame and considerable fortune; Sears
entered the Colonial Police and was now an Assistant Superintendent in charge of traffic.

Edward Sears stood like a pillar in the witness box, erect,
straight, and with steady eyes. He spoke in a quiet, confident
manner, a man sure of what he could tell. He was squarely
built, with smooth dark hair, deep-set slate-gray eyes, a thin
line for a mouth that implied determination.

It was shortly before midnight, possibly a little after, when
he was driving his police car south on George Street, by the
old Island Bookshop. He looked across at the approaching
station wagon going north on George Street and recognized
Harold Christie as the passenger in the right front seat. It
was as simply said as that; but of all those connected with
the case, only Christie and the white driver knew that Sir
Harry's battered body lay *face down* in the back on the
vehicle's floor.

Under Eric Hallinan's cross-examination, Sears admitted
that it was raining at the time he identified Christie, but the
cars passed under a street light and this flash of illumination
was all he needed to recognize the man he had known all his
life in Nassau. He admitted that the two vehicles were going
in opposite directions and traveling perhaps as fast as twenty
miles an hour. He could not identify the driver of the station wagon but could tell that he was white. As traffic in
Nassau flows on the left in the British fashion, Sears and
Christie were within two or three feet of each other when
the two vehicles passed under the street light, not over three
blocks from the cabin cruiser where Sir Harry was struck
down.

Eric Hallinan could not shake Sears from his story. "I'm
satisfied I saw Harold Christie that night in that station

wagon," Sears repeated in his quiet, forceful voice, the words of a man who would never budge from a position he thought right and correct. Everyone in the courtroom knew that if Captain Edward Sears did not see Harold Christie in the station wagon on that Nassau street at around midnight, he certainly believed that he saw him; and being convinced in his own mind he saw him, he would say so no matter what his fellow officers might think, or what the Crown's attorney might hope or wish.

The jurors now thought back to a portion of Godfrey Higgs' cross-examination of Major Pemberton days earlier:

Mr. Higgs: "Did you notice Mr. Christie's bed on Thursday morning at Westbourne?"

"Yes."

Mr. Higgs: "Did it appear to have been slept in?"

"It was not heavily rumpled, but someone had certainly lain on it. There was an indentation on the pillow and the bed itself."

Mr. Higgs: "Were the sheets rumpled up?"

"Very little."

Mr. Higgs: "Did you examine Mr. Christie's car or his station wagon?"

"I did not."

Mr. Higgs: "Did you see Mr. Christie's clothes in his bedroom?"

"I do not remember."

The jurors also remembered the bloody prints on both sides of the south doors to the bedroom in which Christie was supposed to have slept.

Obviously, the testimony of Police Captain Edward Sears was at cross-purposes with Christie's protests that he and Sir Harry never once left Westbourne after their guests departed around eleven in the evening. It was another conflict which the jury would have to resolve; it no longer involved de Marigny directly, but no one at the time could really interpret its true significance.

30

The Support of
a Loyal Wife

It was not so much *what* Nancy Oakes de Marigny had to say—her vigor lay in the fact that she would appear at all as witness for the defense.

She stood in the witness box dressed in a black suit with small white dots, a white "pancake" hat, a white dickey at her throat. She wore a white glove on her left hand but held the other glove in her right, a sort of pacifying comforter that she rolled between questions. The minute the questions came, however, her hand became motionless as she responded without hesitancy in a firm, loud voice. Her elevated chin, in model's pose, exuded confidence but not defiance.

Technically, Godfrey Higgs called her to negate the Crown's two principal elements of motive: hatred and desire for financial gain. Psychologically, her mere appearance screamed out to all the world her firm belief in her husband's innocence, a stance that cleaved her from her mother and siblings. This sad-eyed schoolgirl, the epitome of dogged, unfailing loyalty, glanced into the prisoner's dock from time to time, a silent reassurance to the man she loved, as though trying to send him strength and comfort. Her actions were not lost on the jury.

For the better part of an hour, Godfrey Higgs led her skillfully through a recital of her first meeting with Alfred de Marigny, the courtship in New York, the California trip, the Mexican honeymoon, her many and serious illnesses, finally the estrangement from both her father and her mother.

Mr. Higgs: "And to what do you attribute this estrangement between you, your husband and your parents?"

"I attribute it solely to the attitude of my parents. My husband and I tried hard to change that attitude, and we had still hoped to change it."

Nancy glanced once more to the prisoner's dock where de Marigny sat completely immobile, his eyes transfixed on the attractive girl whose love for him rent her from her parents.

Mr. Higgs: "Did you at any time ever hear your husband make any expression of hatred toward your father?"

"No, never. He never spoke ill of my father at all. When the differences and disagreeable episodes occurred, he was always sympathetic toward my father, attributing it to his age and health."

Mr. Higgs: "At any time during your married life, did the accused ever try to obtain money from you?"

"No, never."

Mr. Higgs: "Did the accused at any time make any offer to you in connection with any money you had?"

"No. I invested three thousand pounds sterling in the chicken farm. This was from my savings account, and I made my own decision to make the investment after he and I talked it over. I became half owner in the chicken farm. It was not a loan of my money to him."

Mr. Higgs: "What money did you and your husband use to live on after your marriage?"

"He had some money of his own, several thousand pounds. I had some savings funds. My mother gave us some money for the Mexican honeymoon trip. We were not destitute or dependent upon my parents or anyone else. We had planned to make our own way, and the chicken farm appeared to be a profitable enterprise."

Higgs next led the witness back to her initial contacts with Captain Melchen and Captain Barker. First she talked to them over the telephone, and then saw them when they visited her mother and other family members in Bar Harbor, the day of her father's funeral.

Mr. Higgs: "Did Captain Melchen and Captain Barker tell you anything about who murdered your father?"

"Yes. Both on the telephone and at Bar Harbor, they gave me to understand it was my husband."

Mr. Higgs: "Did they tell you why they thought it was your husband?"

"Yes. They said there could be no doubt about it. His fingerprints had been found on the screen next to my father's bed."

Mr. Higgs: "Did they say fingerprint or fingerprints?"

"They definitely said fingerprints. I understood there were several or many of my husband's fingerprints on the screen."

Mr. Higgs: "Did they imply any doubt as to whether these fingerprints had positively been identified as your husband's?"

"There was no doubt whatsoever; as a matter of fact, they assured me that the prints positively were those of my husband."

The jurors scowled at the recital of this unfair, some thought underhanded, attempt to drive a wedge between husband and wife, perhaps an attempt to influence her testimony in the courtroom against him, on nothing more positive than the then nebulous Exhibit J which, by Barker's own testimony, was not positively identified until July 19, some four days after the conversation with Nancy Oakes de Marigny and her mother in Bar Harbor. The jurors thought "foul," and nothing rises up to penalize a side more viciously than the jury's deduction of unfair tactics.

Godfrey Higgs could not ask Nancy Oakes de Marigny point-blank if she thought her husband innocent. This would be a conclusion of the witness on the ultimate fact which the jury must decide. Having negated the Crown's two principal items of motive, and having shown the "foul" action of Melchen and Barker, he turned his witness over to the Attorney General for cross-examination.

Eric Hallinan recognized his own delicate psychological position: He could not overattack the witness without driving her into the embrace of the jury's sympathy. He decided to open on what should have been a relatively safe ground, but it backfired.

The Attorney General: "Where were you when you first learned of your father's death?"

"I was in Miami, and I received a telegram from my husband telling me to go to my mother, and I. . . ."

This effort to relate probably the most traumatic event in her life was too much. Suddenly, her pent-up emotions of months, perhaps years, exploded. Her sobs came silently, but her tears gushed in torrents, bouncing off her clasped hands, the rail surrounding the witness box, even down onto the crier's desk below. The Chief Justice showed concern and sympathy.

The Chief Justice: "Perhaps we should take a brief recess?"

"No! No! I'll be all right in a few moments!" Nancy Oakes de Marigny pleaded to Sir Oscar through contorted face and spattering tears. "I'm sorry. I'll be all right in just a moment."

Tears now flooded the eyes of Alfred de Marigny as he sat paralyzed in the witness box, helpless to save his wife or give her comfort. As the tears flowed down the sides of his face, he paid them no notice, watching only the ordeal of his wife.

The Attorney General: "My lord, I have here a rather lengthy letter which I propose to read to the jury. Perhaps this would be a good time to do it."

The Chief Justice: "You may proceed."

Hallinan now turned to face the jury, his left side to the witness and Sir Oscar. He began to read Nancy's letter to her mother dated May 26, 1943:

> Dearest Mother,
>   Several days ago I received a letter from the bank, advising me that you had instructed them to purchase two thousand pounds worth of British War Loan Bonds in my name. These certificates have not arrived as yet from London; but as soon as they do, I will request the bank to return them to you. Nothing is more natural than for a

family to give their children gifts on such occasions, but under the circumstances it is impossible for me to accept from either you or Father such gifts that have the smell of charity to a poor relative.

At the time that you and Father left Mexico, you both seemed to hold my husband in high esteem. In fact, you both took him into your confidence in many matters of a personal nature, indeed, much more so than you had ever done with your own child. As things were then, even you were very happy and looking forward to a normal family life of trust and good fellowship. However, since our return from Mexico, the picture has changed erratically. You choose to believe the insinuations of third parties, in preference to inquiring frankly the truth and facts of certain matters of your own people, and, when an attempt was made by us to show you how you had been misled, you refused to co-operate with our lawyer.

In addition, when Father came to Nassau with Sydney, he was most insulting in his behavior toward us. At that time, he expressed in the most forceful terms his desire for us to sever further connections with the Oakes family. Painful as it was, I was forced to choose between my parents and my husband. Under the circumstances, there could be no question in my mind as to where my decision lay.

For this wholly unnecessary and unhappy situation, I place the responsibility on Walter Foskett, who has been, I believe, deliberately misguiding your judgment. His conduct throughout has been most unethical. It is not the duty of a man to pass judgment on a man's integrity, based merely on such fantastic and flimsy evidence. Instead of frankly inquiring into the matter and discussing the whole business with Alfred, his lawyer, and other responsible persons, he chose to accuse without reason. It is unforgivable that he should have acted in such a manner as to create disharmony and hate amongst the family. I can now see the truth behind the gossip and stories that I have heard about him, and which I had, until recently, disregarded.

I am enclosing certain documents and letters which should show you that the whole matter was really very simple and could have been cleared up in five minutes with no unpleasantness. This separation agreement was arranged privately to the satisfaction of both parties at the time and could, of course, have been obtained by Walter Foskett for your inspection had he acted in a responsible manner.

I want you to know that both of us can forgive this whole painful affair if you and Father can wash away your prejudices against my husband, and you can regard him with respect and trust to which he is entitled. Otherwise, I can never again feel any love or respect for you or Father or accept any of the natural advantages usually given to children by their parents. Sincerely, I am praying that you will not misunderstand the plain language of this letter, it may appear hard at first reading, but no insulting or bitter feeling is intended. It is simply the bare truth as seen through my eyes. I pray God that you will also see the truth and justice in these statements.

Your loving daughter, *Nancy*

Eric Hallinan carefully folded the letter and placed it on the registrar's desk. By this time, Nancy Oakes de Marigny, pale, tear-stained, and frail, was once more in complete charge of herself. She twisted the white glove in her right hand as she waited for the Attorney General's next question.

The Attorney General: "That was a pretty hard letter for a girl to write to her mother, was it not?"

"You might think so; but you were not mixed up in all of this."

The Chief Justice: "Did you wish to sever relations with your father and mother?"

"Not if I could help it. I had earnestly hoped that it would not come to that."

Sir Oscar shook his head gently in a deliberate effort to convey his sympathy, and Nancy's pale face and black dress stood out in marked contrast to his white wig and scarlet robe. They were father and daughter comforting each other.

The Attorney General: "If it [the letter] would not cause your father and mother to regard your husband with respect and confidence, then you would sever relations with them?"

"I was afraid that I probably would have to sever relations with my father and mother, but I was hoping that they would change their attitude."

The Attorney General: "After you wrote that letter to your mother, did either your mother or father send you any communication in an effort on their part to make friends?"

"I did not receive any communication whatsoever again from either my father or my mother."

The Attorney General: "I take it then that you were cut off by your parents?"

"I do not consider myself cut off by them or from them. We just had no more relations afterwards."

Jury Foreman Sands asked Nancy if she knew whether her parents had changed their wills the preceding February. Her reply was straightforward.

"They might have, but I did not know anything about it."

Foreman Sands: "Did you ever discuss the question of your parents' wills with your husband?"

"No, never. That would not be a proper subject for us to talk about."

As Nancy Oakes de Marigny stepped slowly from the witness box, Godfrey Higgs announced to all that "The defense rests, my lord!"

Nancy Oakes de Marigny, the loyal wife, served as theatrical finale to a dramatically scripted case for the defense.

31

The Verdict

The great oratory of the English language does not occur in the House of Commons, in the House of Lords, in Congressional and legislative chambers across the United States, or on lecture podia. It takes place in English-speaking courtrooms in the form of perorations by British barristers as they sum up the evidence for their side of the case to the British juries who must find the facts. It is an oratory designed to persuade, to move the listener to favorable action; but to be effective, it must also enrapture and entertain.

There are skeptics who claim that the British barrister is a downright dangerous instrumentality. He is such a hypnotic spellbinder that he mesmerizes audiences through the force of his words so that they do not critically analyze his assertions. The countering argument, of course, is that for every barrister advancing the Crown's case, an equally distinguished and effective man sums up for the defense.

Godfrey Higgs spoke first, for two hours and twenty minutes altogether, in precise, logical tones devoid of histrionics. First he tore apart the Crown's case, calling "the American police" liars who fabricated the fingerprint evidence. He urged the jury to comply with the ancient precept of reasonable doubt and conclude, in the light of all the evidence, that Exhibit J did not come from the Chinese screen by Sir Harry's bed but was a fake and forgery through and through.

Point by point, he ridiculed the fourteen points outlined by Alfred Adderley in his opening address to the jury twenty days earlier. Lady Oakes, he reminded the jury, admitted that her accused son-in-law had not exhibited ill will toward Sir Harry nor obtained any money from him. Delicately, he emphasized Nancy Oakes' loyalty in standing by her husband, an open testimonial to his innocence far more forceful than words alone could proclaim. Then Higgs appealed to the jurors not to be swayed by "prejudice" that stemmed from the fact that de Marigny was a "foreigner" "whose social and moral concepts on sex and marital relations may differ drastically from ours."

Higgs insisted that de Marigny's alibi was proved beyond question, and even though the jurors might not approve of de Visdelou's relationship with Betty Roberts, the stories each told about de Marigny's return to the Victoria Avenue house after taking Mrs. Clark and Mrs. Ainsley home rang with an aura of truth.

Eric Hallinan ridiculed the credibility of the alibi witnesses: They were his friends, either employees or spongers living under his roof. Why would they not testify that he was home at the critical hour? It was soon apparent that Eric Hallinan's great forte was ridicule, the sarcastic implication that witnesses testified falsely. After all, did not the jury need to take into account the moral and social attitudes of de Visdelou and Betty Roberts to properly appraise their probable honesty?

Then Hallinan launched into a broadside attack that characterized de Marigny as an unscrupulous fortune hunter who "held a pistol to the heads of both Sir Harry and Lady Oakes, the pistol being their daughter, Nancy Oakes." The attack against de Marigny, with detailed mention of his two previous marriages and his episodes with second wife, Ruth, made even the most stoic in the courtroom squirm. If the jurors chose not to believe all the Crown's witnesses, they could at least believe some who described de Marigny's hatred for his father-in-law and his threats to do him grave bodily harm. De Marigny satiated his hatred of Sir Harry by the murder which most conveniently also put the Oakes fortune within his grasp, control and ultimate dissipation.

"From January to July," Hallinan implored, "there was a steadily increasing crescendo of events until finally he was confronted with the failure of his attempt to get access to the Oakes fortune, therefore resorting to murder as his only way to do it."

Sir Oscar summed up the evidence in his charge to the jury, and it was considered a summation "against the Crown." He castigated the performance of Captains Melchen and Barker and suggested that it would be well for the Royal Governor to institute an investigation of the Colonial Police. When, however, he came to Exhibit J, he said he could find no evidence of its fabrication, that this was merely an insinuation by the defense without proof. For the moment, it seemed that the Chief Justice was almost putting his imprimatur on this controlling bit of evidence. But he hastened on to remind the jurors that they were the sole determiners of the genuineness of Exhibit J. If they chose to believe the defense experts that it could not have come from the screen, that was the jury's prerogative.

It was 5:25 on a sunless, blustery afternoon when the jury went out for its deliberations. De Marigny was led back by two constables to his vermin-infested jail room, across the lawn from the courthouse. Nancy waited nervously at home, hopeful that Raymond Schindler's call would come early in the evening, although he had advised her that the jury might well be out for as long as forty-eight or seventy-two hours. It was not considered an easy case, certainly not one for rapid decision.

At 7:18, Nancy Oakes de Marigny began her frantic rush back to the courtroom in her chauffeur-driven car: Schindler's call explained that the jury was coming back.

Alfred de Marigny sat in the prisoner's dock, tense and almost quivering, by the time Nancy fought her way into the crowded room. Thousands of blacks and a handful of whites milled around Rawson Square; it was the atmosphere of a football afternoon in the States.

As Sir Oscar Daly ascended the bench in white wig and scarlet robe, he did not anticipate that the jury had reached its verdict; rather, he thought they might be there to request additional instructions on the law or the evidence, or even to ask about the procedures of their discussions.

The robed court crier asked the jury foreman whether they had reached a verdict, but no one in the room expected his answer.

"We have," Foreman Sands replied.

"What is your verdict?" the crier asked.

"Not guilty," Sands announced in a loud voice.

A pall of silence engulfed the room for several seconds until realization dawned. Then a tumultuous shout went up, de Marigny grinned broadly in the prisoner's dock, and Nancy pushed and shoved her way through the well of the court in de Marigny's direction.

She was forced to wait until the constables raised the hinged lid so that de Marigny could step out, a free man who could never again be tried for this offense. She reached him first, before anyone else, and slipped her arm around his waist. He shook hands quickly with Callender and Higgs, and then the girl who stood by him led him out of the screaming room to the car where the chauffeur waited with motor running.

It was a sufficient excuse for a carnival celebration for the throngs milling outside around the square. Bedlam broke loose and the police finally called for fire hoses to disperse the cheering, dancing, celebrating crowds who adopted de Marigny's victory as their own.

A few minutes later in downtown Nassau, hotels and bars filled with people who also elected to celebrate the victory. Champagne flowed for the rest of the night.

At de Marigny's Victoria Avenue home, the reunited couple made their way through hundreds of cheering blacks who completely surrounded the house. Half-a-dozen police officers were required to maintain order while Alfred de Marigny, Nancy Oakes de Marigny, Betty Roberts, and Georges de

Visdelou were served a leisurely dinner by candlelight, de Marigny himself lighting the candles in the hurricane lamp shades.

It was not until the following day that Nancy and Alfred de Marigny learned of the jury's "further recommendation." It read: "The jury recommends that de Marigny be deported immediately."

When the Chief Justice finally heard this recommendation through the noise of the shrieking crowds, he said, "That's something I cannot contend with, but no doubt the proper authorities will take proper cognizance of your recommendation."

It was a most unusual verdict, but it proved the validity of the Common Law jury system. This jury of peers and equals, a cross-section of the Nassau community, obviously was prejudiced against de Marigny, enough to recommend that he be sent away from the colony; still, they could transcend that bias to say that the Crown's evidence did not prove him guilty of murder. Perhaps no greater testimonial to independent jury action can be found in any case.

The following night there was a defense victory celebration at the home of Baroness Marie af Trolle, Nancy Oakes' longtime friend from the boarding schools of Europe. Raymond Schindler and Leonarde Keeler were staying at the Trolle home, and someone insisted that Keeler bring out his polygraph. For forty-five minutes, he amused the guests by catching them in "lies" as his machine recorded changes in their blood pressure, respiration, pulse amplitude, and electrical skin response. Keeler showed half-a-dozen of the ladies that they could not "beat" the machine by having them pick a card from a deck, showing it to everyone in the room but Keeler, and replacing it. He instructed them to lie about the card when questioned after the attachments from the machine were placed around their chests, on their upper arms, and on their middle fingers. When the guests lied about the critical card, the needles on the machine invariably fluctuated, some widely and some less severe. Keeler explained that while the guest attached to the machine might be perfectly in control of his voluntary motions, he could not master the pounding of his heart, the rise in his blood pressure, the alteration of his respiration, and the flow of resistance through his skin, as he attempted his deception. The pens of the machine recorded uncontrollable physiological responses brought about by the fear or excitement of being detected in a lie.

On and on, Keeler captivated the guests with this new diversion; suddenly, Alfred de Marigny released his arm from Nancy's waist and said, "Test me in connection with the Oakes murder. I am willing to take your polygraph test."

Nancy looked up at him hesitantly but he returned a reassuring smile.

"It's all right. It's all right. I want the test. I've always wanted the test," de Marigny insisted in his French accent, displaying all his charm.

Schindler and Keeler were jubilant over the possibility. Ever since becoming attached to the defense, they desperately hoped to get de Marigny on the polygraph. Keeler was somewhat disturbed at the format and suggested that it might be better if the test was made in private instead of in front of this group of friends.

"No, go ahead right here. Ask me anything about the case! I have no fears about the case. Just don't ask me anything about my past!" de Marigny insisted.

Keeler agreed to the stipulation. All the questions would be related to the Oakes murder. Everyone in the room tensed as Keeler adjusted the blood-pressure cuff, the chest cable, and the finger cup. He began in the electrically charged room, so quiet that the only sounds were the oscillations of the recording pens on the rolling graph paper. Keeler spoke softly but clearly, interspersing his relevant with irrelevant questions, the standard polygraph technique.

"Is your name Alfred de Marigny?"

"Yes."

"Do you live in Nassau?"

"Yes."
"Do you know who killed Sir Harry Oakes?"
"No."
"Have you had something to eat today?"
"Yes."
"Did you kill Sir Harry Oakes yourself?"
"No."
"Were you born in Nassau?"
"No."
"Did you put your hand on that screen?"
"No."
Keeler found de Marigny to be somewhat nervous and high-strung, a "good reactor," which meant that he would expect a strong physiological response if de Marigny lied. His graphs were even, showing no lesser physiological response to the question "Is your name de Marigny?" than to the questions "Do you know who killed Sir Harry Oakes?" and "Did you kill Sir Harry yourself?"

In the opinion of Leonarde Keeler, one of the great pioneers in scientific crime detection, even allowing for the fact that the test was administered in front of a group of people, de Marigny registered no evidence whatsoever of lying or deception. Keeler wrote him a clean bill of health.

A little over six months elapsed and Nancy de Marigny again contacted Raymond Schindler, now back in New York. Her husband still labored under a horrendous cloud. While all knew the jury had acquitted him, the vote of nine to three implied that at least one-fourth of that body thought de Marigny guilty.

On June 26, 1944, Schindler wrote to the Royal Governor:

Your Royal Highness:
Knowing your deep concern for the welfare of the citizens of the Bahamas, and for the good repute of your Government, I take the liberty of addressing you on a matter of grave importance. It is my considered opinion that the murderer of Sir Harry can be found, identified, convicted and brought to justice. . . . During the incarcera-

tion and trial of de Marigny, no adequate investigation was possible. . . . Statements which failed to point toward the defendant were ignored. It goes without saying that I, and my associate, Leonarde Keeler, would welcome an opportunity to work on the case. We would willingly offer our services without compensation.

Schindler received a perfunctory acknowledgment of the letter from one of the Duke's secretaries; but no invitation to reopen the Sir Harry Oakes case came with it.

There the matter has fomented for twenty-eight years, a blurred blot of violence in a violent land, an episode that residents of the Bahamas even now discuss only with close friends and in guarded whispers.

As soon as possible after the close of World War II, the Duke and Duchess of Windsor returned to Europe from their despised exile in the Bahamas. No one dares to mention the Oakes case to him.

Alfred de Marigny has lived out his years under a cloak of suspicion impossible to imagine.

32

Attorney General Hallinan
Looks Back

Attorney General Eric Hallinan, now Sir Eric, who recently wound up an illustrious judicial career as Chief Justice of the Windward and Leeward Islands, can look back with incredibly objective detachment to the most highly publicized case of his career.

On board I.S. *Geesthaven*
at Dominica, West Indies

GOOD FRIDAY
9th April '71
Dear Mr. Houts:

I've been preoccupied pulling up my roots in Barbados (after 11 years) preparatory to going to live in Spain. But I now have some spare moments to reply to your letters requesting some information from me concerning the Oakes case.

I fear you will be disappointed in what I have to offer. I am not sufficiently interested in the case to recollect and record all that went on.

I think the attitude of a prosecutor in a British court (such as I was) may be somewhat different to one in an American court. Something you said in your letters (not with me as I write) gave me the impression that I should have been very concerned at the failure of the prosecution in this Oakes case. . . .

In British practice, the prosecutor in an Assize Court

[district or superior court] is a barrister whose task is *not* to conduct the criminal investigation or even supervise it, but to present the evidence which the Crown has in its possession against the accused. A magistrate at the Preliminary Inquiry decides whether the Crown has a prima facie case to go to a judge and jury at the Assize. If the accused is returned for trial, then it is the duty of the prosecutor (myself in the Oakes case as Attorney General) to present the evidence for the Crown as cogently and *at the same time as fairly* as possible. It is *not* the function or duty of a prosecutor to try and obtain a conviction by every means in his power or to make the case appear stronger than it is. On the other hand, he must lead the evidence for the Crown even though he may consider it weak; he must leave it to the jury to assess its value.

The only part of the Oakes case to which you specifically referred in your letters was the fingerprint evidence. I have no objection in letting you have my recollection of this part of the case which perhaps may be of some interest. You must remember that, once the trial was over, I never pursued the matter further; many things may have transpired since then. I only know what happened before and at the trial.

The Duke of Windsor, then Governor of the Bahamas, thought the investigation into the murder of Sir Harry Oakes was too big for the local police headed by Colonel Erskine-Lindop—in this, the Governor may well have been right. But his request for aid from the Miami City Police was unfortunate. The Duke had been impressed with the efficiency of their arrangements when he passed through Miami on his journeys to and from the United States. Two officers were sent over from Miami, Melchen and Barker. Melchen was the non-technical C.I.D. officer. I do not recollect his making any very material contribution to the investigation. Barker was the fingerprint and photographic expert.

Barker took photographs of Oakes corpse, and of the bedroom where he was murdered. I remember seeing the imprints of a hand on the wall as if someone had groped his way round the room. Barker took photographs of these which I thought was important. He then announced that he had found the accused's fingerprint on a screen besides Oakes bed. He did not photograph it in situ (the usual practice) but stated that he had taken it off on to a "scotch tape" which he later produced in court.

He informed me that proper facilities for developing photographs, making enlargements etc. were not available in Nassau, so he flew over to Miami to do it there. I was then informed by the police that Barker had sent a message to say that light had got into the plates on the way over and had spoilt them.

Sir Harry Oakes' body (which had been embalmed and was being flown to Bar Harbour, Maine, for burial) had to be intercepted in mid-air and flown back to Nassau. The cerements were again removed and the ghastly business of photographs gone through again. I enquired what had happened about the hand prints on the wall of Oakes bedroom but was told they were "negative." I regard the way in which the investigation of these hand prints was covered as one of the most sinister and mysterious features of the case.

When Barker's evidence of the fingerprints was brought up to me, I had misgivings as to the method he had used in obtaining it. I wrote to the Federal C.I.D. [FBI] of the United States asking them to send an expert as a "second opinion" to Barker. I was informed that once the police of a U.S. city had been called in, the Federal C.I.D. would not join the investigation. I then applied to the New York City police who sent down a most reliable officer, Dec. Inspector Conway. Conway confirmed my doubts as to Barker's procedure: the fingerprints should have been photographed in situ and not taken off on a "scotch-tape."

My position at the trial was perfectly clear. I had to lead Barker's evidence and *let the jury decide* whether or not they believed him when he said he had taken the fingerprint from the screen beside Oakes bed. I also put Dec. Inspector Conway in the witness box to give his opinion of the fingerprint and the method in which Barker had dealt with it.

It is now over 27 years since the trial, and I have no

record, diary or notes of the case. What I have stated is
my recollection. However, I am confident that what I
have written is correct.

Yours sincerely,
Eric Hallinan

10th April

P.S.—I have read what I wrote last night. From the point
of view of an American about to write a book on a British
criminal trial, perhaps the most useful contribution I can
make at this distance of time and without notes, is to emphasize the function of a prosecutor in a British Court.

He is not "out to win"; and he is not an investigator.
The police conduct the investigation and the prosecutor
orders and presents the evidence, which the investigation
has adduced, to a judge and jury. At the end of a criminal
trial where I was the prosecutor, I never felt that the
Crown had "lost" its case, if the accused person was
acquitted. If the Crown's case had been cogently and
fairly presented, then I was satisfied—whatever the outcome. In the Oakes case, I was satisfied the Crown had
done its duty. The judge had summed-up strongly against
the Crown as he was entitled to do, and the jury had
acquitted."

I would that we all knew our place in the Common Law
scheme of things as well as Sir Eric.

33

Could de Marigny Survive
a Civil Law Trial?

Now, twenty-eight years later, we can consider a game of *Suppose,* hopefully with Sir Eric Hallinan's objectivity:

Suppose that Sir Harry were killed during one of his journeys about the world in Cuba or Venezuela, the French Riviera or Mexico City, China or Japan, Rio or Biarritz, Sarajevo or the Holy City, in a country whose formula for justice is the Civil (Roman) Law system. Suppose that Alfred and Nancy de Marigny were traveling in that same city, Alfred having the same access to Sir Harry as he had in Nassau and at Westbourne. Suppose that for some reason, the governor and police were under tremendous pressures to "solve" the murder. All the evidence is the same, only the *location* of the murder and trial is different.

Could de Marigny survive the Civil Law trial?

To begin with, the burden would be on Alfred de Marigny to prove his innocence, not on the state to prove him guilty. What an unbelievable difference this makes! The comparatively hapless and insignificant accused, often without friends and funds, is matched against the awesome power of the state; even if the evidence is equally balanced in the eyes of the Civil Law judges, the defendant loses since he must establish his innocence beyond a reasonable doubt. The psychological advantage to the state of the burden of proof is real and substantial; most defendants find it impossible to

overcome; the conviction rate in the Civil Law courts is almost 100 percent, which means that anyone accused by the
police of a crime is almost automatically convicted of that
crime.

Next, Alfred de Marigny's fate would be determined by a
single judge or a panel of judges, not by a jury of his peers
and equals, although in a few Civil Law countries two or
three carefully selected laymen do sit with the professional
judges, who always form the majority and dominate the
laymen.

These judges in the Civil Law country who would try
Alfred de Marigny are little more than civil-service bureau-
crats, subject to the whim of the Minister of Justice and
through him the Presidente, Committee, Junta, Premier, or
President, elected or otherwise, who rules at the moment.
Immediately after leaving law school, some graduates elect
to become judges instead of practicing lawyers. Their first
assignments are normally to small, provincial communities,
where they begin their slow, competitive, perilous climb up
the bureaucratic judicial ladder, just as a labor commissioner, postal employee, customs inspector, agriculture super-
visor, army officer, public-works administrator, or policeman.
There is practically no way for experienced practicing lawyers to enter the judging profession laterally, since they are
bound for a lifetime by their choice to become lawyers instead of judges upon graduation from law school.

These judges in the Civil Law system are far from independent.

In many of the Civil Law countries, de Marigny would
never see or hear Captains Melchen or Barker, Lieutenant
Douglas or Harold Christie, Doctors Quackenbush or Fitzmaurice, Detective Frank Conway or Lady Oakes, or any of
the other witnesses against him. Their evidence would be
submitted informally to the judge in the form of sworn affidavits carefully worked out in advance in front of a notary
public.

Since these written affidavits would be the only way for
the judges to learn of Sir Harry's head wounds, the "fire,"

de Marigny's opportunity, the motive of hatred, and Exhibit J, there would be no opportunity for a Godfrey Higgs or Ernest Callender to get at the truth through cross-examination. A Higgs' only weapon of challenge would be a counter-affidavit, the only format for attack on Exhibit J the disputing affidavit of a Detective O'Neil; but the Captain O'Neils brave enough to challenge the state's police witnesses are hard to find. There is little doubt that Exhibit J would be accepted as offered by Barker without the slightest hesitation: The judges would undoubtedly decide that it was lifted from the No. 5 area of the Chinese screen near Sir Harry's bed.

Even in those Civil Law countries where the accused does see and hear the witnesses testify against him in court, if a Higgs or Callender wanted to ask them further questions, he must request permission of the presiding judge, who would put the question himself to the witness. There is no possible way for a hard-hitting, lie-shattering, truth-finding cross-examination to develop as the one Higgs gave Harold Christie or Captain Barker.

Instead of sitting like Sir Oscar as an independent presiding officer who can "sum up against the Crown" if need be, but whose ideas on the evidence the jury can ignore, the Civil Law judge sits as inquisitor, investigator, prosecutor, defender, interrogator, legal arbiter, and fact-finder all in one. The laymen who sit with the judges (in some countries) are most often afraid to vote against the will of the executive as expressed by the prosecutor; the laymen really do not temper the rigid attitudes of the subservient, professional, bureaucratic judges.

De Marigny's chances for acquittal in a Civil Law trial must be written off as nil.

How then did this Civil Law system come about?

Instead of rising from the custom and usage of the people as did the Common Law, the Civil Law rests upon one basic tenet of political power: There is no rule of law but that which is spelled out in the form of a statute. These statutes were promulgated by kings or emperors, all-powerful and far removed by station and perspective from the subjects the statute was to regulate and regiment.

Since the statute represented the will of the emperor, the judges were compelled to apply it like automatons to a given case. The judge was specifically forbidden to "make law" through his rulings and opinions since this derogated the will of the emperor; so the precedent of prior case decisions could play no controlling role in present and future cases.

Without the use of the precedent of Supreme Court decisions in prior cases, different trial judges interpreted the same statute in different ways as they attempted to apply it to different cases. The fate of the accused rested upon his luck in landing before a judge who *might* but who was not *bound* to construe the statute in his favor. Guilt or innocence fluctuated widely upon the subjective biases of the individual judges. The concept of a "rule of law" instead of the "rule of man" could not develop as the Common Law world knows it.

From the viewpoint of the political power structure that evolved in the Civil Law countries, the arrangement precluded the development of a strong, independent judiciary who could call back the emperor to legality when he erred into a path of repression and oppression.

When king or emperor granted a modicum of individual liberty to his subjects through a statute or edict, it came as a condescending sop to quell the periodic clamor of the subjects, a tactical palliative to shore up the throne. Since the subjects' personal rights were a gift of the king, the magnanimity of one king could be taken back by a future monarch under the same guise of political expediency that caused the rights to be grudgingly granted by the first king. There were no independent judges like Sir Oscar to rise up and act as buffer between king and subjects; and as there was no group to oppose the king and enforce the rights of the subjects, the concept of inalienable personal liberties did not develop. Even today, since the idea of habeas corpus is

not known, a subject can be arrested by the king's agents
(the police) on nothing more than suspicion or "slander
against the state," and confined indefinitely without trial.
Coerced confessions of guilt are routinely received as competent evidence.

The first loyalty of the Civil Law judges remains clearly
to the king, and when a conflict exists over where the line
in a specific case must be drawn, the subject is penalized and
not the king. Without the shield of independent judges between subject and king, personal freedom for the subject
never became *off limits to the king.*

The controlling tradition that *both* king and subject are
ruled by the *same* law did not permeate the philosophy of
the people. The king remained all-powerful. When a subject
asked for a redress of a grievance, his application was to the
king's own judges, who might or might not turn a sympathetic ear. If a particular king was overly aggressive, the
judges were afraid to act in the subject's behalf, just when the
subject most needed the protection of independent judges.

The situation today continues basically unchanged. The
king or emperor is called *presidente, jefe, generalissimo, premier, leader, party boss,* even *president,* but his role and
power remain the same, and the police still and always will
be his loyal agents.

When the modern emperors rose and reigned between the
two World Wars, the Civil Law judges could offer the subject
no help whatsoever. In Germany, they caved in almost immediately under the Nazi storm troopers and actually joined
in enforcing Hitler's most noxious decrees.

In Russia, the Civil Law judges of the imperial Romanovs
were never given an opportunity to shift functions under
Stalin's brand of communism, although they were actually
replaced for a brief period after the Revolution by the
peoples' courts, instruments of cruelty that rivaled, perhaps
surpassed, those of the French Revolution.

Some limited few judges held out valiantly for several

short years against Mussolini's fascism; but without the tradition of judicial independence to sustain them, their noble
gestures perished tragically and too soon.

Today no embers of personal liberty on a permanent,
generation-after-generation time perspective really glow
brightly throughout the continent of South America, across
the broad sweep of Asia, behind the Iron and Bamboo Cur-
tains or on the continent of Europe; only a few transitory
clutches at freedom exist since no independent judges are
available to impose themselves between the citizens and the
harsh realities of the potential despot.

The most common question to be decided in any case
reaching the court in either Civil or Common Law system is
whether the king (through the police) drew a line in the
right place. In the Common Law world, if the courts think
not, the king is penalized, and not the subject. The mere fact
that a line needs to be drawn automatically implies choice,
and choice suggests differences of opinion among reasonable
men who act from differing frames of reference. In the
Common Law system, the *independent judges,* instead of
king or subject, have the final say of where the line will fall.
Not so in the Civil Law world.

By the very nature of the scheme, the Common Law
judges sit in judgment on the king's actions—and thank God
they do! No thinking man possessed of historical perspective
would will it otherwise.

As Henry de Bracton's * Common Law maxim expressed
it: The king must recognize the 'law that made him king.' "
Translated differently it reads, "The king is below no man;
but he is below God *and the law!*"

The unique features of the Common Law system that dis-
tinguish it from the Civil Law are the historical independence
of its judges and their attempt to balance the interests and
rights of the citizen against his king at all times. Although
now called *president, governor, mayor,* or *bureaucrat* in

* Thirteenth-century English judge and the first writer of any real
stature on English law.

Washington, he is still the king with tremendous power, or potential power, over the citizen; and if the king steps out of line to flail away at a citizen without due process, the independent judges, supported by the philosophy of the people, are strong enough to call him back to a standard of accountability.

As an accidental blueprint of political structure, the Common Law system has served us well. Democratic government, with enforceable personal rights for all citizens, can thrive only where four basic conditions coexist: (1) geographical integrity of the country's borders so that the threat of foreign invasion does not press the state into a permanent posture of military dominance—democracy cannot long endure a war! (2) the economic, social, and cultural assets must be enjoyable by a vast majority of the people, not just a privileged few; (3) an overwhelming percentage of the people must be literate; and (4) historically, *independent judges* must exist to act as buffer between king and subjects.

Only the Common Law sphere is blessed with this last fundamental ingredient. The chances of permanent, stable, constitutional, democratic government remaining long in any other place in the world must be rated dismal, and this means that no inalienable personal rights exist to protect the falsely accused Alfred de Marignys. Even though these rights read well and convincingly on paper in written constitutions in the Civil Law countries, no judges are available to enforce them against the king, whether the crime alleged is murder or rape, slander against the state or capitalistic deviation, a rejection of state doctrine or libel against the Leader.

34

A Call To Save the Common Law System in America

In the impersonal, dehumanizing urban centers where 145 million people out of a total of 204 million live, our Common Law system is perilously close to extinction. Time is frighteningly short, and unless we can leap forward all the components within the system two hundred years in a single decade, personalized justice and individual liberty in this country cannot endure. The two concepts are so intimately interwoven that one cannot survive without the other.

In many cities, the right to a "speedy trial" in criminal matters guaranteed in *every* constitution means a delay of between sixteen and twenty-four months after arrest before the trial can be held because of clogged court calendars. In noncriminal matters—personal injury actions, suits to collect money owed from a debtor, landlord-tenant disputes, and business litigation—delays of four, five, and six years before a case can be heard are commonplace.

Farseeing Meyer Lansky and his Mafia and Cosa Nostra associates have already entered the judicial void and stand ready to come on with a rush as the system stagnates further. A few case examples illustrate exactly what is already occurring:

Case 1: A housewife in Los Angeles receives calls that border on blackmail from a man in Chicago with whom she was sexually intimate before her marriage. Reaching a nervous breaking point, she finally explains her predicament to her husband, who consults a Los Angeles lawyer, who in turn calls an attorney in Chicago. After two weeks of fruitless discussion while the threatening calls continue, the two lawyers advise the husband that "it is a difficult case" because the man has not quite violated the extortion laws; and besides, it would be several weeks, maybe months, before an application to a Chicago judge for a restraining order could be heard.

In desperation the husband spills out his problem to his associates at work and one of them comes up with a solution. For a thousand dollars, there is "a man" in Los Angeles who can arrange for the man in Chicago to "have the hell beaten out of him," which "for damn sure" will put a stop to the calls.

This sounds like the only salvation to the harassed Los Angeles couple, so they pay the thousand dollars. The Syndicate in Chicago, working in close liaison with their associates in Los Angeles, send out two strong-arm men who do teach the Chicago caller a severe, almost fatal lesson, and the calls stop.

Case 2: A manufacturer's representative in Miami is owed $23,000 by a merchant in Manhattan. After spending several hundred dollars futilely on lawyers' fees, he is told that if he decides to sue for collection, it may be five years before the case can be heard in the New York courts.

The manufacturer's representative is also led to "a man" in Miami who can arrange the collection of the $23,000 from the New York merchant for $5,000, substantially less than the lawyer's contingent fee would be, even assuming that the full $23,000 is collected five years later.

Two Cosa Nostra "goons" from a "family" in New York, under threats of violence to the merchant and his real, blood family, force the payment of the $23,000, even though the merchant claims that the merchandise delivered was shoddy and unmarketable.

Case 3: A lieutenant general at one of the air bases in the western part of the United States is bucking hard for his

fourth star, but he has a serious competitor for the only slot
open. His intelligence sources advise him that his competitor's base is running as smoothly as most flights to the moon;
but suddenly, a labor walkout on his own base threatens to
throw an expansion program completely off date, which may
reflect adversely on the general's chances for promotion.

The general reaches "a man" and two powerful Cosa
Nostra "families" swing into co-operative attack. The money
necessary to force the settlement of the labor dispute within
twenty-four hours comes from the general's wealthy wife,
who would gladly pay ten times the cost to guarantee her
husband's fourth star.

Case 4: A substantial building contractor is indicted for
fraud against the government on a one hundred-million-
dollar construction contract. The government's chief witness
is the former comptroller of the company, whose records
shout fraud so clearly that the greenest law student the first
day after his admission to the bar could produce the contractor's conviction. It costs the contractor $50,000, but "a
man" arranges for the comptroller to become tongue-tied
from fear so that the United States Attorney is forced to
accept a guilty plea to a relatively insignificant offense which
carries with it almost no penalty.

These are but a few representative examples of what is
now happening.

Frighteningly enough, most of the reform proposals for
our Common Law system are totally lacking in historical
perspective and threaten to move us dangerously close to
the Civil Law system with all its totalitarian possibilities.
Unless these reforms are historically sound, they can produce a cure far worse than the present illness.

The thrust of our effective reforms to save the Common
Law system in America must be in two separate but interlocking areas: the courts *and* the police.

In the courtrooms, we are now reaping the bitter harvest of
three full centuries of wanton recklessness. The early colonists

from England were a rebellious breed who attempted to throw off all vestiges of pomp and formality. With the rallying cry of equality and democracy permeating the professions, particularly the law, they abolished the British distinction between *barrister*—the men like Higgs, Callender, Adderley, and Hallinan, who try the cases in the courtroom—and *solicitor,* the office lawyers who prepare the cases. Regardless of professional experience or personal abilities, any lawyer was welcome to rush into the courtroom to see what he could accomplish for himself and his client.

We blundered along, not well but passably, under this unspecialized, "democratic" arrangement until World War II. Until then, the incredible shifts from rural to urban society did not take place. Enough lawyers were still trained through the apprentice route in law offices where they could learn the art of courtroom advocacy on a preceptor basis from older men who had performed the barrister roles in United States courtrooms. These men are now gone, leaving us with lawyers trained only in the law schools, by professors who have never seen the inside of a courtroom, professors incestuously inbred by several uninterrupted generations of so-called research scholars, who can track down an obtuse legal problem in the law books like a monitoring station following the flight of an astronaut, but who are as pathetic in the field of advocacy as deaf-mutes.

Trying to operate an adversary system in the courtroom without able barristers who know the art of advocacy is like attempting to drive a gasoline engine by circulating distilled water through its cylinders. This is one main reason why a Charles Manson trial in Los Angeles can sputter along for nine-and-a-half months and produce nausea in all who see or hear anything about it.

Our judges need not even be drawn from this group of law-school-trained lawyers who bumble their way through courtrooms without any knowledge of the art of advocacy. Often the *office* lawyers, as a political party or political bar-association reward, suddenly find themselves on the bench. They may require from several hours to several days to rule

on an objection or motion which Sir Oscar Daly, himself a
great barrister before ascending the bench, would dispose
of as quickly as he could say "Sustained" or "Overruled."
Even with Godfrey Higgs' objection to the admission of
Exhibit J, a completely novel legal question without any
prior cases for precedent, Sir Oscar took the problem with
him at adjournment time and ruled with assurance at the
opening of court the following morning. Most American
judges would have vacillated between uncertainty and fear
of reversal on appeal for hours or days before daring to make
a cautious, perhaps ambiguous, ruling on the admissibility of
the fingerprint lift.

With the courtroom requirements of 145 million urban people to be served, our Common Law system will die from the
asphyxia of its own delays unless drastic reform, as distinguished from revolutionary programs are launched immediately.

Step 1 is for all bar associations to initiate a rigorous Cer-
tification Program. (The Specialty Boards in medicine now
certify doctors as specialists in cardiology, neurology, ortho-
pedics, obstetrics, and sixteen other fields of medicine. The
quality of the practice of medicine across the country has
improved tremendously since the inauguration of the Specialty Boards a little over a generation ago.) No lawyer will
be permitted to go into the courtroom to try a case until
certified as courtroom-ready by the Bar Association Certifica-
tion Board.

Step 2 is a crash program in the art of advocacy to develop
a crop of courtroom barristers who can articulate and persuade, and who can serve as the source of supply for our
future Sir Oscar Dalys, men who will move along a Manson
trial to completion in a few weeks at the most.

Step 3 is the return to the British concept of where the
lawyer's duty first lies. Under the British philosophy, the first
loyalty of Godfrey Higgs and Ernest Callender, Eric Hallinan and Alfred Adderley, was to Sir Oscar Daly. The American philosophy is that the lawyer's first duty is to his client,
which means that he can do *anything* under the sun to gain

tactical advantage so long as it is not specifically prohibited by law, or rule of court, or legal ethics.

What a difference this makes! The shift to *and enforcement of* this new image of duty will eliminate many of the nefarious practices now clogging the courts and seriously threatening their survival.

Even the thought by the barristers involved in the de Marigny trial of a delaying motion to gain a tactical advantage for their side would have been utterly abhorrent to them. Their single joint goal was to get all of the evidence to the jury as forcefully and quickly as possible, to permit a rapid and correct verdict, so that all could move on to the next case of the next citizen seeking redress from the court.

If these barristers had attempted delaying tactics, or the use of Sir Oscar's court as a political forum as in the Angela Davis case, some of the other Black Panther trials, the trial of the Chicago Seven, and the evangelical cases of the New Left, Sir Oscar would have stopped it short within the first thirty seconds. The barrister who attempted it would have been thought mad by his solicitor contacts, who would respond effectively by never bringing him another brief.

Step 4 is a stringent bar-association review of all pretrial and trial motions, something that has not been attempted rigorously in three hundred years. Many of these motions can be eliminated altogether, and most of the others can be drastically revised. The thrust of the revision must be the elimination of delay, and any motion that can be used to delay must be ruthlessly restricted. Every pretrial motion must pass a single test: Will it help determine whether the police have accused the right man? If not, we can do without it.

All pretrial motions can be made *orally* at one time, within ten days after the arraignment at a great saving of time and no loss of effectiveness.

Step 5 is a shift in jury-selection procedures. The quality of the jury panel must be improved so that we again draw our "cross-section of the community" to apply its practical standards to the conduct of the defendants.

Throughout the fifty-one jurisdictions in the United States today, we find some thirty-eight occupational classifications of persons exempt from jury service: doctors, dentists, veterinarians, chiropractors, lawyers, accountants, undertakers, federal employees, state employees, members of the National Guard, teachers—almost any group with enough political influence to lobby an exemption statute through its legislative body. Some citizens are so well shielded from jury service that they can claim exemption under not one but three or four separate categories. Tens of millions of citizens cannot be called for jury duty; and when a jury boils down to housewives, wage-earners, or retired citizens only, our goal to obtain a true cross-section of the community is not within sight.

The courtroom process of jury selection, which required a scant fifty-five minutes of Sir Oscar's time in the de Marigny case, must be taken away from the lawyers and given exclusively to the judges, as is now done in the Federal Courts.

The selection of a Manson jury can take five weeks only because the lawyers, who readily admit it in their own seminars and textbooks, use the jury-selection process as a conditioning, reinforcement, teaching technique to impress their theory of the case on the jury. Each prospective juror may be asked: "Now if it develops that the defendant found his wife and her boyfriend nude in bed when he came home unexpectedly, and if the evidence shows that the defendant was emotionally unstable and tended to fly off the handle easily when provoked by minor matters, and if the evidence further shows that upon discovering his wife and her boyfriend nude together in bed he went immediately to the bureau drawer where he kept his loaded .38 revolver, and while still looking at these two people cowering in bed nude he pointed that revolver and, by his own statement to the police, pointed it first at the man and pulled the trigger two or three times—he does not remember how many, so great was his shock—and then pointed it at the head of his dearly beloved nude wife who had betrayed him, and pulled the trigger several times—so great was his shock that he does not remember how many—would you take this into consideration when you get out there in that jury room to begin your deliberations?"

That same question is endlessly repeated in a droning monotone day upon day to every prospective member of the jury so that the poor unfortunate man first chosen for jury service sits helplessly imprisoned in the jury box, hearing it several hundred times before eleven other members of the community are dubbed jurors. The victorious lawyer then gloats to his brethren at the bar: "You know, by God, I didn't win that case during the trial! I won it during my jury selection. By the time I had those twelve people in the box—sure, it took three-and-a-half weeks—they were better conditioned to my theory of the case than a seven-year-old kid after watching a bunch of TV commercials for Mother's cookies. Bartender, bring us another round of drinks! This is my celebration!"

Trial by jury should never be limited or curtailed even to the point of reducing the number from twelve to nine or six. The cost of a trial jury is a negligible, infinitesimal fraction of 1 percent of what we spend on other facets of our criminal-justice system. Trial by jury is the only truly democratic form of participation left in the justice process, and we dare not destroy it. In the de Marigny case, we have every reason to conclude that while Sir Oscar "summed up against the Crown" in that he severely castigated the police, he indicated that he might well have accepted Exhibit J as legitimate. Fact-finding is too tenuous and human to take from a lay jury, who approach it from twelve differing but interlocking perspectives, to give it to a single individual whose biases and blind spots in a particular case cannot be counterbalanced by eleven other frames of reference. Perhaps the closest approach to objective truth on this earth is the conclusion reached by twelve members of the community, each with his own built-in prejudices, partisanship and favoritism, who argue without rule or restriction within the confines of the jury room, and counterbalance each other.

We can quickly obtain our goal of bringing every criminal case to trial within sixty days of arraignment, and we can control appeals so that all are finished within ninety days of the verdict if we but demand it of our lawyers and legislators.

With the police, our options are seriously limited. We either improve our present system, or we go to a highly nationalized, military-police table of organization, or we return to the private-vigilante concept of the old watches-and-wards, which obviously cannot function in today's populous, urbanized congestion. We can and must win the fight to professionalize the police so that we eliminate the Melchens and the Barkers.

Step 1 is the realization by each citizen that the policeman is his direct agent: "The policeman is my substitute! If that policeman were not out there keeping the peace and preventing crime, I would be compelled to join with a group of neighbors to attempt it ourselves; or the governor would send in a military unit to operate a system of martial law, although it would not be labeled as such."

There are no alternatives.

Each citizen, therefore, must feel that when a policeman is attacked by gun or knife, the citizen is also attacked because the policeman is, in practical reality, only an extension of the citizen himself. If the policeman does not have the tools or the philosophy to combat crime, it is because he has not received them from his principal, the citizen.

Step 2 is the recognition that the police are the sun around which the planets of the judges, prosecutors, defense lawyers, parole officers, probation officers, and penologists revolve. Everything starts with the police, and what they do during the initial stages of a case controls its final disposition. The police are the hub of the justice wheel from which all other components both originate and converge as spokes. This can only mean that the most drastic and pressing of our reforms must be with the police.

Step 3 is the admission that at the present time, the police simply do not have the tools to combat and solve crime.

There has been almost zero progress in scientific crime detection in the last fifty years, detective writers to the contrary notwithstanding. When all is said and done, the police are still left with only the two basic tools of the centuries: the *informant* and the *confession.* Law enforcement has simply not enjoyed the technological developments of the Space Age. The police must be advanced forward a thousand years in this single decade.

Step 4 is the formal invitation to the police to come into the Common Law system as a principal partner. They are no longer to be the abandoned, castigated bastards whose presence is reluctantly permitted but never really graciously accepted.

Step 5 is for the police to recognize their role in this Common Law system as fact-gatherer as distinguished from fact-finder. Just as lawyers must alter their philosophy as to where their first duty lies, police must cease to perform "trial by policemen" in which they prejudge a suspect's guilt and set about to collect *only* the evidence consistent with their theory of guilt while ignoring or suppressing evidence consistent with the suspect's innocence. The fabrication of an Exhibit J should shock the community with the same impact as the release of an Organized Crime murderer by a corrupt judge.

The police must understand that the nature of the Common Law scheme requires the independent judges and lay jurors to pass judgment on the policeman's work. If the judge finds it defective, he must cast it out.

Once the police understand their role as a major partner in the Common Law formula, their innate hostility toward judges, prosecutors, defense attorneys, penologists, and jurors will substantially abate. The police will know that it is not up to them to "do it all"; they are but part of the team, though granted, theirs is the starring role. They will come to take pride in their work, and like Sir Eric Hallinan can say: "at the end of a criminal trial where I was the prosecutor, I never felt that the Crown had 'lost' its case, if the accused person was acquitted. If the Crown's case had been cogently and fairly presented, then I was satisfied—whatever the outcome."

Time is critically short for all of us. We either rush through these reforms of the courts and the police, or as our Common Law system winds down to a stoppage, we see the totalitarian "efficiencies" of a Civil Law system emerge, while Meyer Lansky and his Mafia and Cosa Nostra associates gleefully await their own profitable takeover.

Index